WILLIAM JAMES
ON
PSYCHICAL RESEARCH

WILLIAM JAMES
ON
PSYCHICAL RESEARCH

Compiled and Edited

by

GARDNER MURPHY

and

ROBERT O. BALLOU

With an Introduction and concluding remarks
by Gardner Murphy

NEW YORK • THE VIKING PRESS

VIKING COMPASS EDITION
Issued in 1969 by The Viking Press, Inc.
625 Madison Avenue, New York, N.Y. 10022

Distributed in Canada by
The Macmillan Company of Canada Limited

Library of Congress catalog card number: 60-11807

Printed in U.S.A.

Acknowledgment is made to Paul R. Reynolds and Son for permission
to reprint selections from the following works: *Memories and Studies*
by William James, published by Longmans, Green & Co., copyright
1911 by Henry James, Jr.; *The Letters of William James*, edited by
Henry James, published by the Atlantic Monthly Press, copyright 1920
by Henry James; and *The Thought and Character of William James*,
by Ralph Barton Perry, published by Little, Brown & Co., copyright
1935 by Henry James.

The publishers and editors acknowledge their debt to the American Society for Psychical Research and the Society for Psychical Research (London) for permission to reprint the material from their *Proceedings* and *Journals* which forms the bulk of this work, and to The American Society for Psychical Research for permission to publish for the first time letters from William James which are in their possession. Thanks are especially due to Mrs. Laura Abbott Dale and Miss Rhea White of the American Society for the valuable help so cheerfully given by them both.

CONTENTS

WILLIAM JAMES
ON
PSYCHICAL RESEARCH

INTRODUCTION[1]

By Gardner Murphy

Everything conspired to make William James a pioneer in psychical research. One could almost see it coming a hundred years ahead. One might look first at his ancestry and early rearing; then at his more formal education; then at his career in medicine and in philosophy, and his integration of these studies with psychology; at his determination to investigate the margins and edges of all that is known; and at his consequent discovery, in psychical research, of a kind of inquiry that fulfilled the cravings accumulated from all these many areas of experience.

The family history usually begins with "William of Albany," his grandfather, who made a fortune and enabled his many children to start off in life with some degree of freedom from the current struggle to exist. Among his sons, Henry James, Sr., the father of William James and of Henry James the novelist, early chose for himself a life of study, contemplation, speculation. He was a "seeker," who in the nineteenth-century effort to find a new, solid

---

[1] Much of this essay has appeared in the *Journal of the American Society for Psychical Research*, July 1949.

ground to stand on, explored one philosophy or religious movement after another. Having as a child suffered a series of amputa-
tions upon a leg, he had been deprived to some degree of normal
social intercourse; yet he managed to preserve a vivid, earnest,
hearty enthusiasm and a real gift for friendship with all sorts of
fellow seekers. His warm response to the teachings of Swedenborg
—who, against the background of an amazing scientific achievement, had nevertheless seen fit to identify himself with his great
vision of the beyond—was characteristic of his deep sympathies,
though he never joined the Swedenborgian fold. He created in the
home atmosphere an exhilarating sense of the worth-whileness of
pursuing problems of cosmic dimensions, of asking forever one
more question as to the place of man in this world and as to the
real basis for ethics and religion; everybody in the family was apparently always ready for a debate which wound up with humor
and with agreement to live and let live.

William (born in 1842) and Henry (born in 1843) shared this
atmosphere. As their letters show, there was a rugged intensity of
fellowship despite their profound temperamental differences. The
contrast appears in the fact that while Henry James had sought
the meanings of life in introspection and in the subtleties of self-
observation, it was William James's determination to look for
answers in the new scientific world of the evolutionary period, and
to attempt to support his personal faith with the knowledge and
wisdom of empirical inquiry. Both were empiricists, but in a very
different sense, Henry James looking for the shadings and over-
tones of daily experience, William trying always to accumulate
more facts from every quarter.

The freedom of the family to roam about reached its richest
values for William James during the journeys to England, France,
Switzerland, and Germany. A special importance should perhaps be
attached to a year in Geneva, in which, as he entered upon adoles-
cence, William James found his enthusiasm fired by a mixture of
science and art. He loved, for example, to draw the skeletons in the
Geneva museum. Soon he was thinking of becoming a painter.

After returning to the United States, he entered upon his studies at Harvard (1861). Ill health dogged him all during these years. He was obviously unfit for military service, and his chemistry professor noted the long hours in which he had to lie still and rest, being unable to stand at his table and his test tubes as most students did. His interest in science, especially biology, led into medicine. Medicine meant, however, much more for him than the continuation of scientific studies. Indeed, his one attempt to be a pure scientist, his journey with Agassiz to the Amazon to collect and barrel fishes, resulted in a tremendous breakdown and a long illness. Medicine, however, he could ultimately master, with hopes, as he said, that he could not only "support W. J., but Mrs. W. J. as well."

During these medical years, moreover, he was carrying forward the kinds of thinking which another journey to Europe had set going within him. He had exposed himself to the physiological psychology of Helmholtz, and the other giants of the period, and wrote to his brother that he hoped that these beginnings of a new experimental science of psychology had something to offer, and he wanted to see what he could do in this area too.

After finishing medical school (1869), and going on into further studies in physiology, he attracted the attention of President Eliot of Harvard, who asked him to teach physiology to Harvard undergraduates. This led rapidly to experimental psychology, where James rapidly rose to fame through a series of brilliant publications which began in 1876. As a matter of fact, during these years he had made a contract with Henry Holt for his *Principles of Psychology,* and over a twelve-year period, from 1878 to 1890, he turned out chapter after chapter of this monumental work.

As he began his Harvard career, he had been married to Alice Gibbens, and a quiet and happy home life in Cambridge made possible a period of relative freedom from the strain and illness which had frequently been his lot.

The question has often been debated as to what factors, other than his marriage and his steady work at Harvard, had turned the semi-invalid into such a productive and effective teacher and writer. The answer which he himself apparently emphasized most was that the restitution of his health came from the study of the evolutionary philosophy of the French philosopher Renouvier, who taught that *spontaneity, genuine freedom,* is available to the individual who strikes out on a new path for himself. He can creatively remake his personal life, including his health as well as his intellectual and spiritual goals. Evidently James's long sufferings, his backaches, his eye-aches, his periods of semi-invalidism, his pathetic and futile journeys to the mud-baths in Bohemia, all of which left him still an invalid, were things of the past when once he realized, in the language of Renouvier, that he could spontaneously, arbitrarily re-create his own life. Though he never became really rugged, his physical and intellectual vitality were in some measure a response to this new conviction.

Of his introduction to Renouvier's philosophy and its effect upon him he wrote this in a diary under date of April 30, 1870:

> I think that yesterday was a crisis in my life. I finished the first part of Renouvier's second "Essais" and see no reason why his definition of Free Will—"the sustaining of a thought *because I choose to* when I might have other thoughts"—need be the definition of an illusion. At any rate, I will assume for the present—until next year—that it is no illusion. My first act of free will shall be to believe in free will. For the remainder of the year, I will abstain from the mere speculation and contemplative *Grübelei* in which my nature takes most delight, and voluntarily cultivate the feeling of moral freedom, by reading books favorable to it, as well as by acting. After the first of January, my callow skin being somewhat fledged, I may perhaps return to metaphysical study and skepticism without danger to my powers of action. For the present then remember: care little for speculation; much for the *form* of my action; recollect that only when habits of order are formed can we advance to really interesting fields of action—and consequently accumulate grain on grain of willful choice like a very miser; never forgetting how one link dropped undoes an indefinite number. *Principiis obsta*—Today has furnished the exceptionally passionate initiative which Bain posits as needful for the acquisition of habits. I will see to the sequel. Not in

maxims, not in *Anschauungen,* but in accumulated *acts* of thought lies salvation. *Passer outre.* Hitherto, when I have felt like taking a free initiative, like daring to act originally, without carefully waiting for contemplation of the external world to determine all for me, suicide seemed the most manly form to put my daring into; now, I will go a step further with my will, not only act with it, but believe as well; believe in my individual reality and creative power. My belief, to be sure, *can't* be optimistic—but I will posit life (the real, the good) in the self-governing *resistance* of the ego to the world. Life shall be built in doing and suffering and creating.[2]

Three years later (March 18, 1873) his father commented on Renouvier's effect on William in a letter to Henry James, Jr.:

[William] said several things: the reading of Renouvier (particularly his vindication of the freedom of the will) and of Wordsworth, whom he has been feeding on now for a good while; but more than anything else, his having given up the notion that all mental disorder requires to have a physical basis. This had become perfectly untrue to him. He saw the mind does act irrespectively of material coercion, and could be dealt with therefore at first hand, and this was health to his bones. It was a splendid declaration, and though I had known from unerring signs of the fact of the change, I never had been more delighted than by hearing of it so unreservedly from his own lips. He has been shaking off his respect for men of mere science as such, and is even more universal and impartial in his mental judgments than I have known him before.[3]

His somewhat later interest, then, in "mental healing" is not surprising, and is obviously closely related to his eagerness to test every phenomenon which seemed to have some other than strictly materialistic and mechanistic causation. Indeed as early as 1864, when he was a young man of twenty-two, he wrote, "A doctor does more by the moral effect of his presence on the patient and family than anything else."[4]

[2] *The Letters of William James,* edited by his son, Henry James (Boston: Atlantic Monthly Press, 1920), Vol. I, pp. 147–48.
[3] Ibid., Vol. I, pp. 169–70.
[4] *The Thought and Character of William James,* by Ralph Barton Perry (Boston: Little, Brown, 1935).

It was somewhat later than this that he became actively interested in professional practitioners in "mental healing," and, as he so often did in controversial matters which interested him, tried to put their theories to the test in subjecting himself to one of them. On February 5, 1887, he wrote to his sister Alice:

> I have been paying ten or eleven visits to a mind-cure doctress, a sterling creature, resembling the "Venus of Medicine," Mrs. Lydia E. Pinkham; made solid and veracious-looking. I sit down beside her and presently drop asleep, whilst she disentangles the snarls out of my mind. She says she never saw a mind with so many, so agitated, so restless, etc. She said my *eyes*, mentally speaking, kept revolving like wheels in front of each other and in front of my face, and it was four or five sittings ere she could get them *fixed*. I am now, *unconsciously to myself*, much better than when I first went, etc. I thought it might please you to hear an opinion of my mind so similar to your own. Meanwhile what boots it to be made unconsciously better, yet all the while consciously to lie awake o' nights, as I still do? [5]

The fact that his "mind-cure doctress" did him little or no good in no way diminished James's interest in what he considered the important experiment being conducted by the "mind-cure" practitioners and its potential value to therapy and the long, slow task of learning more about the human mind and personality. The nineties found him actively engaged in opposing bills before the Massachusetts Legislature designed to end the practice of mental healers by requiring licenses based upon medical examinations. His point of view is expressed in the following letter to James P. Putnam:

> Dear Jim, —On page 7 of the *Transcript* tonight you will find a manifestation of me at the State House, protesting against the proposed medical license bill.
> If you think I *enjoy* that sort of thing you are mistaken. I never did anything that required as much moral effort in my life. My vocation is to treat of things in an all-round manner and not make *ex-parte* pleas to influence (or seek to) a peculiar jury. *Aussi*, why do the medical brethren force an unoffending citizen like

---

[5] Henry James, ed., op. cit., Vol. I, p. 261.

me into such a position? Legislative license is sheer humbug—
mere abstract paper thunder under which every ignorance and
abuse can still go on. Why this mania for more laws? Why seek
to stop the really extremely important experiences which these
peculiar creatures are rolling up?

Bah! I'm sick of the whole business, and I well know how all my
colleagues at the Medical School, who go only by the label, will
view me and my efforts. But if Zola and Col. Picquart can face
the whole French army, can't I face their disapproval?—Much
more easily than that of my own conscience!

You, I fancy, are not one of the fully disciplined demanders of
more legislation. So I write to you, as on the whole my dearest
friend hereabouts, to explain just what my state of mind is.
Ever yours,

W. J.[6]

On William James's attitude his son comments:

James was not indulging in empty rhetoric when he said that
his conscience drove him to face the disapproval of his medical
colleagues. Some of them never forgave him, and to this day
references to his "appearance" at the State House in Boston are
marked by partisanship rather than understanding.

What happened cannot be understood without recalling that
thirty-odd years ago the licensing of medical practitioners was
just being inaugurated in the United States. Today it is evident
that everyone must be qualified and licensed before he can be
permitted to write prescriptions, to sign statements upon which
public records, inquests, and health statistics are to be based, and
to go about the community calling himself a doctor. On the other
hand, experience has proved that those people who do not pretend to be physicians, who do not use drugs or the knife, and who
attempt to heal only by mental or spiritual influence, cannot be
regulated by the clumsy machinery of the criminal law. But either
because the whole question of medical registration was new, or
because professional men are seldom masters of the science of
lawmaking, the sponsors of the bills proposed to the Massachusetts Legislature in 1894 and 1898 ignored these distinctions.
James did not name them, although his argument implied them
and rested upon them. The bills included clauses which attempted
to abolish the faith-curers by requiring them to become Doctors

[6] Ibid., Vol. II, p. 66.

of Medicine. The "Spiritualists" and Christian Scientists were a numerous element in the population and claimed a religious sanction for their beliefs. The gentlemen who mixed an anti-spiritualist program in their effort to have doctors examined and licensed by a State Board were either innocent of political discretion or blind to the facts. For it was idle to argue that faith-curers would be able to continue in their own ways as soon as they had passed the medical examinations of the State Board, and that accordingly the proposed law could not be said to involve their suppression. Obviously, medical examinations were barriers which the faith-curers could not climb over. This was the feature of the proposed law which roused James to opposition, and led him to take sides for the moment with all the spokesmen of all the -isms and -opathies.

"I will confine myself to a class of diseases" (he wrote to the *Boston Transcript* in 1894) "with which my occupation has made me somewhat conversant. I mean the diseases of the nervous system and the mind. . . . Of all the new agencies that our day has seen, there is but one that tends steadily to assume a more and more commanding importance, and that is the agency of the patient's mind itself. Whoever can produce effects there holds the key of the situation in a number of morbid conditions of which we do not yet know the extent; for systematic experiments in this direction are in their merest infancy. They began in Europe fifteen years ago, when the medical world so tardily admitted the facts of hypnotism to be true; and in this country they have been carried on in a much bolder and more radical fashion by all those 'mind-curers' and 'Christian Scientists' with whose results the public, and even the profession, are growing gradually familiar.

"I assuredly hold no brief for any of these healers, and must confess that my intellect has been unable to assimilate their theories, so far as I have heard them given. But their *facts* are patent and startling; and anything that interferes with the multiplication of such facts, and with our freest opportunity of observing and studying them, will, I believe, be a public calamity. The law now proposed will so interfere, simply because the mind-curers will not take the examinations. . . . Nothing would please some of them better than such a taste of imprisonment as might, by the public outcry it would occasion, bring the law rattling down about the ears of the mandarins who should have enacted it.

"And whatever one may think of the narrowness of the mind-curers, their logical position is impregnable. They are proving by the most brilliant new results that the therapeutic relation may be what we can at present describe only as a relation of one person to another person; and they are consistent in resisting to the uttermost any legislation that would make 'examinable' information the root of medical virtue, and hamper the free play of personal force and affinity by mechanically imposed conditions."

James knew as well as anyone that in the ranks of the healers there were many who could fairly be described as preying on superstition and ignorance. "X—— personally is a rapacious humbug" was his privately expressed opinion of one of them who had a very large following. He had no reverence for the preposterous theories with which their minds were befogged; but "every good thing like *science* in medicine," as he once said, "has to be imitated and grimaced by a rabble of people who would be at the required height; and the folly, humbug and mendacity is pitiful." Furthermore he saw a quackery quite as odious and much more dangerous than that of the "healers" in the patent-medicine business, which was allowed to advertise its lies and secret nostrums in the newspapers and on the billboards, and which flourished behind the counter of every apothecary and village storekeeper at that time. (The Federal Pure Food and Drug Act was still many years off.)

The spokesmen of the medical profession were ignoring what he believed to be instructive phenomena. "What the real interests of medicine require is that mental therapeutics should *not* be stamped out, but studied, and its laws ascertained. For that the mind-curers must at least be suffered to make their experiments. If they cannot interpret their results aright, why then let the orthodox M.D.s follow up their facts, and study and interpret them. But to force the mind-curers to a State examination is to kill the experiments outright." But instead of the open-minded attitude which he thus advocated, he saw doctors who "had no more exact science in them than a fox terrier" invoking the holy name of Science and blundering ahead with an air of moral superiority.

"One would suppose," he exclaimed again in the 1898 hearing, "that any set of sane persons interested in the growth of medical truth would rejoice if other persons were found willing to push out their experiences in the mental-healing direction, and provide a mass of material out of which the conditions and limits of such therapeutic methods may at last become clear. One would suppose that our orthodox medical brethren might so rejoice; but instead of rejoicing they adopt the fiercely partisan attitude of a powerful trades-union, demanding legislation against the competition of 'scabs.' . . . The mind-curers and their public return the scorn of the regular profession with an equal scorn, and will never come up for the examination. Their movement is a religious or quasi-religious movement; personality is one condition of success there, and impressions and intuitions seem to accomplish more than chemical, anatomical or physiological information. . . . Pray do not fail, Mr. Chairman, to catch my point. You are not to ask yourselves whether these mind-curers do really achieve the successes that are claimed. It is enough for you as legislators to ascertain that a large number of our citizens, persons as intelligent and well educated as yourself, or I, persons whose number seems daily to increase, are convinced that they do achieve them, are persuaded that a valuable new department of medical experience is by them opening up. Here is a purely medical question, regarding which our General Court, not being a well-spring and source of medical virtue, not having any private test of therapeutic truth, must remain strictly neutral under penalty of making the confusion worse . . . Above all things, Mr. Chairman, let us not be infected with the Gallic spirit of regulation and reglementation for their own abstract sakes. Let us not grow hysterical about law-making. Let us not fall in love with enactments and penalties because they are so logical and sound so pretty, and look so nice on paper." [7]

The relationship of mental healing, psychical research, and religion in James's attitude is a clear one. To him all of them were similar manifestations of vastly important and little-understood areas of the human mind and its powers, which must be investigated by any means at our disposal if progress in understanding was to be achieved. To his own consideration of all of them he brought his pragmatic philosophy and his insistence that a thing was not necessarily untrue simply because it conflicted with known principles of science. In psychic phenomena *something* happened even

[7] Ibid., Vol. II, pp. 67 ff.

though it was still impossible to know exactly what or how. In mental healing there were undeniably cases in which healing occurred through the influence of mind over matter—whether the mind was that of the healer or the patient. In religion there were realities to the one who experienced it deeply which bore fruits in a good and satisfying life.

Renouvier's philosophy of spontaneity was an aspect of a still larger movement of thought within him. He was more and more convinced that the threadbare abstractions which characterized German idealistic philosophy and British idealistic philosophy almost to the same degree could make no real contact with the tough, vital, throbbing, everyday realities with which our immediate life is concerned. Always give us realities, give us facts, give us concreteness. In later years, for example, when asked to tell what "pragmatism" was really about, he stressed the fact that it dealt with the practical *and the concrete,* and that if one must choose between the two, to be concrete was even more important than to be practical. He was moving toward "radical empiricism," the habit of thrusting oneself forward into the world of experience, to make the richest possible contact with the concrete, the immediate, the real.

The extraordinary series of lectures that he gave at Edinburgh in 1901, which appeared in the volume *The Varieties of Religious Experience,* is a consummation of this faith in the importance of the concrete and the personal. Religion is to be judged not in terms of the abstract representation of an invisible world, but in terms of the living fiber of its substance as we feel it moving through us; and even the mystic is to be understood in terms of the kinds of reality with which he makes contact, the "window" into an unseen world, said James, upon which one's own personal vision depends. As R. B. Perry put it in his final evaluation of James, James always "knew there was more." [8] No summary, no scheme can ever contain the creative totality of the real. Indeed, those last extraordinary ten years of his life from 1900 to 1910, in which he turned out such

[8] Op. cit., Vol. II, p. 704.

14   WILLIAM JAMES ON PSYCHICAL RESEARCH

a series of epoch-making philosophical contributions, represent the
constantly changing, many-faceted expression of his determination
to make contact everywhere with the concrete and the vital. He
never constructed a *system* of philosophy. He wrote many psy-
chologies and many philosophies; it was evidently his wish to let
posterity decide what it could use.

The interest in psychical research came, then, as a perfectly
normal and "predictable" response to this kind of attitude toward
life. In the home environment one did not laugh at the claims of
Swedenborg. One studied them, played with them, tossed them
about, rejected some aspects of them, took other aspects more
seriously, just as one did with regard to Christian Science, or any
of the other new winds of doctrine that swept through the intellectual atmosphere. Questions about telepathy or survival were
just as reasonable as any other kind of question. Such questions
were not to be decided *a priori*, or in deferential regard for authority, but by recourse to rigorous investigation. When, therefore,
the Society for Psychical Research was founded in London in 1882
under the able leadership of scholars of the stature of Henry Sidgwick, Sir William Barrett, and Frederic Myers, he shared warmly
in the whole enterprise. Shortly thereafter he played a leading
part in forming an American Society for Psychical Research, which
after a few years became the American Branch of the London Society. (The present American Society for Psychical Research later
replaced this American Branch.)

During these years William James was eagerly and actively concerned with the investigations by these societies into alleged
hauntings, apparitions, and communications with the deceased. He
himself was drawn as early as 1885 to investigate the extraordinary
phenomena of Mrs. L. E. Piper, who was purported while in deep
trance to give information to sitters regarding which she could
have had no normal knowledge. In the first sittings which he held,
sometimes in the company of his wife, highly personal material was
given which he and his wife were morally certain could never have
been known normally to Mrs. Piper—indeed some of which was

apparently known to no living person but themselves. Other sitters
had similar success. His impressions of these early sittings were reported in 1890 to his friend Frederic Myers in a letter which is
reprinted in this book.

The evidence furnished by Mrs. Piper did not establish for William James any *prima facie* case for survival as such, but it indicated, as he said over and over again, a "lightning stroke" of conviction that there were received by the medium's mind many items
which she had never normally acquired. He continued to have
sittings through his life. He did not hesitate to go out to Concord
to see the curious physical phenomena produced by Mr. Foss, in
whose home the table charged about in the darkness like a wild
beast, and he made it his business to keep informed regarding
Mrs. Piper, through the extensive reports offered by Richard Hodgson. He was in the meantime closely following the studies of
phantasms of the living and of the dead, and the whole realm of
phenomena to which his friend Frederic Myers was applying the
conception of the "subliminal self." In his review of Myers's post-
humous treatise, *Human Personality and Its Survival of Bodily
Death*, he wrote: "Anyone with a healthy sense for evidence, a
sense not methodically blunted by the sectarianism of 'Science,'
ought now, it seems to me, to feel that exalted sensibilities and
memories, veridical phantasms, haunted houses, trances with supernormal faculty, and even experimental thought-transference, are
natural kinds of phenomenon which ought, just like other natural
events, to be followed up with scientific curiosity." [9]

In 1905 Richard Hodgson suddenly died. It soon became James's
task to edit and report upon the long series of communications
purporting to come from the deceased Hodgson through the trance
communications of Mrs. Piper. Here he poured himself into a
systematic and critical task of editing and evaluation, in which
both the strength and the weakness of the evidence for the surviving personality of Hodgson were carefully appraised.

---

[9] *Proceedings of the Society for Psychical Research*, Vol. XVIII, 1903. The
review is reprinted elsewhere in this book.

Since Hodgson had been very well known to psychical research and to Mrs. Piper personally, the problem of evidential communication regarding his continued existence beyond death was an extraordinarily difficult one. Let us hasten to add that the Hodgson-control is by no means one of the strongest in terms of evidence for survival; there is not a great deal of first-class material, and there is a great deal of sheer talking which the living Hodgson would certainly not have taken seriously as survival evidence.

The final verdict (see pp. 197–210) was that the representation of his deceased friend, and the evidence given of his personal identity, was of such a sort as to suggest that Richard Hodgson himself, or a "spirit counterfeit" of him, was there. But James's whole concluding statement should be noted; it reads as follows:

Fechner in his *Zend-Avesta* and elsewhere assumes that mental and physical life run parallel, all memory-processes being, according to him, coordinated with material processes. If an act of yours is to be consciously remembered hereafter, it must leave traces on the material universe such that when the *traced parts of the said universe systematically enter into activity together* the act is consciously recalled. During your life the traces are mainly in your brain; but after your death, since your brain is gone, they exist in the shape of all the records of your actions which the outer world stores up as the effects, immediate or remote, thereof, the cosmos being in some degree, however slight, made structurally different by every act of ours that takes place in it. Now, just as the air of the same room can be simultaneously used by many different voices for communicating with different pairs of ears, or as the ether of space can carry many simultaneous messages to and from mutually attuned Marconi-stations, so the great continuum of material nature can have certain tracts within it thrown into emphasized activity whenever activity begins in any part or parts of a tract in which the potentiality of such sysmatic activity inheres. The bodies (including of course the brains) of Hodgson's friends who come as sitters, are naturally parts of the material universe which carry some of the traces of his ancient acts. They function as receiving stations, and Hodgson (at one time of his life at any rate) was inclined to suspect that the sitter himself acts "psychometrically," or by his body being what, in the trance-jargon, is called an "influence," in attracting the right spirits and eliciting the right communications from the other side. If, now, the *rest* of the system of physical traces left behind by Hodgson's acts were, by some sort of mutual induction throughout its extent, thrown into gear and made to vibrate all at once, by the presence of such human bodies to the medium, we should have a Hodgson-system active in the cosmos again, and the "conscious aspect" of this vibrating system might be Hodgson's spirit redivivus, and recollecting and willing in a certain momentary way. There seems fair evidence of the reality of psychometry; [10] so that this scheme covers the main phenomena in a vague general way. In particular, it would account for the "confusion" and "weakness" that are such prevalent features: the system of physical traces corresponding to the given spirit would then be only imperfectly aroused. It tallies vaguely with the analogy of energy finding its way from higher to lower levels. The sitter, with his desire to receive, forms, so to speak, a drainage-opening or sink; the medium, with her desire to personate, yields the nearest lying material to be drained off; while the spirit desiring to communicate is shown the way by the current set up, and swells the latter by its own contributions.

It is enough to indicate these various possibilities, which a serious student of this part of nature has to weigh together, and between which his decision must fall. His vote will always be cast (if ever it be cast) by the sense of the dramatic probabilities of nature which the sum total of his experience has begotten in him. *I myself feel as if an external will to communicate were probably there,* that is, I find myself doubting, in consequence of my whole acquaintance with that sphere of phenomena, that Mrs. Piper's dream-life, even equipped with "telepathic" powers, accounts for all the results found. But if asked whether the will to communicate be Hodgson's, or be some mere spirit-counterfeit of Hodgson, I remain uncertain and await more facts, facts which may not point clearly to a conclusion for fifty or a hundred years.[11]

---

[10] Myers defined this as: "The use of an object associated with the communicator, usually held in the sensitive's hand, to bring the communicator closer or to facilitate communication from him."

[11] "Report on Mrs. Piper's Hodgson-Control," in *Proceedings of the Society for Psychical Research,* Vol. XXVIII, 1909. The report is reprinted elsewhere in this book.

Thus, while he had early and repeatedly expressed his conviction regarding the reality of telepathy, he apparently never reached conviction on the question of the evidence for survival. One finds, nevertheless, a constant insistence on the legitimacy and importance of the inquiry. Indeed, he had published a little book on *Human Immortality* in 1898 [12] in which he had suggested that perhaps the brain acts as a transmitter rather than an originator of mental processes, so that the deceased may perfectly well be able to carry on a trans-physical existence. He believed, however, that Frederic Myers's studies of the "subliminal consciousness" showed such a vast array of paranormal powers possessed by the deeper strata of the living personality that it is difficult to tell which, if any, phenomena of trance mediumship, or of psychical research in general, may require an interpretation transcending the action of these deeper subliminal powers.

But it was not simply the research that James carried on, nor the views he expressed, which gave him the permanent place which he holds in psychical research. It was in large measure the courage and energy with which he stressed the importance of these inquiries; his eager insistence upon the definitive nature of the evidence that at least telepathy exists; his demand that the instruments of such research, such as spiritualist mediums, be respected, honored, and studied with an open mind; his emphatic recognition and *insistence* that an organized type of research enterprise must be set up, with continuity over the years; his deep conviction that a long-range empirical investigation, rather than anybody's religious or philosophical opinion, was the only guide which a thoughtful and literate public could accept. He believed that, regardless of the question whether the demonstration of continued existence beyond death is ever possible, psychical research has epoch-making implications for the extension of our understanding about the deeper levels of personality, and of the relation of personality to the universe in which it is placed.

---

[12] *Human Immortality: Two Supposed Objections to the Doctrine.* Boston: Houghton Mifflin and Company, 1898. Reprinted elsewhere in this book.

I

---•---

EARLY IMPRESSIONS

On March 22, 1869, William James wrote to his brother Henry: "I wrote a notice of a book on spiritualism (Planchette) *for the* Advertiser *and got $10.00!" James was then twenty-seven years old and a senior in the Harvard Medical School.*

It was not until seventeen years later, in 1885, after his first meeting with the famous Boston medium Mrs. Piper, that his serious interest in psychical research was aroused and reflected in research and contributions to literature on the subject.

The review of Planchette, *which appeared in the* Boston Daily Advertiser *on March 10, 1869, could scarcely be called a contribution to the literature of psychical research, but it is included here as the first public expression of interest and as a fragmentary expression of a point of view which was later to be stated more eloquently and with greater profundity.*

REVIEW OF "PLANCHETTE"

The pretty little book whose title we give [here], and of which Mr. Epes Sargent is known as the author, is a brief general history or treatise of so-called spiritualistic phenomena, the particular

19

instrument, planchette, which gives the name to the whole, being disposed of in very few lines.

The work is entertaining, and characterized by a perfect freedom from extravagance of manner or opinion, its contents mainly consisting of quotations from other writers—either reports of "manifestations," or discussions polemical and speculative as to their cause. The author himself, to be sure, appears at intervals, corroborating "things seen and heard," or applauding and reinforcing, sometimes with a good deal of epigrammatic force, the theoretic arguments of the authorities on whose shoulders he seems to have preferred to rest the burden of his cause; but his mind is not felt through the book, as if it had grasped the subject as a whole with any degree of energy. This feebleness of handling, although in a literary point of view a defect, is nevertheless probably fitted to render the book all the more popular. A reader of scientific habits of thought would have been more interested by a very few cases described by the author over his own signature, and with every possible detail given, in which pedantically minute precautions had been taken against illusion of the senses or deceit. Of course it is quite natural that people who are comfortably in possession of a season ticket over the Stygian ferry, and daily enjoying the privileges it confers of correspondence with the "summer-land," should grow out of all sympathy with the critical vigilance and suspicion about details which characterize the intellectual condition of the "Sadducees," as our author loves to call the earthbound portion of the community. From his snug home in an atmosphere in which pianos float, "soft warm hands" bud forth from vacant space, and lead pencils write alone, the spiritualist has a right to feel a personal disdain for the "scientific man" who stands inertly aloof in his pretentious enlightenment. Scientific men seem to demand that spiritualists should *come* and demonstrate to them the truth of their doctrine, by something little short of a surgical operation upon their intellects. But the spiritualist, from his point of view, is quite justified in leaving them forever on their "laws of nature," unconverted, since he no way needs their countenance.

But an author writing avowedly for purposes of propagandism should have recognized more fully the attitude of this class, and recollected that one narrative personally vouched for and *minutely* controlled would be more apt to fix their attention than a hundred of the striking but comparatively vaguely reported second-hand descriptions which fill many of the pages of this book. The present attitude of society on this whole question is as extraordinary and anomalous as it is discreditable to the pretensions of an age which prides itself on enlightenment and the diffusion of knowledge. We see tens of thousands of respectable people on the one hand admitting as facts of everyday certainty what tens of thousands of others equally respectable claim to be abject and contemptible delusion; while other tens of thousands are content to stand passively in the dark between these two hosts and in doubt, the matter meanwhile being—rightfully considered—one of really transcendent interest. In this state of things recrimination is merely lost time. Those people who have the interests of truth at heart should remember that personal dignity is of very little comparative consequence. If our author, in concert with some good mediums, had instituted some experiments in which everything should be protected from the possibility of deceit, remembering that the morality of no one in such a case is to be taken for granted, and that such personal precautions cannot be offensively construed, he would probably have made a better contribution to clearing up the subject than he has now done.

Perhaps after all, though, even such evidence would be ineffectual. The attitude of the average carnal mind toward the "manifestations" seems to be pretty well expressed by the words quoted from a Mr. Bell, who described some of Home's wonders in the *Cornhill Magazine:* "I refuse to believe such things upon the evidence of other people's eyes; and I may possibly go so far as to protest that I would not believe them even on the evidence of my own. *When I have seen them,* however, I am compelled to regard the subject from an entirely different point of view." Our author probably considers that if what has already been published is not sufficient to convince, no possible addition to it could help it, ocular evidence being alone adequate. It is pretty certain that a mere admission of the facts in dispute on the testimony of others would bear little scientific fruit. If true they should be actively embraced in one conception with the other facts of the universe, and no one can at present conceive of them in this vivid natural way without much personal familiarity. As the book before us is written from a much less esoteric point of view than most other publications dealing with the same subject, it will doubtless awaken the curiosity of many outsiders, the very looseness of the treatment forming a part of its attractiveness.

To the "*cui bono*" objection to spiritualism the author in many places replies, and often with much sarcastic point. "What is the use"—he quotes from Franklin—"of a new-born baby?" Certainly, *from the scientific point of view,* few things can be imagined more idiotic than Faraday's demand, in a letter fixing the preliminary conditions of an interview which some persons tried to bring about between him and the medium Home: "If the effects are miracles, or the work of spirits, does he [Home] admit the utterly contemptible character both of them and their results, up to the present time, in respect either of yielding information or instruction, or supplying any force or action of the least value to mankind?" But, *from the point of view of ordinary human interest,* and as opposed to the jubilation which the spiritualist circles themselves keep up, we must confess to a certain sympathy with the dictum of the *Saturday Review:* "If this is the spirit-world, it is much better to be a respectable pig and accept annihilation, than to be cursed with such an immortality." The existence of the phenomena as a class once being granted, we fail to discover among all the facts given in *Planchette* a single one possessing either aesthetic beauty, intellectual originality, or material usefulness.

The latter half of the book is occupied by quotations from various authors, concerning the philosophy of spiritualism, much of it being that serene, optimistic musing "into the blue," in which the sect seems chiefly to delight, and which the reader may obtain by the

bucketful, if he wish, in the *Banner of Light*. It remains quite detached from the other scientific and philosophical problems of the
day, except perhaps in the case of a single extract from Mr. S. G.
Finney, "one of the most eloquent of American mediums"; but we
are not told whether the words quoted from him were delivered
in the trance state or not.

To sum up, we hope sincerely that this little book will succeed in
waking up a few capable and critical people, whose authority will
help along a reconciliation. The phenomena seem in their present
state to pertain more to the sphere of the disinterested student of
nature than to that of the ordinary layman. It is certain that, if once
admitted, they must make a great revolution in our conception of
the physical universe; but that being done, they would seem to
have no more claim on the attention of each particular individual,
than any of the special problems of organic chemistry, for instance,
or of pathological anatomy.

II

---•---

GENERAL STATEMENTS

William James's interest in psychical research, once it had been aroused by his contact with Mrs. Piper and researchers whom he respected, ranged over the entire field. Nothing was too trivial to escape his attention; nothing too fantastic to warrant his examination and the testing of his keenly analytical mind. His contributions to the literature of the subject consist of both general statements (with illustrations to illustrate specific remarks) and detailed reports on individual manifestations.

The three major contributions which follow, and the letters, are chosen as general statements to give the reader an over-all view of the subject and an understanding of William James's comprehensive consideration of it.

WHAT PSYCHICAL RESEARCH HAS ACCOMPLISHED [1]

"The great field for new discoveries," said a scientific friend to me the other day, "is always the unclassified residuum." Round about the accredited and orderly facts of every science there ever floats

[1] This essay is formed of portions of an article in *Scribner's* magazine for March 1890, of an article in the *Forum* for July 1892, and of the President's Address before the Society for Psychical Research, published in the *Proceedings* for June 1896 and in *Science.*—W. J. It was first published in the present form in 1897, in *The Will to Believe and Other Essays.*—ED.

25

a sort of dust-cloud of exceptional observations, of occurrences minute and irregular and seldom met with, which it always proves more easy to ignore than to attend to. The ideal of every science is that of a closed and completed system of truth. The charm of most sciences to their more passive disciples consists in their appearing, in fact, to wear just this ideal form. Each one of our various *ologies* seems to offer a definite head of classification for every possible phenomenon of the sort which it professes to cover; and so far from free is most men's fancy, that, when a consistent and organized scheme of this sort has once been comprehended and assimilated, a different scheme is unimaginable. No alternative, whether to whole or parts, can any longer be conceived as possible. Phenomena unclassifiable within the system are therefore paradoxical absurdities, and must be held untrue. When, moreover, as so often happens, the reports of them are vague and indirect; when they come as mere marvels and oddities rather than as things of serious moment—one neglects or denies them with the best of scientific consciences. Only the born geniuses let themselves be worried and fascinated by these outstanding exceptions, and get no peace till they are brought within the fold. Your Galileos, Galvanis, Fresnels, Purkinjes, and Darwins are always getting confounded and troubled by insignificant things. Anyone will renovate his science who will steadily look after the irregular phenomena. And when the science is renewed, its new formulas often have more of the voice of the exceptions in them than of what were supposed to be the rules.

No part of the unclassified residuum has usually been treated with a more contemptuous scientific disregard than the mass of phenomena generally called *mystical*. Physiology will have nothing to do with them. Orthodox psychology turns its back upon them. Medicine sweeps them out; or, at most, when in an anecdotal vein, records a few of them as "effects of the imagination"—a phrase of mere dismissal, whose meaning, in this connection, it is impossible to make precise. All the while, however, the phenomena are there, lying broadcast over the surface of history. No matter where you open its pages, you find things recorded under the name of divinations, inspirations, demoniacal possessions, apparitions, trances, ecstasies, miraculous healings and productions of disease, and occult powers possessed by peculiar individuals over persons and things in their neighborhood. We suppose that "mediumship" originated in Rochester, New York, and animal magnetism with Mesmer; but once look behind the pages of official history, in personal memoirs, legal documents, and popular narratives and books of anecdote, and you will find that there never was a time when these things were not reported just as abundantly as now. We college-bred gentry, who follow the stream of cosmopolitan culture exclusively, not infrequently stumble upon some old-established journal, or some voluminous native author, whose names are never heard of in *our* circle, but who number their readers by the quarter-million. It always gives us a little shock to find this mass of human beings not only living and ignoring us and all our gods, but actually reading and writing and cogitating without ever a thought of our canons and authorities. Well, a public no less large keeps and transmits from generation to generation the traditions and practices of the occult; but academic science cares as little for its beliefs and opinions as you, gentle reader, care for those of the readers of the *Waverley* and the *Fireside Companion*. To no one type of mind is it given to discern the totality of truth. Something escapes the best of us—not accidentally, but systematically, and because we have a twist. The scientific-academic mind and the feminine-mystical mind shy from each other's facts, just as they fly from each other's temper and spirit. Facts are there only for those who have a mental affinity with them. When once they are indisputably ascertained and admitted, the academic and critical minds are by far the best fitted ones to interpret and discuss them—for surely to pass from mystical to scientific speculations is like passing from lunacy to sanity; but on the other hand if there is anything which human history demonstrates, it is the extreme slowness with which the ordinary academic and critical mind acknowledges facts to exist which present themselves as wild facts, with no stall or pigeonhole, or as facts which

threaten to break up the accepted system. In psychology, physiology, and medicine, wherever a debate between the mystics and
the scientifics has been once for all decided, it is the mystics who
have usually proved to be right about the *facts,* while the scientifics
had the better of it in respect to the theories. The most recent and
flagrant example of this is "animal magnetism," whose facts were
stoutly dismissed as a pack of lies by academic medical science the
world over, until the non-mystical theory of "hypnotic suggestion"
was found for them—when they were admitted to be so excessively
and dangerously common that special penal laws, forsooth, must
be passed to keep all persons unequipped with medical diplomas
from taking part in their production. Just so stigmatizations, invul-
nerabilities, instantaneous cures, inspired discourses, and demoniacal
possessions, the records of which were shelved in our libraries but
yesterday in the alcove headed "superstitions," now, under the
brand-new title of "cases of hystero-epilepsy," are republished, re-
observed, and reported with an even too credulous avidity.

Repugnant as the mystical style of philosophizing may be (especially when self-complacent), there is no sort of doubt that it goes
with a gift for meeting with certain kinds of phenomenal experience. The writer of these pages has been forced in the past few
years to this admission; and he now believes that he who will pay
attention to facts of the sort dear to mystics, while reflecting upon
them in academic-scientific ways, will be in the best possible position to help philosophy. It is a circumstance of good augury that
certain scientifically trained minds in all countries seem drifting
to the same conclusion. The Society for Psychical Research has been
one means of bringing science and the occult together in England
and America; and believing that this Society fulfills a function
which, though limited, is destined to be not unimportant in the
organization of human knowledge, I am glad to give a brief account
of it to the uninstructed reader.

According to the newspaper and drawing-room myth, soft-headed-
ness and idiotic credulity are the bond of sympathy in this Society,
and general wonder-sickness its dynamic principle. A glance at

the membership fails, however, to corroborate this view. The president is Professor Henry Sidgwick,[2] known by his other deeds as the most incorrigibly and exasperatingly critical and skeptical mind in England. The hard-headed Arthur Balfour is one vice-president, and the hard-headed Professor J. P. Langley, secretary of the Smithsonian Institution, is another. Such men as Professor Lodge, the eminent English physicist, and Professor Richet, the eminent French physiologist, are among the most active contributors to the Society's *Proceedings;* and through the catalogue of membership are sprinkled names honored throughout the world for their scientific capacity. In fact, were I asked to point to a scientific journal where hard-headedness and never-sleeping suspicion of sources of error might be seen in their full bloom, I think I should have to fall back on the *Proceedings of the Society for Psychical Research.* The common run of papers, say on physiological subjects, which one finds in other professional organs, are apt to show a far lower level of critical consciousness. Indeed, the rigorous canons of evidence applied a few years ago to testimony in the case of certain "mediums" led to the secession from the Society of a number of spiritualists. Messrs. Stainton Moses and A. R. Wallace, among others, thought that no experiences based on mere eyesight could ever have a chance to be admitted as true, if such an impossibly exacting standard of proof were insisted on in every case.

The S. P. R., as I shall call it for convenience, was founded in 1882 by a number of gentlemen, foremost among whom seem to have been Professors Sidgwick, W. F. Barrett, and Balfour Stewart, and Messrs. R. H. Hutton, Hensleigh Wedgwood, Edmund Gurney, and F. W. H. Myers. Their purpose was twofold—first, to carry on systematic experimentation with hypnotic subjects, mediums, clairvoyants, and others; and, secondly, to collect evidence concerning apparitions, haunted houses, and similar phenomena which are incidentally reported, but which, from their fugitive character, admit of no deliberate control. Professor Sidgwick, in his introductory address, insisted that the divided state of public opinion on all

---

[2] Written in 1891.—W. J.

these matters was a scandal to science—absolute disdain on
a priori grounds characterizing what may be called professional
opinion, while indiscriminate credulity was too often found among
those who pretended to have a first-hand acquaintance with the
facts.

As a sort of weather bureau for accumulating reports of such
meteoric phenomena as apparitions, the S. P. R. has done an immense amount of work. As an experimenting body, it cannot be
said to have completely fulfilled the hopes of its founders. The
reasons for this lie in two circumstances: first, the clairvoyant and
other subjects who will allow themselves to be experimented upon
are few and far between; and, secondly, work with them takes an
immense amount of time, and has had to be carried on at odd intervals by members engaged in other pursuits. The Society has not
yet been rich enough to control the undivided services of skilled
experimenters in this difficult field. The loss of the lamented Edmund Gurney, who more than anyone else had leisure to devote,
has been so far irreparable. But were there no experimental work
at all, and were the S. P. R. nothing but a weather bureau for catching sporadic apparitions, etc., in their freshness, I am disposed to
think its function indispensable in the scientific organism. If any
one of my readers, spurred by the thought that so much smoke must
needs betoken fire, has ever looked into the existing literature of
the supernatural for proof, he will know what I mean. This literature is enormous, but it is practically worthless for evidential purposes. Facts enough are cited, indeed; but the records of them are
so fallible and imperfect that at most they lead to the opinion that
it may be well to keep a window open upon that quarter in one's
mind.

In the S. P. R.'s *Proceedings,* on the contrary, a different law pre-
vails. Quality, and not mere quantity, is what has been mainly kept
in mind. The witnesses, where possible, have in every reported case
been cross-examined personally, the collateral facts have been
looked up, and the story appears with its precise coefficient of
evidential worth stamped on it, so that all may know just what its

weight as proof may be. Outside of these *Proceedings,* I know of
no systematic attempt to *weigh* the evidence for the supernatural.
This makes the value of the volumes already published unique; and
I firmly believe that as the years go on and the ground covered
grows still wider, the *Proceedings* will more and more tend to
supersede all other sources of information concerning phenomena
traditionally deemed occult. Collections of this sort are usually best
appreciated by the rising generation. The young anthropologists
and psychologists who will soon have full occupancy of the stage
will feel how great a scientific scandal it has been to leave a great
mass of human experience to take its chances between vague tradition and credulity on the one hand and dogmatic denial at long
range on the other, with no body of persons extant who are willing
and competent to study the matter with both patience and rigor.
If the Society lives long enough for the public to become familiar
with its presence, so that any apparition, or house or person in-
fested with unaccountable noises or disturbances of material objects, will as a matter of course be reported to its officers, we shall
doubtless end by having a mass of facts concrete enough to theorize
upon. Its sustainers, therefore, should accustom themselves to the
idea that its first duty is simply to exist from year to year and per-
form this recording function well, though no conclusive results of
any sort emerge at first. All our learned societies have begun in
some such modest way.

But one cannot by mere outward organization make much progress in matters scientific. Societies can back men of genius, but can
never take their place. The contrast between the parent Society and
the American Branch illustrates this. In England, a little group of
men with enthusiasm and genius for the work supplied the nucleus;
in this country, Mr. Hodgson had to be imported from Europe before any tangible progress was made. What perhaps more than
anything else has held the Society together in England is Professor
Sidgwick's extraordinary gift of inspiring confidence in diverse sorts
of people. Such tenacity of interest in the result and such absolute
impartiality in discussing the evidence are not once in a century

found in an individual. His obstinate belief that there is something
yet to be brought to light communicates patience to the discouraged;
his constitutional inability to draw any precipitate conclusion re-
assures those who are afraid of being dupes. Mrs. Sidgwick—a sister,
by the way, of the great Arthur Balfour—is a worthy ally of her
husband in this matter, showing a similarly rare power of holding
her judgment in suspense, and a keenness of observation and capacity for experimenting with human subjects which are rare in either
sex.

The *worker* of the Society, as originally constituted, was Edmund
Gurney. Gurney was a man of the rarest sympathies and gifts. Although, like Carlyle, he used to groan under the burden of his
labors, he yet exhibited a colossal power of dispatching business
and getting through drudgery of the most repulsive kind. His two
thick volumes on *Phantasms of the Living,* collected and published
in three years, are a proof of this. Besides this, he had exquisite
artistic instincts, and his massive volume on *The Power of Sound*
was, when it appeared, the most important work on aesthetics in
the English language. He had also the tenderest heart and a mind
of rare metaphysical power, as his volumes of essays, *Tertium
Quid,* will prove to any reader. Mr. Frederic Myers, already well
known as one of the most brilliant of English essayists, is the *in-
genium praefervidum* of the S. P. R. Of the value of Mr. Myers's
theoretic writings I will say a word later. Dr. Hodgson, the American secretary, is distinguished by a balance of mind almost as rare
in its way as Sidgwick's. He is persuaded of the reality of many of
the phenomena called spiritualistic, but he also has uncommon
keenness in detecting error; and it is impossible to say in advance
whether it will give him more satisfaction to confirm or to smash
a given case offered to his examination.

It is now time to cast a brief look upon the actual contents of
these *Proceedings*. The first two years were largely taken up with
experiments in thought-transference. The earliest lot of these were
made with the daughters of a clergyman named Creery, and con-

vinced Messrs. Balfour Stewart, Barrett, Myers, and Gurney that the girls had an inexplicable power of guessing names and objects thought of by other persons. Two years later, Mrs. Sidgwick and Mr. Gurney, recommencing experiments with the same girls, detected them signaling to each other. It is true that for the most part the conditions of the earlier series had excluded signaling, and it is also possible that the cheating may have grafted itself on what was originally a genuine phenomenon. Yet Gurney was wise in abandoning the entire series to the skepticism of the reader. Many critics of the S. P. R. seem out of all its labors to have heard only of this case. But there are experiments recorded with upwards of thirty other subjects. Three were experimented upon at great length during the first two years: one was Mr. G. A. Smith; the other two were young ladies in Liverpool in the employment of Mr. Malcolm Guthrie.

It is the opinion of all who took part in these latter experiments that sources of conscious and unconscious deception were sufficiently excluded, and that the large percentage of correct reproductions by the subjects of words, diagrams, and sensations occupying other persons' consciousness were entirely inexplicable as results of chance. The witnesses of these performances were in fact all so satisfied of the genuineness of the phenomena that "telepathy" has figured freely in the papers of the *Proceedings* and in Gurney's book on phantasms as a *vera causa* on which additional hypotheses might be built. No mere reader can be blamed, however, if he demand, for so revolutionary a belief, a more overwhelming bulk of testimony than has yet been supplied. Any day, of course, may bring in fresh experiments in successful picture-guessing. But meanwhile, and lacking that, we can only point out that the present data are strengthened in the flank, so to speak, by all observations that tend to corroborate the possibility of other kindred phenomena, such as telepathic impression, clairvoyance, or what is called "test-mediumship." The wider genus will naturally cover the narrower species with its credit.

Gurney's papers on hypnotism must be mentioned next. Some of them are less concerned with establishing new facts than with analyzing old ones. But omitting these, we find that in the line of pure observation Gurney claims to have ascertained in more than one subject the following phenomenon: The subject's hands are thrust through a blanket, which screens the operator from his eyes, and his mind is absorbed in conversation with a third person. The operator meanwhile points with his finger to one of the fingers of the subject, which finger alone responds to this silent selection by becoming stiff or anesthetic, as the case may be. The interpretation is difficult, but the phenomenon, which I have myself witnessed, seems authentic.

Another observation made by Gurney seems to prove the possibility of the subject's mind being directly influenced by the operator's. The hypnotized subject responds, or fails to respond, to questions asked by a third party according to the operator's silent permission or refusal. Of course, in these experiments all obvious sources of deception were excluded. But Gurney's most important contribution to our knowledge of hypnotism was his series of experiments on the automatic writing of subjects who had received post-hypnotic suggestions. For example, a subject during trance is told that he will poke the fire in six minutes after waking. On being waked he has no memory of the order, but while he is engaged in conversation his hand is placed on a planchette, which immediately writes the sentence, "P., you will poke the fire in six minutes." Experiments like this, which were repeated in great variety, seem to prove that below the upper consciousness the hypnotic consciousness persists, engrossed with the suggestion and able to express itself through the involuntarily moving hand.

Gurney shares, therefore, with Janet and Binet, the credit of demonstrating the simultaneous existence of two different strata of consciousness, ignorant of each other, in the same person. The "extra-consciousness," as one may call it, can be kept on tap, as it were, by the method of automatic writing. This discovery marks a new era in experimental psychology, and it is impossible to overrate its importance. But Gurney's greatest piece of work is his laborious *Phantasms of the Living*. As an example of the drudgery stowed away in the volumes, it may suffice to say that in looking up the proofs for the alleged physical phenomena of witchcraft, Gurney reports a careful search through two hundred and sixty books on the subject, with the result of finding no first-hand evidence recorded in the trials except the confessions of the victims themselves; and these, of course, are presumptively due to either torture or hallucination. This statement, made in an unobtrusive note, is only one instance of the care displayed throughout the volumes. In the course of these, Gurney discusses about seven hundred cases of apparitions which he collected. A large number of these were "veridical," in the sense of coinciding with some calamity happening to the person who appeared. Gurney's explanation is that the mind of the person undergoing the calamity was at that moment able to impress the mind of the percipient with a hallucination.

Apparitions, on this "telepathic" theory, may be called "objective" facts, although they are not "material" facts. In order to test the likelihood of such veridical hallucinations being due to mere chance, Gurney instituted the "census of hallucinations," which has been continued with the result of obtaining answers from over twenty-five thousand persons, asked at random in different countries whether, when in good health and awake, they had ever heard a voice, seen a form, or felt a touch which no material presence could account for. The result seems to be, roughly speaking, that in England about one adult in ten has had such an experience at least once in his life, and that of the experiences themselves a large number coincide with some distant event. The question is, Is the frequency of these latter cases too great to be deemed fortuitous, and must we suppose an occult connection between the two events? Mr. and Mrs. Sidgwick have worked out this problem on the basis of the English returns, seventeen thousand in number, with a care and thoroughness that leave nothing to be desired. Their conclusion is that the cases where the apparition of a person is seen on the day of his death are four hundred and forty times too numerous to be ascribed to chance. The reasoning employed to calculate this number is simple enough. If there be only a fortuitous connection between the death of an individual and the occurrence of his apparition to someone at a distance, the death is no more likely to fall on the same day as the apparition than it is to occur on the same day with any other event in nature. But the chance-probability that any individual's death will fall on any given day marked in advance by some other event is just equal to the chance-probability that the individual will die at all on any specified day; and the national death-rate gives that probability as one in nineteen thousand. If, then, when the death of a person coincides with an apparition of the same person, the coincidence be merely fortuitous, it ought not to occur oftener than once in nineteen thousand cases. As a matter of fact, however, it does occur (according to the census) once in forty-three cases, a number (as aforesaid) four hundred and forty times too great. The American census, of some seven thousand answers, gives a remarkably similar result. Against this conclusion the only rational answer that I can see is that the data are still too few; that the net was not cast wide enough; and that we need, to get fair averages, far more than twenty-four thousand answers to the census question. This may, of course, be true, though it seems exceedingly unlikely; and in our own twenty-four thousand answers veridical cases may possibly have heaped themselves unduly.

The next topic worth mentioning in the *Proceedings* is the discussion of the physical phenomena of mediumship (slate-writing, furniture moving, and so forth) by Mrs. Sidgwick, Mr. Hodgson, and "Mr Davey." This, so far as it goes, is destructive of the claims of all the mediums examined. "Mr Davey" himself produced fraudulent slate-writing of the highest order, while Mr. Hodgson, a "sitter" in his confidence, reviewed the written reports of the series of his other sitters—all of them intelligent persons—and showed that in every case they failed to see the essential features of what was done before their eyes. This Davey-Hodgson contribution is probably the most damaging document concerning eye-witnesses' evidence that has ever been produced. Another substantial bit of work based on personal observation is Mr. Hodgson's report on Madame Blavatsky's claims to physical mediumship. This is adverse to the lady's pretensions; and although some of Madame Blavatsky's friends make light of it, it is a stroke from which her reputation will not recover.

Physical mediumship in all its phases has fared hard in the *Proceedings*. The latest case reported on is that of the famous Eusapia Paladino, who being detected in fraud at Cambridge, after a brilliant career of success on the Continent, has, according to the Draconian rules of method which govern the Society, been ruled out from a further hearing. The case of Stainton Moses, on the other hand, concerning which Mr. Myers has brought out a mass of unpublished testimony, seems to escape from the universal condemnation, and appears to force upon us what Mr. Andrew Lang calls the choice between a moral and a physical miracle.

In the case of Mrs. Piper, not a physical but a trance medium, we seem to have no choice offered at all. Mr. Hodgson and others have made prolonged study of this lady's trances, and are all convinced that supernormal powers of cognition are displayed therein. These are *prima facie* due to "spirit-control." But the conditions are so complex that a dogmatic decision either for or against the spirit hypothesis must as yet be postponed.

One of the most important experimental contributions to the *Proceedings* is the article of Miss X. on "Crystal Vision." Many persons who look fixedly into a crystal or other vaguely luminous surface fall into a kind of daze, and see visions. Miss X. has this susceptibility in a remarkable degree, and is, moreover, an unusually intelligent critic. She reports many visions which can only be described as apparently clairvoyant, and others which beautifully fill a vacant niche in our knowledge of subconscious mental operations. For example, looking into the crystal before breakfast one morning she reads in printed characters of the death of a lady of her acquaintance, the date and other circumstances all duly appearing in type. Startled by this, she looks at the *Times* of the previous day for verification, and there among the deaths are the identical words which she has seen. On the same page of the *Times* are other items which she remembers reading the day before; and the only explanation seems to be that her eyes then inattentively observed, so to speak, the death items, which forthwith fell into a special corner of her memory, and came out as a visual hallucination when the peculiar modification of consciousness induced by the crystal-gazing set in.

Passing from papers based on observation to papers based on narrative, we have a number of ghost stories, etc., sifted by Mrs. Sidgwick and discussed by Messrs. Myers and Podmore. They form the best ghost literature I know of from the point of view of emotional interest. As to the conclusions drawn, Mrs. Sidgwick is rigorously noncommittal, while Mr. Myers and Mr. Podmore show themselves respectively hospitable and inhospitable to the notion that such stories have a basis of objectivity dependent on the continued existence of the dead.

I must close my gossip about the *Proceedings* by naming what, after all, seems to me the most important part of its contents. This is the long series of articles by Mr. Myers on what he now calls the "subliminal self," or what one might designate as ultramarginal consciousness. The result of Myers's learned and ingenious studies in hypnotism, hallucinations, automatic writing, mediumship, and the whole series of allied phenomena is a conviction which he expresses in the following terms:

> Each of us is in reality an abiding psychical entity far more extensive than he knows—an individuality which can never express itself completely through any corporeal manifestation. The self manifests itself through the organism; but there is always some part of the self unmanifested, and always, as it seems, some power of organic expression in abeyance or reserve.

The ordinary consciousness Mr. Myers likens to the visible part of the solar spectrum; the total consciousness is like that spectrum prolonged by the inclusion of the ultra-red and ultra-violet rays. In the psychic spectrum the "ultra" parts may embrace a far wider range, both of physiological and of psychical activity, than is open to our ordinary consciousness and memory. At the lower end we have the *physiological* extension, mind-cures, "stigmatization" of ecstatics, etc.; in the upper, the hyper-normal cognitions of the medium-trance. Whatever the judgment of the future may be on Mr. Myers's speculations, the credit will always remain to them of being the first attempt in any language to consider the phenomena of hallucination, hypnotism, automatism, double personality, and mediumship as connected parts of one whole subject. All constructions in this field must be provisional, and it is as something provisional that Mr. Myers offers us his formulations. But, thanks to him, we begin to see for the first time what a vast interlocked and graded system these phenomena, from the rudest motor-automatisms to the most startling sensory apparition, form. Quite apart from Mr. Myers's conclusions, his methodical treatment of them by classes and series is the first great step toward overcoming the distaste of orthodox science to look at them at all.

One's reaction on hearsay testimony is always determined by one's own experience. Most men who have once convinced themselves, by what seems to them a careful examination, that any one species of the supernatural exists, begin to relax their vigilance as to evidence, and throw the doors of their minds more or less wide open to the supernatural along its whole extent. To a mind that has thus made its *salto mortale*, the minute work over insignificant cases and quiddling discussion of "evidential values" of which the Society's reports are full seem insufferably tedious. And it is so; few species of literature are more truly dull than reports of phantasms. Taken simply by themselves, as separate facts to stare at, they appear so devoid of meaning and sweep that, even were they certainly true, one would be tempted to leave them out of one's universe for being so idiotic. Every other sort of fact has some context and continuity with the rest of nature. These alone are contextless and discontinuous.

Hence I think that the sort of loathing—no milder word will do —which the very words "psychical research" and "psychical researcher" awaken in so many honest scientific breasts is not only natural, but in a sense praiseworthy. A man who is unable himself to conceive of any *orbit* for these mental meteors can only suppose that Messrs. Gurney, Myers, & Company's mood in dealing with them must be that of silly marveling at so many detached prodigies. And such prodigies! So science simply falls back on her general *non-possumus;* and most of the would-be critics of the *Proceedings* have been contented to oppose to the phenomena recorded the simple presumption that in some way or other the reports *must* be fallacious—for so far as the order of nature has been subjected to really scientific scrutiny, it always has been proved to run the other way. But the oftener one is forced to reject an alleged sort of fact by the use of this mere presumption, the weaker does the presumption itself get to be; and one might in course of time use up one's presumptive privileges in this way, even though one started (as our anti-telepathists do) with as good a case as the great induction of psychology that all our knowledge comes by the use of our eyes and ears and other senses. And we must remember also that this undermining of the strength of a presumption by reiterated report of facts to the contrary does not logically require that the facts in question should all be well proved. A lot of rumors in the air against a business man's credit, though they might all be vague, and no one of them amount to proof that he is unsound, would certainly weaken the *presumption* of his soundness. And all the more would they have this effect if they formed what Gurney called a fagot and not a chain—that is, if they were independent of one another, and came from different quarters. Now, the evidence for telepathy, weak and fitting, taken just as it comes, forms a fagot and not a chain. No one item cites the content of another item as part of its own proof. But taken together the items have a certain general consistency; there is a method in their madness, so to speak. So each of them adds presumptive value to the lot; and cumulatively, as no candid mind can fail to see, they subtract presumptive force from the orthodox belief that there can be nothing in anyone's intellect that has not come in through ordinary experiences of sense.

But it is a miserable thing for a question of truth to be confined to mere presumption and counter-presumption, with no decisive thunderbolt of fact to clear the baffling darkness. And, sooth to say, in talking so much of the merely presumption-weakening value of our records, I have myself been willfully taking the point of view of the so-called "rigorously scientific" disbeliever, and making an *ad hominem* plea. My own point of view is different. For me the thunderbolt *has* fallen, and the orthodox belief has not merely had its presumption weakened, but the truth itself of the belief is decisively overthrown. If I may employ the language of the professional logic-shop, a universal proposition can be made untrue by a particular instance. If you wish to upset the law that all crows are black, you must not seek to show that no crows are; it is enough if you prove one single crow to be white. My own white crow is Mrs. Piper. In the trances of this medium, I cannot resist the conviction that knowledge appears which she has never gained by the ordinary waking use of her eyes and ears and wits. What the source of this knowledge may be I know not, and have not the glimmer of an explanatory suggestion to make; but from admitting the fact of such knowledge I can see no escape. So when I turn to the rest of the evidence, ghosts and all, I cannot carry with me the irreversibly negative bias of the "rigorously scientific" mind, with its presumption as to what the true order of nature ought to be. I feel as if, though the evidence be flimsy in spots, it may nevertheless collectively carry heavy weight. The rigorously scientific mind may, in truth, easily overshoot the mark. Science means, first of all, a certain dispassionate method. To suppose that it means a certain set of results that one should pin one's faith upon and hug forever is sadly to mistake its genius, and degrades the scientific body to the status of a sect.

We all, scientists and non-scientists, live on some inclined plane of credulity. The plane tips one way in one man, another way in another; and may he whose plane tips in no way be the first to cast a stone! As a matter of fact, the trances I speak of have broken down for my own mind the limits of the admitted order of nature. Science, so far as science denies such exceptional occurrences, lies prostrate in the dust for me; and the most urgent intellectual need which I feel at present is that science be built up again in a form in which such things may have a positive place. Science, like life, feeds on its own decay. New facts burst old rules; then newly divined conceptions bind old and new together into a reconciling law.

And here is the real instructiveness of Messrs. Myers and Gurney's work. They are trying with the utmost conscientiousness to find a reconciling conception which shall subject the old laws of nature to the smallest possible strain. Mr. Myers uses that method of gradual approach which has performed such wonders in Darwin's hands. When Darwin met a fact which seemed a poser to his theory, his regular custom, as I have heard an able colleague say, was to fill in all round it with smaller facts, as a wagoner might heap dirt round a big rock in the road, and thus get his team over without upsetting. So Mr. Myers, starting from the most ordinary facts of inattentive consciousness, follows this clue through a long series which terminates in ghosts, and seeks to show that these are but extreme manifestations of a common truth—the truth that the invisible segments of our minds are susceptible, under rarely realized conditions, of acting and being acted upon by the invisible segments of other conscious lives. This may not be ultimately true (for the theosophists, with their astral bodies and the like, may, for aught I now know, prove to be on the scientifer trail), but no one can deny that it is in good scientific form—for science always takes a known kind of phenomenon, and tries to extend its range.

I have myself, as American agent for the census, collected hundreds of cases of hallucination in healthy persons. The result is to make me feel that we all have potentially a "subliminal" self, which may make at any time irruption into our ordinary lives. At its lowest, it is only the depository of our forgotten memories; at its highest, we do not know what it is at all. Take, for instance, a series of cases. During sleep, many persons have something in them which measures the flight of time better than the waking self does. It wakes them at a preappointed hour; it acquaints them with the moment when they first awake. It may produce a hallucination— as in a lady who informs me that at the instant of waking she has a vision of her watch-face with the hands pointing (as she has often verified) to the exact time. It may be the feeling that some physiological period has elapsed; but, whatever it is, it is subconscious.

A subconscious something may also preserve experiences to which we do not openly attend. A lady taking her lunch in town finds herself without her purse. Instantly a sense comes over her of rising from the breakfast table and hearing her purse drop upon the floor. On reaching home she finds nothing under the table, but summons the servant to say where she has put the purse. The servant produces it, saying: "How did you know where it was? You rose and left the room as if you didn't know you'd dropped it." The same subconscious something may recollect what we have forgotten. A lady accustomed to taking salicylate of soda for muscular rheumatism wakes one early winter morning with an aching neck. In the twilight she takes what she supposes to be her customary powder from a drawer, dissolves it in a glass of water, and is about to drink it down, when she feels a sharp slap on her shoulder and hears a voice in her ear saying, "Taste it!" On examination, she finds she has got a morphine powder by mistake. The natural interpretation is that a sleeping memory of the morphine powders awoke in this quasi-explosive way. A like explanation offers itself as most plausible for the following case: A lady, with little time to catch the train, and the expressman about to call, is excitedly looking for the lost key of a packed trunk. Hurrying upstairs with a bunch of keys, proved useless, in her hand, she hears an "objective" voice distinctly say, "Try the key of the cake-box." Being tried, it fits. This also may well have been the effect of forgotten experience.

Now, the effect is doubtless due to the same hallucinatory mecha-

nism; but the source is less easily assigned as we ascend the scale
of cases. A lady, for instance, goes after breakfast to see about one
of her servants who has become ill overnight. She is startled at distinctly reading over the bedroom door in gilt letters the word
"smallpox." The doctor is sent for, and ere long pronounces smallpox to be the disease, although the lady says, "The thought of
the girl's having smallpox never entered my mind till I saw the apparent inscription." Then come other cases of warning; for example, that of a youth sitting in a wagon under a shed, who suddenly
hears his dead mother's voice say, "Stephen, get away from here
quick!" and jumps out just in time to see the shed roof fall.

After this come the experiences of persons appearing to distant
friends at or near the hour of death. Then, too, we have the trance
visions and utterances, which may appear astonishingly profuse and
continuous, and maintain a fairly high intellectual level. For all
these higher phenomena, it seems to me that while the proximate
mechanism is that of "hallucination," it is straining a hypothesis
unduly to name any ordinary subconscious mental operation—
such as expectation, recollection, or inference from inattentive
perception—as the ultimate cause that starts it up. It is far better
tactics, if you wish to get rid of mystery, to brand the narratives
themselves as unworthy of trust. The trustworthiness of most of
them is to my own mind far from proved. And yet in the light of the
medium-trance, which *is* proved, it seems as if they might well all
be members of a natural kind of fact of which we do not yet know
the full extent.

Thousands of sensitive organizations in the United States today
live as steadily in the light of these experiences, and are as indifferent to modern science, as if they lived in Bohemia in the twelfth
century. They are indifferent to science, because science is so cal-
lously indifferent to their experiences. Although in its essence
science only stands for a method and for no fixed belief, yet as
habitually taken, both by its votaries and outsiders, it is identified
with a certain fixed belief—the belief that the hidden order of nature is mechanical exclusively, and that non-mechanical categories

are irrational ways of conceiving and explaining even such things as human life. Now, this mechanical rationalism, as one may call it, makes, if it becomes one's only way of thinking, a violent breach with the ways of thinking that have played the greatest part in human history. Religious thinking, ethical thinking, poetical thinking, teleological, emotional, sentimental thinking, what one might call the personal view of life to distinguish it from the impersonal and mechanical, and the romantic view of life to distinguish it from the rationalistic view, have been, and even still are, outside of well-drilled scientific circles, the dominant forms of thought. But for mechanical rationalism, personality is an insubstantial illusion. The chronic belief of mankind, that events may happen for the sake of their personal significance, is an abomination; and the notions of our grandfathers about oracles and omens, divinations and apparitions, miraculous changes of heart and wonders worked by inspired persons, answers to prayer and providential leadings, are a fabric absolutely baseless, a mass of sheer *un*truth.

Now, of course, we must all admit that the excesses to which the romantic and personal view of nature may lead, if wholly unchecked by impersonal rationalism, are direful. Central African Mumbo-Jumboism is one of unchecked romanticism's fruits. One ought accordingly to sympathize with that abhorrence of romanticism as a sufficient world-theory; one ought to understand that lively intolerance of the least grain of romanticism in the views of life of other people, which are such characteristic marks of those who follow the scientific professions today. Our debt to science is literally boundless, and our gratitude for what is positive in her teachings must be correspondingly immense. But the S. P. R.'s *Proceedings* have, it seems to me, conclusively proved one thing to the candid reader; and that is that the verdict of pure insanity, of gratuitous preference for error, of superstition without an excuse, which the scientists of our day are led by their intellectual training to pronounce upon the entire thought of the past, is a most shallow verdict. The personal and romantic view of life has other roots besides wanton exuberance of imagination and perversity of heart. It is perennially fed by *facts of experience,* whatever the ulterior interpretation of those facts may prove to be; and at no time in human history would it have been less easy than now—at most times it would have been much more easy—for advocates with a little industry to collect in its favor an array of contemporary documents as good as those which our publications present. These documents all relate to real experiences of persons. These experiences have three characters in common: They are capricious, discontinuous, and not easily controlled; they require peculiar persons for their production; their significance seems to be wholly for personal life. Those who preferentially attend to them, and still more those who are individually subject to them, not only easily may find, but are logically bound to find, in them valid arguments for their romantic and personal conception of the world's course. Through my slight participation in the investigations of the S. P. R. I have become acquainted with numbers of persons of this sort, for whom the very word "science" has become a name of reproach, for reasons that I now both understand and respect. It is the intolerance of science for such phenomena as we are studying, her peremptory denial either of their existence or of their significance (except as proofs of man's absolute innate folly), that has set science so apart from the common sympathies of the race. I confess that it is on this, its humanizing mission, that the Society's best claim to the gratitude of our generation seems to me to depend. It has restored continuity to history. It has shown some reasonable basis for the most superstitious aberrations of the foretime. It has bridged the chasm, healed the hideous rift that science, taken in a certain narrow way, has shot into the human world.

I will even go one step farther. When from our present advanced standpoint we look back upon the past stages of human thought, whether it be scientific thought or theological thought, we are amazed that a universe which appears to us of so vast and mysterious a complication should ever have seemed to anyone so little and plain a thing. Whether it be Descartes' world or Newton's, whether it be that of the materialists of the last century or that of the Bridgewater treatises of our own, it always looks the same to us—incredibly perspectiveless and short. Even Lyell's, Faraday's, Mill's, and Darwin's consciousness of their respective subjects are already beginning to put on an infantile and innocent look. Is it then likely that the science of our own day will escape the common doom; that the minds of its votaries will never look old-fashioned to the grandchildren of the latter? It would be folly to suppose so. Yet if we are to judge by the analogy of the past, when our science once becomes old-fashioned, it will be more for its omissions of fact, for its ignorance of whole ranges and orders of complexity in the phenomena to be explained, than for any fatal lack in its spirit and principles. The spirit and principles of science are mere affairs of method; there is nothing in them that need hinder science from dealing successfully with a world in which personal forces are the starting-point of new effects. The only form of thing that we directly encounter, the only experience that we concretely have, is our own personal life. The only complete category of our thinking, our professors of philosophy tell us, is the category of personality, every other category being one of the abstract elements of that. And this systematic denial on science's part of personality as a condition of events, this rigorous belief that in its own essential and innermost nature our world is a strictly impersonal world, may, conceivably, as the whirligig of time goes round, prove to be the very defect that our descendants will be most surprised at in our own boasted science, the omission that to their eyes will most tend to make *it* look perspectiveless and short.

ON MEDIUMSHIP [1]

In *"mediumships"* or *"possessions"* the invasion and the passing away of the secondary state are both relatively abrupt, and the duration of the state is usually short—i.e., from a few minutes to a

[1] From *The Principles of Psychology*, Vol. I, pp. 393–400. Reprinted by arrangement with Henry Holt & Company.—ED.

few hours. Whenever the secondary state is well developed no memory for aught that happened during it remains after the primary consciousness comes back. The subject during the secondary consciousness speaks, writes, or acts as if animated by a foreign person, and often names this foreign person and gives his history. In old times the foreign "control" was usually a demon, and is so now in communities which favor that belief. With us he gives himself out at the worst for an Indian or other grotesquely speaking but harmless personage. Usually he purports to be the spirit of a dead person known or unknown to those present, and the subject is then what we call a "medium." Mediumistic possession in all its grades seems to form a perfectly natural special type of alternate personality, and the susceptibility to it in some form is by no means an uncommon gift, in persons who have no other obvious nervous anomaly. The phenomena are very intricate, and are only just beginning to be studied in a proper scientific way. The lowest phase of mediumship is automatic writing, and the lowest grade of that is where the subject knows what words are coming, but feels impelled to write them as if from without. Then comes writing unconsciously, even whilst engaged in reading or talk. Inspirational speaking, playing on musical instruments, etc., also belong to the relatively lower phases of possession, in which the normal self is not excluded from conscious participation in the performance, though their initiative seems to come from elsewhere. In the highest phase the trance is complete, the voice, language, and everything are changed, and there is no after-memory whatever until the next trance comes. One curious thing about trance utterances is their generic similarity in different individuals. The "control" here in America is either a grotesque, slangy, and flippant personage ("Indian" controls, calling the ladies "squaws," the men "braves," the house a "wigwam," etc., etc., are excessively common); or, if he ventures on higher intellectual flights, he abounds in a curiously vague optimistic philosophy-and-water, in which phrases about spirit, harmony, beauty, law, progression, development, etc., keep recurring. It seems exactly as if one author composed more than half of the trance messages, no matter by whom they are uttered. Whether all subconscious selves are peculiarly susceptible to a certain stratum of the *Zeitgeist* and get their inspiration from it, I know not; but this is obviously the case with secondary selves which become "developed" in spiritualist circles. There the beginnings of the medium trance are indistinguishable from effects of hypnotic suggestion. The subject assumes the role of a medium simply because opinion expects it of him under the conditions which are present; and carries it out with a feebleness or a vivacity proportionate to his histrionic gifts. But the odd thing is that persons unexposed to spiritual traditions will so often act in the same way when they become entranced, speak in the name of the departed, go through the motions of their several death-agonies, send messages about their happy home in the summer-land, and describe the ailments of those present. I have no theory to publish of these cases, several of which I have personally seen.

As an example of the automatic writing performances I will quote from an account of his own case kindly furnished me by Mr. Sidney Dean of Warren, Rhode Island, member of Congress from Connecticut from 1855 to 1859, who has been all his life a robust and active journalist, author, and man of affairs. He has for many years been a writing subject, and has a large collection of manuscript automatically produced.

Some of it [he writes us], is in hieroglyph, or strange compounded arbitrary characters, each series possessing a seeming unity in general design or character, followed by what purports to be a translation or rendering into mother English. I never attempted the seemingly impossible feat of copying the characters. They were cut with the precision of a graver's tool, and generally with a single rapid stroke of the pencil. Many languages, some obsolete and passed from history, are professedly given. To see them would satisfy you that no one could copy them except by tracing.

These, however, are but a small part of the phenomena. The "automatic" has given place to the *impressional*, and when the work is in progress I am in the normal condition, and seemingly two minds, intelligences, persons, are practically engaged. The writing is in my own hand but the dictation not of my own mind and will, but that of another, upon subjects of which I can have no knowledge and hardly a theory; and I, myself, consciously criticise the thought, fact, mode of expressing it, etc., while the hand is recording the subject-matter and even the words impressed to be written. If *I* refuse to write the sentence, or even the word, the impression instantly ceases, and my willingness must be mentally expressed before the work is resumed, and it is resumed at the point of cessation, even if it should be in the middle of a sentence. Sentences are commenced without knowledge of mine as to their subject or ending. In fact, I have never known in advance the subject of disquisition.

There is in progress now, at uncertain times, not subject to my will, a series of twenty-four chapters upon the scientific features of life, moral, spiritual, eternal. Seven have already been written in the manner indicated. These were preceded by twenty-four chapters relating generally to the life beyond material death, its characteristics, etc. Each chapter is signed by the name of some person who has lived on earth—some with whom I have been personally acquainted, others known in history. . . . I know nothing of the alleged authorship of any chapter until it is completed and the name impressed and appended. . . . I am interested not only in the reputed authorship—of which I have nothing corroborative —but in the philosophy taught, of which I was in ignorance until these chapters appeared. From my standpoint of life—which has been that of biblical orthodoxy—the philosophy is new, seems to be reasonable, and is logically put. I confess to an inability to successfully controvert it to my own satisfaction.

It is an intelligent *ego* who writes, or else the influence assumes individuality, which practically makes of the influence a personality. It is *not* myself, of that I am conscious at every step of the process. I have also traversed the whole field of claims of "unconscious cerebration," so called, so far as I am competent to critically examine it, and it fails, as a theory, in numberless points, when applied to this strange work through me. It would be far more reasonable and satisfactory for me to accept the silly hypothesis of re-incarnation—the old doctrine of metempsychosis— as taught by some spiritualists to-day, and to believe that I lived a former life here, and that once in a while it dominates my intellectual powers, and writes chapters upon the philosophy of life, or opens a post-office for spirits to drop their effusions, and have them put into English script. No; the easiest and most natural solution to me is to admit the claim made, i.e., that it is a decarnated intelligence who writes. But *who?* that is the question. The names of scholars and thinkers who once lived are affixed to the most ungrammatical and weakest of *bosh.* . . .

It seems reasonable to me—upon the hypothesis that it is a person using another's mind or brain—that there must be more or less of that other's style or tone incorporated in the message, and that to the unseen personality, i.e., the power which impresses, the thought, the fact, or the philosophy, and not the style or tone, belongs. For instance, while the influence is impressing my brain with the greatest force and rapidity, so that my pencil fairly flies over the paper to record the thoughts, I am conscious that, in many cases, the vehicle of the thought, i.e., the language, is very natural and familiar to me, as if, somehow, *my* personality as a writer was getting mixed up with the message. And, again, the style, language, everything, is entirely foreign to my own style.

I am myself persuaded by abundant acquaintance with the trances of one medium that the "control" may be altogether different from any *possible* waking self of the person. In the case I have in mind, it professes to be a certain departed French doctor; and is, I am convinced, acquainted with facts about the circumstances, and the living and dead relatives and acquaintances, of numberless sitters whom the medium never met before, and of whom she has never heard the names. I record my bare opinion here unsupported by the evidence, not, of course, in order to convert anyone to my view, but because I am persuaded that a serious study of these trance phenomena is one of the greatest needs of psychology, and think that my personal confession may possibly draw a reader or two into a field which the *soi-disant* "scientist" usually refuses to explore.

Many persons have found evidence conclusive to their minds that in some cases the control is really the departed spirit whom it pretends to be. The phenomena shade off so gradually into cases where this is obviously absurd, that the presumption (quite apart from *a priori* "scientific" prejudice) is great against its being true.

The case of Lurancy Vennum is perhaps as extreme a case of "possession" of the modern sort as one can find. Lurancy was a young girl of fourteen, living with her parents at Watseka, Illinois, who (after various distressing hysterical disorders and spontaneous trances, during which she was possessed by departed spirits of a more or less grotesque sort) finally declared herself to be animated by the spirit of Mary Roff (a neighbor's daughter, who had died in an insane asylum twelve years before) and insisted on being sent "home" to Mr. Roff's house. After a week of "homesickness" and importunity on her part, her parents agreed, and the Roffs, who pitied her, and who were spiritualists into the bargain, took her in. Once there, she seems to have convinced the family that their dead Mary had exchanged habitations with Lurancy. Lurancy was said to be temporarily in heaven, and Mary's spirit now controlled her organism, and lived again in her former earthly home.

The girl, now in her new home, seemed perfectly happy and content, knowing every person and everything that Mary knew when in her original body, twelve to twenty-five years ago, recognizing and calling by name those who were friends and neighbors of the family from 1852 to 1865, when Mary died, calling attention to scores, yes, hundreds of incidents that transpired during her natural life. During all the period of her sojourn at Mr. Roff's she had no knowledge of, and did not recognize, any of Mr. Vennum's family, their friends or neighbors, yet Mr. and Mrs. Vennum and their children visited her and Mr. Roff's people, she being introduced to them as to any strangers. After frequent visits, and hearing them often and favorably spoken of, she learned to love them as acquaintances, and visited them with Mrs. Roff three times. From day to day she appeared natural, easy, affable, and industrious, attending diligently and faithfully to her household duties, assisting in the general work of the family as a faithful, prudent daughter might be supposed to do, singing, reading, or conversing as opportunity offered, upon all matters of private or general interest to the family.

The so-called Mary whilst at the Roffs' would sometimes "go back to heaven," and leave the body in a "quiet trance," i.e., without the original personality of Lurancy returning. After eight or nine weeks, however, the memory and manner of Lurancy would sometimes partially, but not entirely, return for a few minutes. Once Lurancy seems to have taken full possession for a short time. At last, after some fourteen weeks, conformably to the prophecy which "Mary" had made when she first assumed "control," she departed definitively and the Lurancy-consciousness came back for good. Mr. Roff writes:

She wanted me to take her home, which I did. She called me Mr. Roff, and talked with me as a young girl would, not being acquainted. I asked her how things appeared to her—if they seemed natural. She said it seemed like a dream to her. She met her parents and brothers in a very affectionate manner, hugging and kissing each one in tears of gladness. She clasped her arms around her father's neck a long time, fairly smothering him with kisses. I saw her father just now (eleven o'clock). He says she has been perfectly natural, and seems entirely well.

Lurancy's mother writes, a couple of months later, that she was perfectly and entirely well and natural. For two or three weeks after her return home, she seemed a little strange to what she had been before she was taken sick last summer, but only, perhaps, the natural change that had taken place with the girl, and except it seemed to her as though she had been dreaming or sleeping, etc. Lurancy has been smarter, more intelligent, more industrious, more womanly, and more polite than before. We give the credit of her complete cure and restoration to her family, to Dr. E. W. Stevens, and Mr. and Mrs. Roff, by their obtaining her removal to Mr. Roff's, where her cure was perfected. We firmly believe that, had she remained at home, she would have died, or we would have been obliged to send her to the insane asylum; and if so, that she would have died there; and further, that I could not have lived but a short time with the care and trouble devolving on me. Several of the relatives of Lurancy, including ourselves, now believe she was cured by spirit power, and that Mary Roff controlled the girl.

Eight years later, Lurancy was reported to be married and a mother, and in good health. She had apparently outgrown the mediumistic phase of her existence.

On the condition of the sensibility during these invasions, few observations have been made. I have found the hands of two automatic writers anesthetic during the act. In two others I have found this not to be the case. Automatic writing is usually preceded by shooting pains along the arm nerves and irregular contractions of the arm muscles. I have found one medium's tongue and lips apparently insensible to pin-pricks during her (speaking) trance.

If we speculate on the brain condition during all these different perversions of personality, we see that it must be supposed capable of successively changing all its modes of action, and abandoning the use for the time being of whole sets of well-organized association-paths. In no other way can we explain the loss of memory in passing from one alternating condition to another. And not only this, but we must admit that organized systems of paths can be thrown out of gear with others, so that the processes in one system give rise to one consciousness, and those of another system to another *simultaneously* existing consciousness. Thus only can we understand the facts of automatic writing, etc., whilst the patient is out of trance, and the false anesthesias and amnesias of the hysteric type. But just what sort of dissociation the phrase "thrown out of gear" may stand for, we cannot even conjecture; only I think we ought not to talk of the doubling of the self as if it consisted in the failure to combine on the part of certain systems of *ideas* which usually do so. It is better to talk of *objects* usually combined, and which are now divided between the two "selves," in the hysteric and automatic cases in question. Each of the selves is due to a system of cerebral paths acting by itself. If the brain acted normally, and the dissociated systems came together again, we should get a new affection of consciousness in the form of a third "self" different from the other two, but knowing their objects together, as the result. . . .

Some peculiarities in the lower automatic performances suggest that the systems thrown out of gear with each other are contained one in the right and the other in the left hemisphere. The subjects, e.g., often write backward, or they transpose letters, or they write mirror-script. All these are symptoms of agraphic disease. The left hand, if left to its natural impulse, will in most people write mirror-script more easily than natural script. Mr. F. W. H. Myers has laid stress on these analogies. He has also called attention to the usual inferior moral tone of ordinary planchette writing. On Hughlings Jackson's principles, the left hemisphere, being the more evolved organ, at ordinary times inhibits the activity of the right one; but Mr. Myers suggests that during the automatic performances the usual inhibition may be removed and the right hemisphere set free to act all by itself. This is very likely to some extent to be the case. But the crude explanation of "two" selves by "two" hemispheres is of course far from Mr. Myers's thought. The selves may be more than two, and the brain systems severally used for each must be conceived as interpenetrating each other in very minute ways.

In 1893 F. W. H. Myers invited William James to become President of the Society for Psychical Research in London. James at first declined on the score of ill health, but when urged (and scolded a little) by Myers he wrote a letter of acceptance. Two letters in the correspondence are printed here, partly because they throw additional light on his interest in mental healing.

James served as President of the English Society for two years. His "Address by the President" which follows the letter to Myers was delivered in 1896 when he retired from the presidency. A part of this address was incorporated later in "What Psychical Research Has Accomplished." The repetitions have been eliminated from the "Address by the President."

Letter from F. W. H. Myers, Cambridge, England, November 16, 1893 [2]

My dear James—

I am very sorry that you are feeling ill; but a touch of something is mixed with my sympathy that I may as well have out. It

[2] *The Thought and Character of William James,* by Ralph Barton Perry (Boston: Little, Brown, 1935), Vol. II, pp. 157–58. Copyright 1935 by Henry James. Permission to reprint granted by Paul R. Reynolds and Son.—ED.

seems to me that your mental and physical disorganization and decay is never by any chance perceptible to anyone but *yourself;* and, moreover, that when you are actually in the presence of friends you are able to make an effort (if such it be) which presents you to them as a source of wisdom and delight—"as light and life communicable"; which makes them rather wish that they were even as you, than grieve over any hidden malaise within you—and yet it seems to me that you lack one touch more of *doggedness* which would render you of even more helpfulness in the world than you are. Why on earth should you not in *public* matters act upon other people's view of you and not on your own? We all wanted you to place your name at our head—we should have been satisfied, however little you had actually *done;* why not have let us have our way? To *underrate* one's own importance in the eyes of others may be (though rarer) as great a nuisance to them as it is to *overrate* it. We must not push you further now; but I warn you that we shall ask you again another year, and that unless we have evidence to your decrepitude from someone besides yourself, we shall then take it somewhat unkind if you won't oblige us!

Mrs. Piper is all right—and the universe is all right—and people will soon pay up more money to S. P. R.—and an eternity of happiness and glory awaits you—and I am sure Mrs. James would agree to much in this letter—and the dear spirits are hovering around us in the Summer Land. Yours always,

F. W. H. Myers

Letter to F. W. H. Myers, Cambridge, December 17, 1893 [3]

My dear Myers—

I telegraphed you this morning "James accepts"—the Presidency of the S. P. R. being understood. This is in consequence of a letter from Pearsall Smith informing me that the Council still desire it and regard it as a matter of importance. They are bent on having a King Log, so they shall be humored. I had no idea, when I got your first invitation, that it was a matter of the slightest

---

[3] Ibid., pp. 158–59.

real *importance,* or so regarded by any of you; and I much regretted to perceive, from your reply to my own letter of declination, that the latter, so far as you were concerned, had been a genuine disappointment. Since however in that reply you treated the refusal as definitive and implied that its consequences were then evolving, I have let the matter drop from my own attention. . . . To tell the truth I supposed the true inwardness of the offer to lie in your friendly wish, yours and the Sidgwicks', to pay me a compliment; which friendly wish I thought almost as well acknowledged by "declined with thanks" as by "accepted."

My state of mind is also revolutionized since that time. I had a pretty bad spell, and know now a new kind of melancholy. It is barely possible that the recovery may be due to a mind-curer with whom I tried eighteen sittings. What makes me think so is that I am enjoying an altogether new kind of *sleep,* or rather an old kind which I have been bereft of for so many years that I had forgotten its existence, and considered myself sleeping as well as I ought to, and told her so, when I went to her, saying my only trouble was my mind. . . . Two . . . other cases of brain trouble, intimate friends of mine, treated simultaneously with me, have entirely recovered. It is a good deal of a puzzle. I should like to get this woman into a lunatic asylum for two months, and have every case of chronic delusional insanity in the house tried by her. That would be a real test, and if successful would *have* to produce some effect. I may possibly bring it about yet!

My college work is all-engrossing, as ever. For a presidential address, even, I should be at a loss for matter. When, by the way, is such a thing due? Here nothing goes on but Mrs. Piper—*toujours* Piper! I wish we could unearth a little variety. I appreciate your strictures . . . as to the absence of doggedness in me, but you must remember that tenacity like *yours* is what puts you in the *immortal galaxy* which I have previously enumerated, and that if it were a common possession, you would lose your distinction! . . .

ADDRESS BY THE PRESIDENT [1]

The Presidency of the Society for Psychical Research resembles a mousetrap. Broad is the path and wide is the way that leadeth thereinto. Flattering bait is spread before the entrance: the distinguished names of one's predecessors in the office; the absence of any active duties; England and America symbolically made one in that higher republic where no disputed frontiers or foreign offices exist—and all the rest of it. But when the moment comes to retrace one's steps and go back to private life, like Cincinnatus to his plow, then comes the sorrow, then the penalty for greatness. The careless presidential mouse finds the wires all pointing now against him, and to get out there is no chance, unless he leave some portion of his fur. So in resigning my office to my worthier successor, I send this address to be read across the ocean as my ransom, not unaware, as I write it, that the few things I can say may well fall short of the dignity of the occasion and the needs of the cause for which our Society exists.

Were psychical research as well organized as the other sciences are, the plan of a presidential address would be mapped out in advance. It could be nothing but a report of progress, an account of such new observations and new conceptions as the interim might have brought forth. But our active workers are so few compared with those engaged in more familiar departments of natural learning, and the phenomena we study so fortuitous and occasional, that two years must, as a rule, prove too short an interval for regular accounts of stock to be taken. Looking back, however, on our whole dozen years or more of existence, one can appreciate what solid progress we have made. Disappointing as our career has doubtless been to those of our early members who expected definite corroboration or the final *coup de grâce* to be given in a

---

[1] *Proceedings, Society for Psychical Research* (London), Part XX, Vol. XII, June 1896.—ED.

few short months to such baffling questions as that of physical mediumship, to soberer and less enthusiastic minds the long array of our volumes of *Proceedings* must suggest a feeling of anything but discouragement. For here, for the first time in the history of these perplexing subjects, we find a large collection of records to each of which the editors and reporters have striven to attach its own precise coefficient of evidential value, great or small, by getting at every item of first-hand evidence that could be attained, and by systematically pointing out the gaps. Only those who have tried to reach conclusions of their own by consulting the previous literature of the occult, as vague and useless, for the most part, as it is voluminous, can fully appreciate the immense importance of the new method which we have introduced. Little by little, through consistently following this plan, our *Proceedings* are extorting respect from the most unwilling lookers-on, and I should like emphatically to express my hope that the impartiality and completeness of record which has been their distinguishing character in the past will be held to even more rigorously in the future. It is not as a vehicle of conclusions of our own, but as a collection of documents that may hereafter be resorted to for testing the conclusions and hypotheses of *anybody*, that they will be permanently important. Candor must be their very essence, and all the hesitations and contradictions that the phenomena involve must appear unmitigatedly in their pages. Collections of this sort are usually best appreciated by the rising generation. The young anthropologists and psychologists who will soon have full occupancy of the stage will feel, as we have felt, how great a scientific scandal it has been to leave a great mass of human experience to take its chances between vague tradition and credulity on the one hand and dogmatic denial at long range on the other, with no body of persons extant who are willing and competent to study the matter with both patience and rigor. There have been isolated experts, it is true, before now. But our Society has for the first time made their abilities mutually helpful.

If I were asked to give some sort of dramatic unity to our history, I should say first that we started with high hopes that the hypnotic field would yield an important harvest, and that these hopes have subsided with the general subsidence of what may be called the hypnotic wave. Secondly, I should say that experimental thought-transference has yielded a less abundant return than that which in the first year or two seemed not unlikely to come in. Professor Richet's supposition that if the unexplained thing called thought-transference be ever real, its causes must, to some degree, work in everybody at all times (so that in any long series of card-guessings, for example, there ought always to be some excess of right answers above the chance number) is, I am inclined to think, not very well substantiated. Thought-transference may involve a critical point, as the physicists call it, which is passed only when certain psychic conditions are realized, and otherwise not reached at all—just as a big conflagration will break out at a certain temperature, below which no conflagration whatever, whether big or little, can occur. We have published records of experiments on at least thirty subjects, roughly speaking, and many of these were strikingly successful. But their types are heterogeneous; in some cases the conditions were not faultless; in others the observations were not prolonged; and generally speaking, we must all share in a regret that the evidence, since it has reached the point it *has* reached, should not grow more voluminous still. For whilst it cannot be ignored by the candid mind, it yet, as it now stands, may fail to convince coercively the skeptic. Any day, of course, may bring in fresh experiments in successful picture-guessing. But meanwhile, and looking that, we can only point out that our present data are strengthened in the flank, so to speak, by all observations that tend to corroborate the possibility of other kindred phenomena, such as telepathic impression, clairvoyance, or what is called "test-mediumship." The wider genus will naturally cover the narrower species with its credit. . . .

In the question of physical mediumship, we have left matters as baffling as we found them, neither more nor less. For if, on the one hand, we have brought out new documents concerning the physical miracles of Stainton Moses, on the other hand we have, by the Hodgson-Davey experiments, and the Paladino episode, very largely increased the probability that testimony based on certain sorts of observation may be quite valueless as proof. Eusapia Paladino has been to us both a warning and an encouragement. An encouragement to pursue unwaveringly the rigorous method in such matters from which our *Proceedings* have never departed, and a warning against drawing any prompt inference whatever from things that happen in the dark. The conclusions to which some of us had been hastily led on "the island" melted away when, in Cambridge, the opportunity for longer and more cunning observation was afforded. Some day, it is to be hoped, our *Proceedings* may be enabled to publish a complete study of this woman's life. Whatever were the upshot of such a study, few documents could be more instructive in all ways for psychical research.

It is pleasant to turn from phenomena of the dark-sitting and rathole type (with their tragi-comic suggestion that the whole order of nature might possibly be overturned in one's own head, by the way in which one imagined oneself, on a certain occasion, to be holding a tricky peasant woman's feet) to the "calm air of delightful studies." And on the credit side of our Society's account a heavy entry must next be made in favor of that immense and patient collecting of miscellaneous first-hand documents that alone has enabled Mr. Myers to develop his ideas about automatism and the subliminal self. In Mr. Myers's papers on these subjects we see, for the first time in the history of men's dealings with occult matters, the whole range of them brought together, illustrated copiously with unpublished contemporary data, and treated in a thoroughly scientific way. All constructions in this field must be provisional, and it is as something provisional that Mr. Myers offers us his attempt to put order into the tangle. But, thanks to his genius, we begin to see for the first time what a vast interlocked and graded system these phenomena, from the rudest motor automatisms to the most startling sensory apparition, form. Mr. Myers's methodical treatment of them by classes and series is the first great step toward overcoming the distaste of orthodox science to look at them at all.

But our *Proceedings* contain still other veins of ore for future working. Ghosts, for example, and disturbances in haunted houses. These, whatever else may be said of them at present, are not without bearing on the common scientific presumption of which I have already perhaps said too much. Of course, one is impressed by such narratives after the mode in which one's impressibility is fashioned. I am not ashamed to confess that in my own case, although my *judgment* remains deliberately suspended, my *feeling* toward the way in which the phenomena of physical mediumship should be approached has received from ghost and disturbance stories a distinctly charitable lurch. Science may keep saying: "Such things are simply impossible"; yet, so long as the stories multiply in different lands, and so few are positively explained away, it is bad method to ignore them. They should at least accrete for future use. As I glance back at my reading of the past few years (reading accidental so far as these stories go, since I have never followed up the subject) ten cases immediately rise to my mind. The Phelps case at Andover, recorded by one of the family, in *McClure's Magazine* for this month; a case in China, in Nevius's *Demon Possession*, published last year; the case in John Wesley's life; the "*Amherst Mystery*" in Nova Scotia (New York, 1888); the case in Mr. Willis's house at Fitchburg, recorded in *The Atlantic Monthly* for August, 1868 (XXII., 129); the Telfair-Mackie case, in Sharpe's *History of Witchcraft in Scotland*, the Morse case, in Upham's *Salem Witchcraft;* the case recounted in the introduction of W. v. Humboldt's *Briefe an eine Freundin;* a case in the *Annales des Sciences Psychiques* for last year (p. 86); the case of the carpenter's shop at Swanland, near Hull, in our *Proceedings*, Vol. VII., Part XX., pp. 383-394. In all of these, if memory doesn't deceive me, material objects are said to have been witnessed by many persons moving through the air in broad daylight. Often the objects were multitudinous—in some cases they were stones showered through windows and down-chimney. More than once it was noted that they fell gently and touched the ground without shock. Apart from the exceptionality of the reputed occurrences, their mutual resemblances suggest a natural type, and I confess that until these records, or others like them, are positively explained away, I cannot feel (in spite of such vast amounts of detected fraud) as if the case against physical mediumship itself as a freak of nature were definitively closed. But I admit that one man's psychological reaction cannot here be like unto another's; and one great duty of our Society will be to pounce upon any future case of this "disturbance" type, catch it while red-handed, and nail it fast, whatever its quality be.

We must accustom ourselves more and more to playing the role of a meteorological bureau, be satisfied for many a year to go without definitive conclusions, confident that if we only keep alive and heap up data, the natural types of them (if there are any) will surely crystallize out; whilst old material that is baffling will get settled as we proceed, through its analogy with new material that will come with the baffling character removed. . . .

But these things lie upon the knees of the gods. I must leave them there, and close now this discourse, which I regret that I could not make more short. If it has made you feel that (however it turn out with modern science) our own Society, at any rate, is not "perspectiveless," it will have amply served its purpose; and the next President's address may have more definite conquests to record.

EXTRACTS FROM LETTERS AND A LECTURE

To Thomas Davidson, February 1, 1885 [1]

As for any "anti-spiritual bias" of our Society, no theoretic basis, or *bias* of any sort whatever, so far as I can make out, exists in it. The one thing that has struck me all along in the men who have

---

[1] *The Letters of William James,* edited by his son, Henry James (Boston: Atlantic Monthly Press, 1920), Vol. I, pp. 249–50. Copyright 1920 by Henry James. Permission to reprint granted by Paul R. Reynolds and Son. The letter was in answer to one from Davidson complaining of the "anti-spiritual bias" of the American Society for Psychical Research.—ED.

had to do with it is their complete colorlessness philosophically. They seem to have no preferences for any general *ism* whatever. I doubt if this could be matched in Europe. Anyhow, it would make no difference in the important work to be done, what theoretic bias the members had. For I take it the urgent thing, to rescue us from the present disgraceful condition, is to ascertain in a manner so thorough as to constitute *evidence* that will be accepted by outsiders, just what the *phenomenal conditions of certain* concrete phenomenal occurrences are. Not till that is done can spiritualistic or anti-spiritualistic theories be even mooted. I'm sure that the more we can steer clear of theories at first, the better. The choice of officers was largely dictated by motives of policy. Not that scientific men are necessarily better judges of all truth than others, but that their adhesion would popularly seem better *evidence* than the adhesion of others, in the matter. And what we want is not only truth, but evidence. We shall be lucky if our scientific names don't grow discredited the instant they subscribe to any "spiritual" manifestations. But how much easier to discredit literary men, philosophers, or clergymen! I think Newcomb, for President, was an uncommon hit—if he believes, he will probably carry others. You'd better chip in, and not complicate matters by talking either of spiritualism or anti-spiritualism. *"Facts"* are what are wanted.

To Shadworth Hodgson, August 16, 1885 [2]

We have been stirred up by the English Society for Psychical Research's example, to start a similar society here, in which I am somewhat interested, though less practically than I could wish. Returns come slowly—I mean stuff to inquire into comes slowly, and altogether my small experience has filled me with a prodigious admiration of the devotion and energy of Gurney, Myers, and others with you. Something solid will come of it all, I am sure. By the way, who is Mr. Richard Hodgson? One of your family? I am glad of his demolition of that jade, Blavatsky, but I must say I think his last article in *Mind* rather muddy and ineffectual. . . .

---

[2] Ralph Barton Perry, op. cit., Vol. I, p. 629.—ED.

To Carl Stumpf, January 1, 1886 [3]

I don't know whether you have heard of the London "Society for Psychical Research," which is seriously and laboriously investigating all sorts of "supernatural" matters, clairvoyance, apparitions, etc. I don't know what you think of such work; but I think that the present condition of opinion regarding it is scandalous, there being a mass of testimony, or apparent testimony, about such things, at which the only men capable of a critical judgment—men of scientific education—will not even look. We have founded a similar society here within the year—some of us thought that the publications of the London society deserved at least to be treated as if worthy of experimental disproof—and although work advances very slowly owing to the small amount of disposable time on the part of the members, who are all very busy men, we have already stumbled on some rather inexplicable facts out of which something may come. It is a field in which the sources of deception are extremely numerous. But I believe there is no source of deception in the investigation of nature which can compare with a fixed belief that certain kinds of phenomenon are *impossible*.

To G. Croom Robertson, August 29, 1886 [4]

I have wasted a good deal of time on "Psychical Research" during the past year, and Gurney and I have scribbled a number of notes to each other in consequence. "Two lost souls!" you will say —but that is what remains to be seen. Our poor little "Society" will very likely break down for lack of a Gurney or a Myers to devote time to it. But I feel quite convinced at the end of my year's work, such as it has been, that this sort of work is as worthy a specialty as a man could take up; only it *is* a specialty, demanding an enormous sacrifice of time, and in which amateurs will be as inferior to experts as they are in most other departments of experience. Believing this, I shall probably give very little time to it next

---

[3] Henry James, ed., op. cit., Vol. I, p. 248.—ED.
[4] Ralph Barton Perry, op. cit., Vol. I, p. 602.—ED.

year, because at the utmost I should be a dabbler and amateur. I
wish that by giving up this, I might get ahead with writing, but
I'm once for all a lame duck, and might as well accept it. The moment I get interested in anything, bang goes my sleep, and I have
to stop for ten days or a fortnight, till everything has grown cold
again and the mood is off. One makes very slow progress at that
rate. I am with wife and babes on a quiet farm in the country—
on the whole in prosperous condition, though I sometimes grow
impatient.

To Shadworth Hodgson, September 12, 1886 [5]

. . . I got successfully through the academic year, in spite of the
fact that I wasted a great deal of time on "psychical research" and
had other interruptions from work which I would fain have done.

To G. Croom Robertson, October 4, 1886 [6]

I mailed you t'other day Part II of the *Proceedings* of the American Society for Psychical Research, a rather sorry "exhibit," from
the "President's" address down. There is no one in the Society who
can give any time to it, and I suspect it will die by the new year.
Farewell! keep a stout heart, and a stiff upper lip. Time and the
hour run through the roughest day! Yours ever,

Wm. James

To His Wife, Alice Gibbens James, 1888 [7]

[Apr. 6.] Hodgson and I started after our baggage arrived, to
find Mr. D———, who, you may have seen by the papers, is making
a scandal by having given himself over (hand and foot) to a
medium, "Madam D——— ," who does most extraordinarily described physical performances. We found the old girl herself, a
type for Alexandre Dumas, obese, wicked, jolly, intellectual, with
no end of go and animal spirits, who entertained us for an hour,

[5] Ibid., Vol. I, p. 638.—ED.
[6] Ibid., Vol. II, pp. 41–42.—ED.
[7] Henry James, ed., op. cit., Vol. I, p. 228.—ED.

gave us an appointment for a sitting on Monday, and asked us to come and see Mr. B. tonight. What will come of it all I don't know. It will be baffling, I suppose, like everything else of that kind.

[Apr. 7.] Mr. B. and Mrs. D. were "too tired" to see us last night! I suspect that will be the case next Monday. It is the knowing thing to do under the circumstances. But that woman is one with whom one would fall *wildly* in love, if in love at all—she is such a fat, *fat* old villain. . . .

[Apr. 24th.] In bed at 11:30, after the most hideously inept psychical night, in Charleston, over a much-praised female medium who fraudulently played on the guitar. A plague take all white-livered, anemic, flaccid, weak-voiced Yankee frauds! Give me a full blooded red-lipped villain like dear old D.—when shall I look upon her like again?

To F. W. H. Myers, January 30, 1891 [8]

My dear Myers,—Your letter of the 12th came duly, but not till now have I had leisure to write you a line of reply. Verily you are the stuff of which world-changers are made! What a despot for psychical research! I always feel guilty in your presence, and am, on the whole, glad that the broad blue ocean rolls between us for most of the days of the year; although I should be glad to have it intermit occasionally, on days when I feel particularly larky and indifferent, when I might meet you without being bowed down with shame.

To speak seriously, however, I agree in what you say, that the position I am now in (professorship, book published and all) does give me a very good pedestal for carrying on psychical research effectively, or rather for disseminating its results effectively. I find however that *narratives* are a weariness, and I must confess that the reading of narratives for which I have no personal responsibility is almost intolerable to me. Those that come to me at first-hand, incidentally to the census, I get interested in. Others much less so; and I imagine my case is a very common case. One page of ex-

[8] Ibid., Vol. I, pp. 305–306.—ED.

perimental thought-transference work will "carry" more than a hundred of *Phantasms of the Living*. I shall stick to my share of the latter, however; and expect in the summer recess to work up the results already gained in an article for *Scribner's* magazine, which will be the basis for more publicity and advertising and bring in another bundle of schedules to report on at the Congress. Of course I wholly agree with you in regard to the *ultimate* future of the business, and fame will be the portion of him who may succeed in naturalizing it as a branch of legitimate science. I think it quite on the cards that you, with your singular tenacity of purpose, and wide look at all the intellectual relations of the thing, may live to be the ultra-Darwin yourself. Only the facts are *so* discontinuous so far that possibly all our generation can do may be to get 'em called facts. I'm a bad fellow to investigate on account of my bad memory for anecdotes and other disjointed details. Teaching of students will have to fill most of my time, I foresee; but of course my weather eye will remain open upon the occult world.

Our "Branch," you see, has tided over its difficulties temporarily; and by raising its fee will enter upon the new year with a certain momentum. You'll have to bleed, though, ere the end, devoted creatures that you are, over there!

From a Lecture before The Lowell Institute, Boston, 1896 [9]

[I am] at the portal of psychical research, into which I said I would not enter. But I suppose that it would be over-cautious in me, and disappoint some of my hearers if I did not say here frankly what I think of the relations of the cases I have dwelt on to these supernormal cases. I put forth my impression merely as such, and with great diffidence; the only thing I am absolutely sure of, being the extreme complication of the facts.

Some minds would see a marvel in the simplest hypnosis—others would refuse to admit that there was anything new even if one rose from the dead. They would either deny the apparition, or say you could find a full explanation of it in Foster's *Physiology*.

---

[9] Ralph Barton Perry, op. cit., Vol. II, p. 169.—ED.

Of these minds one pursues idols of the tribe, another of the cave. Both may be right in respect to a portion of the fact. I myself have no question that the formula of dissociated personality will account for the phenomena I have brought before you. Hypnotism is sleep. Hysteria is obsession, not by demons, but by a fixed idea of the person that has dropped down—Janet's phrase suffices here. But to say that is one thing and to *deny any other range* of *phenomena* is another. Whether supernormal powers of cognition in certain persons may occur, is a matter to be decided by evidence. If they can occur, it may be that there must be a chink. The hypnotic condition is not *in itself* clairvoyant, but is *more favorable* to the cause of clairvoyance or thought-transference than the waking state. So alternate personality, the tendency for the self to break up, may, if there be spirit influences, yield them their opportunity. . . . And if there were real demons, they might possess only hysterics. Thus each side may see a portion of the truth.

To James Sully, March 3, 1901 [10]

Yes! H. Sidgwick is a sad loss, with all his remaining philosophic wisdom unwritten. I feel greatly F. W. H. Myers's loss also. He suffered terribly with suffocation, but bore it stunningly well. He died in this very hotel, where he had been not more than a fortnight. I don't know *how* tolerant (or intolerant) you are toward his pursuits and speculations. I regard them as fragmentary and conjectural—of course; but as most laborious and praiseworthy; and knowing how much psychologists as a rule have counted him out from their profession, I have thought it my duty to write a little tribute to his service to psychology to be read on March 8th, at a memorial meeting of the S. P. R. in his honor. It will appear, whether read or not, in the *Proceedings,* and I hope may not appear to you exaggerated. I seriously believe that the general problem of the subliminal, as Myers propounds it, promises to be one of the *great* problems, possibly even the greatest problem, of psychology.

---

[10] Henry James, ed., op. cit., Vol. II, p. 141.—ED.

To Theodore Flournoy, April 30, 1903 [11]

"Billy" . . . says that you have executed a review of Myers's book,[12] finding it a more difficult task than you had anticipated. I am highly curious to see what you have found to say. I, also, wrote a notice of the volumes, and found it exceeding difficult to know how to go at the job. At last I decided just to skeletonize the points of his reasoning, but on correcting the proof just now, what I have written seems deadly flat and unprofitable and makes me wish that I had stuck to my original intention of refusing to review the book at all. The fact is, such a book need not be *criticized* at all at present. It is obviously too soon for it to be either refuted or established by mere criticism. It is a hypothetical construction of genius which must be kept hanging up, as it were, for new observations to be referred to. As the years accumulate these in a more favorable or in a more unfavorable sense, it will tend to stand or to fall. I confess that reading the volumes has given me a higher opinion than ever of Myers's constructive gifts, but on the whole a lower opinion of the objective solidity of the system. So many of the facts which form its pillars are still dubious.[13]

Bill says that you were again convinced by Eusapia,[14] but that the conditions were not satisfactory enough (so I understood) to make the experiments likely to convince absent hearers. Forever baffling is all this subject, and I confess that I begin to lose my interest. Believe me, in whatever difficulties your review of Myers may have occasioned you, you have my fullest sympathy!

---

[11] Ibid., Vol. II, pp. 185–86.—Ed.

[12] *Human Personality and Its Survival of Bodily Death,* by F. W. H. Myers. —H. J.

[13] "The piles driven into the quicksand are too few for such a structure. But it is essential as a preliminary attempt at methodizing, and will doubtless keep a very honorable place in history." To F. C. S. Schiller, April 8, 1903. —H. J.

[14] Eusapia Paladino, the Italian "medium." The physical manifestations which occurred during her trance had excited much discussion.—H. J.

III

———•———

CLAIRVOYANCE, LEVITATION, AND "THE ASTRAL BODY"

The scope of William James's interest in psychical research is demonstrated in the first volume of Proceedings of the American Society for Psychical Research *(1886–89), containing five contributions from him:* "Report of the Committee on Mediumistic Phenomena" *(reprinted elsewhere in this book),* "Report of the Committee on Hypnotism," "Reaction Time in Hypnotic Trance," "The Consciousness of Lost Limbs," *and* "Notes on Automatic Writing," *as well as a* "Report of the Committee on Trance" *signed by him and Gouverneur M. Carnochan.*

The three pieces which follow evidence his interest in three other types of phenomena. The third, which he called "A Possible Case of Projection of the Double," *is interestingly reminiscent of a letter which James had written forty-two years earlier, at the age of twenty-five, to his sister Alice, some time before he had expressed any interest in psychical research.*

"I see now," he wrote on August 14, 1867, "that an instantaneous transportation of the physical man to any distance for any time, is one of the desiderata which science is bound someday to satisfy. It is necessary—human life without it is an absurdity. At that happy distant day we shall be able for a small fee and the wishing to visit

(with all our sense) and be visited by those we love, even as the eagles stoop unto their nests." *

When he wrote this it was a pleasant, fanciful expression of a twenty-five-year-old young man's desire to be with a dearly loved sister, but it is not surprising that the mind from which this fancy emanated should, years later, be interested in an account of the apparent movement through space of an "astral body."

A CASE OF CLAIRVOYANCE [1]

The following case of the recovery of the body of a drowned person in consequence of indications given by a clairvoyant, has been entrusted to me for publication by Dr. Harris Kennedy, of Roxbury, a cousin of my wife. It should have been published in 1899. Dr. Kennedy (whose brother was staying at Lebanon at the time the events happened) got the depositions of the witnesses while the case was still hot; and delay has added nothing to the data for our judgment.

I first subjoin the summarized account drawn up by Dr. Kennedy.

DR. KENNEDY'S ACCOUNT

On Monday, Oct. 31st, 1898, Miss Bertha Huse left her home at Enfield, N. H., at 6 A.M., before the rest of the family had risen. She took her way down the street toward the so-called Shaker Bridge. On her way she was seen by several people, and by one person when she was on the bridge. Her family, learning of her absence, instituted a search for her, and during the greater part of the day 150 men, more or less, hunted the woods and lake shore in that vicinity. This search proving of no avail, Mr. Whitney, a

---

* Ralph Barton Perry, op. cit., Vol. I, p. 243.—Ed.
[1] *Proceedings, the American Society for Psychical Research*, Vol. I, Part II, 1907, pp. 220 ff. The seeming incongruity of two Volumes I of the *Proceedings*, one covering the years 1886 to 1889, and one the one year 1907, is explained by the history of the society. After the publication of the 1886–89 volume the American Society became amalgamated with the Society for Psychical Research in London and discontinued the publication of its *Proceedings*. When an American Society was re-established it began its new series of proceedings with Volume I, published in 1907.—Ed.

mill owner of Enfield, sent to Boston for divers, with a suitable outfit. A diver named Sullivan worked the better part of all Tuesday, and up to Wednesday noon, without success in the lake.

On Wednesday evening, Nov. 2nd, Mrs. Titus, of Lebanon, N. H., a village about four and one-half miles from Enfield, while dozing after supper, aroused the attention of her husband, who was seated near her, by her noises, and extremely horrified countenance. When he spoke to her, she failed to answer, and it was necessary for him to shake her before arousing her to consciousness. When she was conscious, the first thing she said was, "Why did you disturb me? In a moment I should have found that body." After this she told her husband, "If I behave very peculiarly tonight, or cry out, or seem greatly disturbed, do not on any account awaken me, but leave me to myself." At some time during the night Mr. Titus was aroused by the screams of his wife. He got up, lit a lamp, and waited, obeying his wife's instructions. She, during a following interval, though not awake, spoke in substance as follows:

"She followed the road down to the bridge, and on getting part way across it, stepped out onto that jutting beam which was covered with white frost. There she stood undecided whether to go into the water there or go up over the hill to the pond. While so standing, she slipped on the log, fell backwards, and slid in underneath the timber work of the bridge. You will find her lying, head in, and you will only be able to see one of her rubbers projecting from the timber work."

Early in the morning, at her earnest solicitation, her husband went to Mr. Ayer, an employee of the Mascoma Flannel Co., at Lebanon, and asked him for leave to absent himself from the mill that morning, in order to go with his wife to the Shaker Bridge at Enfield. He then told Mr. Ayer the story, substantially as above. Mr. Titus also told the story to Mr. W. R. Sunderlin, as well as to certain other persons, all in Lebanon, before he went with his wife to Enfield, where he told other parties of this occurrence, and asked Mr. Whitney, who had been foremost in the search, to accompany him and his wife to the spot his wife was desirous of investigating. When they reached the bridge, Mrs. Titus pointed out a certain spot where she said they would find the body in the position as above mentioned. Mr. Whitney, who was then one of quite a number at the spot, sent a messenger to get the diver who had been working in the neighborhood of that spot on the previous days. On his arrival Mrs. Titus pointed out to him the spot where she said the body lay. He said, "I searched there yesterday, and found nothing." She said, "Yes, you searched *there,* and *there* [pointing to certain spots], but you did not search *there,* and if you go down, you will find only the rubber of her shoe projecting from the timber work." To satisfy her, he put on his diving suit, and went down at the spot indicated. After a moment or two, the bonnet of the deceased rose to the surface, and shortly after the diver came up bringing the body. The diver then said, "I did not look in this place yesterday, as the brush and debris were so thick there that I could not see; in fact, all I could feel of the body, was the rubber, projecting from the timber work."

Mrs. Titus's grandmother is said to have had a similar power in her day, but Mrs. Titus is not known to have made any pretense of being a clairvoyant, having never used her trances for any pecuniary reward, or for the sake of any notoriety. On the day following, viz., Nov. 4th, Mrs. Titus was ill.

CORROBORATIVE STATEMENTS

Here follow the statements of several of the persons named in the preceding story. They were written down by Dr. Kennedy from their lips a few days after the occurrences, read by him to them, and signed by them as correct.

Mr. Ayer's Statement

On Thursday, A.M., Nov. 3rd, 1898, Mr. George Titus came to the Mascoma Mills. At about 6.15 A.M. he called Mr. J. C. Ayer to one side to tell him the following:

"My wife had three trances last night, in one she caught hold of me, and I tried to pull her away but could not. She then said,

'I know where the girl is. I can find her. The girl went onto the bridge and walked out on a log and then walked back and forth, looking toward the hills. She slipped off and went down backwards. She did not intend to commit suicide. You will find her in the mud, with one foot out.' "

I, J. C. Ayer, have charge of the mill hands, and know both the sister of the girl, Bertha M. Huse, who was drowned, and Mr. Titus. Both of them worked for me in the mill. This story, which I told Dr. Harris Kennedy on Nov. 10, 1898, is, so far as I know, a correct statement of what was told me by Mr. Titus.

[*Signed*] J. C. AYER

Mr. Sunderlin's Statement

Testimony in the Titus case, given by W. R. Sunderlin, at Lebanon, N. H., Dec. 1st., 1898. The following is as told by Sunderlin to Henry L. Briggs, Nov. 11th., and corrected by Sunderlin in presence of Sinclair Kennedy, Dec. 1st.:

On the morning of Thursday, Nov. 3rd, Geo. A. Titus, who keeps a horse in my barn, came into my barn about 5:20, and looking about said, "What, are we alone here. I want to tell you something, but I don't want anyone to overhear me, and you must say nothing of what I am going to tell you. My wife has had a trance, and declares she can tell where to find the body of Bertha Huse. She says she is in the lake (Mascoma) at the east side of Shaker Bridge."

I naturally laughed at the idea, but Titus stuck to his story. Titus told me that on coming upstairs after supper (he lives in the second-story house), he found his wife sitting in a rocking chair, asleep but gesticulating. He aroused her, whereupon she at once said, "O, George, why did you wake me. In a few minutes I could have told you where that girl is. If I go into another trance tonight or any other time, don't disturb me."

They then retired for the night. Along towards 11 or 12, Titus said he was waked by his wife's groans and mutterings. When he lit a lamp, he found his wife in apparent spasms, though still asleep. While so asleep she declared that Bertha Huse would be found in the lake to the east of the bridge, lying head down between two logs, her body covered by mud and brush; but that one foot would be sticking up, on which was a new rubber. That the girl first appeared to her (Mrs. Titus) on the bridge. That she appeared undecided whether to go in at the spot she was on, or from some point further down the bridge. That while standing on a frost-covered log with her back to the water, her foot slipped, and she went into the lake backwards.

Sunderlin continuing said: "I told Titus, 'Well, George, if you and your wife feel this way, you better hitch up and go out to the bridge. And if your wife thinks she is then sure of the spot, drive up to Enfield and see if you can get Whitney interested in this.'"

When Titus came back later in the day, he told me, "When we arrived at the bridge, she got out of the buggy, and walked along the east side of the bridge, looking intently into the lake. Suddenly she stopped, and said, 'George, she is right down there, between those two logs.' She then got into the buggy, and we drove to Whitney's house.

"Mr. Whitney smiled, on hearing the story, but went to the lake with us. My wife went directly to the spot she had pointed out to me, and told Whitney, 'She is right down there.' As her opinion could not be shaken, Whitney brought the diver. The diver shook his head and said, 'I have been down there.' My wife said, 'No, you have been down there, and there, but not *there*. She is head down in the mud, with one foot sticking up, and a new rubber on it.'

"The diver turned to Whitney, and said, 'I am under your orders, sir.' The diver went down at the spot indicated. In a minute the girl's hat came up. Shortly after the diver brought up the body."

[*Signed*] W. R. SUNDERLIN

In presence of Sinclair Kennedy.

Mr. Titus's Story

Sunday, Oct. 30th, 1898, Mrs. Titus, of Lebanon, said to her husband, "George, something awful is going to happen. I cannot tell you now what it is, but can later on." Monday, Oct. 31st, just about 6:40 A.M., as Mr. Titus was leaving for the mill, his wife said, "That has happened."

At noon Mr. Titus told his wife that the Huse girl (a sister of the one drowned) had gone home, Mr. Titus remarking that her mother was perhaps ill, at least so some of the people at the mill thought. She said, "It is something worse, I can feel it."

Monday evening we heard the girl was missing.

Tuesday, Nov. 1st, Mrs. Titus talked about the matter, and said, "That girl is in the lake."

Wednesday, Nov. 2nd, about 7:30 P.M., after having washed her dishes, Mrs. Titus was in the rocking chair. Mr. Titus spoke to her three times in a low tone and the fourth time loudly, and she woke up. "George, why didn't you let me be, in the morning I could have told you where the girl lay and all about it."

She then got up and walked about the house before she went to bed, which was between 8:30 and 9 P.M. After talking a short time, both Mr. and Mrs. Titus fell asleep.

At 11 P.M. (Wednesday) Mr. Titus woke her up. She was talking in her sleep with the diver, and hit her husband, saying, "She is not down there, but over here to the left." She begged her husband to leave her alone.

At 12.15 A.M. (Thursday) she again went into a trance which lasted until one o'clock. Mr. Titus lit a lamp and watched and talked with her in very low tones; when questioned on this subject she would answer, but did not hear about other things.

She said something about cold, and Mr. Titus said, "Are you cold, Nellie?" She said, "Oh, oh, I am awfully cold." This, Mr. Titus said, referred to the drowned girl.

After she came out of the trance at one o'clock she told it just as she had it in the trance.

In the morning she said it was her duty to go over to the bridge at Enfield, and Mr. Titus asked Mr. Ayer to let him off, which Mr. Ayer did. Mr. and Mrs. Titus drove in a buggy to Enfield, leaving Lebanon at 7, taking about an hour.

When about 5 or 6 rods on the bridge, Mrs. Titus called out to stop and got out and walked over to a certain spot, and looked over and said, "George, she's down there." "Nellie, are you sure?" She said, "Yes."

Then Mr. and Mrs. Titus drove to Mr. Whitney's house, where she told her story. Mr. Whitney laughed, but said he would come down.

Mrs. Titus returned to the same spot, and said, "George, she is down there."

Mr. Whitney arrived a few moments later, about 8:30 or 8:45. Mr. Titus called attention to the spot, and Mr. Whitney said, "Walk down the bridge, and see if there is not another place where she is likely to be."

She, Mrs. Titus, walked down a little way, and came back saying, "George, she is right *there*." She explained that she could see the rubber just as plainly as while in her trance the night before.

Mr. Titus says she located the spot in the night, and that he could and did recognize it from her description.

After the diver came up with the body, he said he was not afraid of the woman in the water, but of the one on the bridge.

Mrs. Titus fights against these trances, as she is usually ill for some time after.

The girl walked down to the bridge, and stood wondering whether she would go there or over to the pasture. She slipped and went down between the logs of the bridge. Went down head first, and was buried in the mud, one foot sticking out. Diver said just anxiously as she said, She knew neither the Huse girl nor was any acquaintance.

Her mother had the power, but wrote. Some days could write nothing, and then again a great deal. Mrs. Titus has no control over the trance which comes on in spite of her efforts to drive it off.

The above story which I told Dr. Harris Kennedy on Nov. 10th, 1898, is, so far as I know, correctly stated.

[*Signed*] GEORGE N. TITUS

Mr. Whitney's Letter

Baltic Mills, Enfield, N. H., Nov. 15th, 1898

My Dear Sir:

There is very little that I can add to the report which you must have in regard to the finding of the body of Miss Huse. Mrs. Titus and her husband called at my house the third morning after the disappearance.

Mrs. Titus said she was positive she could locate the body of Miss Huse in the Muscoma Lake. I went down with her and her husband to the bridge, which crosses the lake, should say the bridge was an eighth of a mile long, we walked along on the bridge together, arriving at a point about three-quarters way across the bridge. Mrs. Titus said, this is the place, she pointed to a place in the water where she said the body would be found. We secured the diver, and he went down and located the body exactly as Mrs. Titus had before said. There is really very little that I can add, Mrs. Titus certainly knew nothing about the circumstances, as she had not been in the town for two or three years previous. The diver's name is Sullivan, and he is from the Boston Tow-Boat Co., 89 State Street.

Yours truly,

[Signed] GEORGE WHITNEY

Mr. Sullivan's Statement

On Nov. 21st, 1898, the diver Sullivan was seen by me [H. Kennedy] and the following drawn up after my chat with him. He signed it on Dec. 1st, at the meeting of the Bowditch Club,[2] at Hotel Nottingham, Boston.

---

[2] The Bowditch Club is a group of assistants and younger instructors at the Harvard Medical School, who meet for purposes of professional enlightenment. Dr. Kennedy was at the time such an assistant.—W. J.

Sullivan's Statement

Nov. 21st, 1898, Mr. Sullivan, the diver in the Enfield case, was seen, at Simpson's dry dock, in East Boston. Being questioned in regard to the finding of Miss Huse, he told the following story:

"I was employed by the Boston Towboat Co., to search the Mascoma Lake. I went up at 7:10 Monday from Boston, arrived at night, and spent the greater part of Tuesday and Wednesday, Nov. 2nd, from 10 A.M. until 3:10 P.M., in searching along the Shaker Bridge. We had given up the idea of diving, and I telephoned to Boston for powder, intending to go down by the early morning train and have the powder meet me at Union Station, and take the next train up, having about 20 minutes in Boston, and return with the powder. In the morning, before I could leave Enfield, Mr. and Mrs. Titus drove over from Lebanon and called on Mr. Whitney. Mr. Titus told Mr. Whitney the story of his wife's trance, and said that altho he did not take much stock in it himself, he felt that on her account he ought to tell Mr. Whitney about it, simply to satisfy his wife. Mr. Whitney laughed, and said that he did not take any stock in it, and at the same time sent for me. We all went to the bridge, and Whitney told me that altho he did not have much faith in it himself, he felt that there might be people in the village who did, and as long as we had started to do all we could to recover the body, we ought at least to give this woman a chance. I said that the villagers up there thought that the missing girl had taken to the woods, and therefore they had had searching parties, while I was dragging the lake; but I told him that I was there, waiting his orders, my business was to find the body, and I was willing to do anything that he said, adding at the same time, that I did not want to be made a fool of by going down in a variety of places that she might point out along the bridge. He said, "No," that she simply would pick out one place, and he thought the least we could do was to go down at the place she picked out, and that would satisfy the villagers.

Mrs. Titus walked along the bridge, and came to a spot and said,

"This looks like the spot I saw in my trance," then after a moment's hesitation she said, "No, not exactly," and walked a little way along and stopped at another point, and said, "This looks very much more like the place that I saw last night." She stood there looking over the rail of the bridge from 20 minutes to half an hour. At last she said she was sure that was the place. I asked Mr. Whitney what I should do, and he said I had my suit, and he thought I had better go down in that spot. I took a guide line with sinker, located the spot from the bridge, threw the sinker over some little way from the bridge, as near as possible to the spot she pointed out. I then placed the ladder, and put on my suit, and went down. Mrs. Titus had told me the body was lying head down, only one foot with a new rubber showing, and lying in a deep hole. I started down the ladder, which extended about five feet under the water. When I swung off the ladder I went sideways and then turned. As I struck the crib work, 10 feet below the ladder, I turned to face the ladder, and my hand struck something. I felt of it, and it felt like a foot. I stopped short where I was: it is my business to recover bodies in the water, and I am not afraid of them, but in this instance I was afraid of the woman on the bridge. I thought to myself, "How can any woman come from four miles away and tell me or any other man where I would find this body?" I investigated and felt of her foot, and made sure that it was a body. She was lying in a deep hole head down. It was so dark that I could not see anything. I had to feel entirely. I pulled her out, carried her up till I could get the light from above, and then arranged her clothing by laying her out on the crib of the bridge. When I had her laid out on the crib, I reached out for my guide line, but found I could not pull it up. I had to take out my knife and cut it as far as I could reach, and then I tied the line under her arms. The line was simply a clothes line (6 thread).

I then came up and asked for Mr. Whitney. I said, "She is down there." Mr. Whitney said, "I know it." I thought Mr. Whitney had been convinced pretty strongly. He said it turned out that when I pulled her out of the hole, her hat came off and rose to the surface, and Martin, who worked the pump for me, came near getting into trouble by being pushed off the bridge when the hat appeared on the surface, because the people rushed for the side of the bridge. Fortunately he was not pushed off.

We had a man there in a little skiff, who pulled her up. Mr. Whitney asked me what I thought of it, and I told him I did not think, I was *stunned*.

There are two statements which Mrs. Titus made that are absolutely correct. She located the place where I was to go down; also told me that the body was lying, head in, in a deep hole, with one foot sticking up, with a new rubber. I was down in about 18 feet of water. It was so dark, nobody could see anything down there. She must have seen the body as it was lying, because she described the position, and she had already pointed out the place I was to go down, and nobody could have known who had not seen the body as it was lying on the bottom. If you ask me how she knew it, I don't know; but if you ask me if I believe in it, why, I have been convinced against my will. If my best friend had told me, I should have thought he had seen a ghost. But if I ever have a similar case and can't find the body, I shall introduce the parties to Mrs. Titus, and she will find it.

[*Signed*] MICHAEL J. SULLIVAN

Witnesses:

Alfred Schaper,	Allen H. Cleghorn,
E. W. Taylor,	Harris Kennedy,
Geo. Burgess Magrath,	Langdon Frothingham,
H. A. Woods,	Alfred W. Balch,
Maynard Ladd,	Henry E. Hewes,
M. A. Potter,	William James.

Mr. Sullivan was cross-examined at the Bowditch Society meeting, where, his story being read to him, he confirmed it, in the presence of the witnesses whose names are signed above. I add some details from the stenographic notes taken on that evening, and from additional information there given by Dr. Kennedy.

The bridge was a straggling structure between an eighth and a quarter of a mile long, originally made by building cribs on the ice. These sank when the ice melted, and were joined by timber. Hardly any current exists; the water is dark, and great quantities of debris and brush have collected in and about the crib work. It was absolutely impossible to see from above either the body, or the place where the body lay. The detail of the Indian rubber shoe (though it adds to the impressiveness of the narration) is unimportant evidentially. Dr. Kennedy says—"The girl was called by her parents at about eight o'clock on the Monday morning. She had been feeling poorly and they had let her sleep. They found she had gone and had taken her rubbers."

At half past 6 on that morning it appears that "the blacksmith's wife," who was in a position to see the bridge, saw a woman upon it. This blacksmith's wife was not interviewed by Dr. Kennedy. The diver had spoken with her. This is what he reports.

Q. Was she an intelligent sort of woman?

A. She seemed so.

Q. She didn't say she saw the woman fall over?

A. No; she said she saw her on the bridge, or thought it was her. She saw some woman there. That was all she could say.

CRITICAL REMARKS

The scientific interpretation of the case is threefold:

1. *The footprint theory.* It appears that there was a light frost on the fatal Monday morning, and that the footprints of the girl were traced from her house to the bridge and thereupon to a distance unrecorded. One of the gentlemen at the Bowditch Club said: "I think that the case is tremendously weakened by the fact that those footprints were seen, and by the fact that people saw her on the bridge. If you can prove that she was seen at a certain point on the bridge before she disappeared, it is not a difficult coincidence to imagine that she fell in at a certain point; and that would surely have been described to Mrs. Titus. It is conceivable that the woman who saw her on the bridge knew Mrs. Titus. Some

people have a power of observation which others have not. Mrs. Titus, with a particularly acute power of observation, might have learned something which others did not."

If this means that footprints and the blacksmith's wife furnished to Mrs. Titus data which the latter's acute powers, either of imagination or observation, completed into an accurate vision of the corpse's position in the water, it seems almost as great a mental miracle as "clairvoyance." The footprints had evidently not led to any spot on the bridge that suggested the girl's having stopped there, for the whole town, knowing of them and in spite of them, was searching the woods; and if they had even indicated one side of the bridge as the more probable side, why should the diver have been allowed to search *both sides, as he did on the Tuesday and Wednesday?* When asked whether he could go back now, and pick out the spot on the bridge where the girl fell off, the diver replied: "I don't think I could pick out that spot." The following questions and answers are from his cross-examination.

Q. How should you know that spot from the one next to it?

A. If there wasn't anything connected with it, I could not pick it out, hardly.

If the diver, who had been there, felt so uncertain, it seems still less likely that Mrs. Titus could have accurately found the spot by a bare hearsay description.

2. This leads to the second naturalistic theory: *Mrs. Titus may have witnessed the accident.* Like the blacksmith's wife, she may have happened to be near the bridge at the fatal hour, and seen what happened. She then probably went home, and with her husband's complicity worked up the trance story, and on Thursday morning pointed out the spot. The husband's alibi of her would necessarily then be false, and would prove him an accomplice on this theory. Mr. Sullivan's remark on having it propounded was, "Yes, but how could she then know the *exact position of the body on the bottom?*"

Another point against this theory is the odd delay until Thursday morning. Why should Mrs. Titus, if she had a perverse desire to win fame as a clairvoyant, have given the diver two free days in which to find the body unaided?

3. Finally, Bertha Huse, intending to commit suicide, might have confided the *intention and the mode of execution to Mrs. Titus, either directly* or through her sister, who, it appears, worked at Lebanon, and was probably known to Mrs. Titus. This third hypothesis is psychologically even more improbable than the two others. Against all three of these explanations stands the fact of the precision of the clairvoyant's direction to the diver. Here are some passages from the latter's cross-examination:

Q. You think that Mrs. Titus pointed to almost the exact spot where the body was found?

A. I know she did. If it wasn't for her, the body would not have been found.

Q. You say it was too dark for you to see?

A. It was total darkness. It is light water, but the crib work cuts off the light.

Again:

Q. You found her with her head down and feet up in almost the exact spot Mrs. Titus indicated?

A. I might say to an inch.

Mr. Sullivan's mind seems to have been quite "stunned," as he expressed it, by the uncanniness of such an exact and immediate verification. "When I put out my hand it came up against something that felt like a foot." . . . "If I had come across the body the day before, or the first day I was there, I would have thought nothing of it. I would say, 'All right for Boston tonight, I guess.' But when I came across her, and felt out what it was, it did actually stun me, and in place of paying attention to the body, I did so to the woman overhead, that picked out the spot, and the way she said it lay. . . . I thought of that, about this Mrs. Titus! I said I never believed in anything like that! Then I commenced to haul her up after I settled that part of it. I had been positive I would not find the body. I had been mad because I would have to go down because of this woman saying, 'There is the spot where the body is.' "

It was evident that the exactness of the description was the striking thing for Sullivan. He was interrogated as to whether the position of the body tallied with Mrs. Titus' account of the way the girl fell over backwards. The body stood vertically, head downwards, in a hole in the cribwork. He thought that a sudden dive backwards was the best explanation of its being caught thus. "She was lying feet up and head down. She was straight up and down." "I take it a woman drowning herself, jumping over feet first, the air would get under her clothes, and she would drift around a little ways; . . . but if a woman goes backwards, she will settle quicker." "Bodies that have drifted, as a general thing, lie horizontal."

It was plain enough that *neither of these three naturalistic explanations has the least plausibility.* A reader to whom the hypothesis of clairvoyance is impossible, had far better explain the case as a very exceptional one of accidental coincidence. I should unhesitatingly do this myself were cognate cases *rarissimi.* But the records of supernormal seership of various types and grades which the *Proceedings* of the S. P. R. are more and more abundantly publishing, make, it seems to me, the scientific *"non-possumus"* absurd. There is an almost identical case, for instance, in Vol. xi, p. 383 ff., where the corpses of two drowned boys named Mason were found in Cochituate Lake, near Natick, Mass., through directions given by a Boston clairvoyant named Mrs. York. See also a similar case on p. 089 of the same volume.

My own view of the Titus case consequently is that it is a decidedly solid document in favor of the admission of a supernormal faculty of seership—whatever preciser meaning may later come to be attached to such a phrase.

I conclude by appending a notice that appeared in the *Granite State Free Press,* of Lebanon, N. H., on Friday, November 11th,

1898, and a letter from a sister of the drowned girl, received by me quite recently.

CARD

The people of Enfield and adjoining towns, who so spontaneously came to our relief and assistance by words of sympathy and kindly and generous acts during the long days and nights of terrible anxiety and suspense, attending search for our dear daughter, sister, and niece; to that kind-hearted man, George E. Whitney, who so generously contributed assistance by personal effort and otherwise; to Mrs. Titus, who voluntarily came to our assistance when all means and efforts had failed, and by the exercise of a, to us mysterious but we believe a God-given power, designated the place where the body could be found and where it was found; to the funeral director, the bearers and singers; to the friends who came from a distance to attend the funeral; and to those who contributed the beautiful flowers; we wish hereby to express to each and all, our deep sense of gratitude and heartfelt thanks for this manifestation of their friendship. The memory of this will always be treasured by us.

[*Signed*]   MR. & MRS. EDWIN E. HUSE.
               LEONA E. HUSE.
               MR. & MRS. GUY E. HUSE.
               MR. & MRS. L. D. DUNBAR.

Enfield, N. H., April 2nd, 1907

Professor William James,
                Cambridge, Mass.

Dear Sir:—

In reply to your letter of recent date received by my mother, I will simply say—we have never had any reason to doubt that the facts of the case you referred to were correctly stated in the papers at the time of the accident.

We do not attempt to explain Mrs. Titus' part in it, but do know she performed a wonderful act for us, for which we shall always be very thankful. We have no reason to doubt either Mr. or Mrs. Titus' statements in regard to it.

In regard to your criticisms, am quite sure if you had been here you would not have advanced them.

We have not seen Mrs. Titus for several years, so can tell you nothing about her.

I judge by your letter that you have the facts of the case, so you will excuse me if I write nothing more—as it is far from pleasant to talk or write about what is to us a great sorrow.

Very truly,

MRS. H. BARROW,

For Mrs. Edwin E. Huse

PHYSICAL PHENOMENA AT A PRIVATE CIRCLE [1]

A fortnight ago I heard that, at a private circle of spiritualists in a New England town, a table had been bodily lifted from the floor with no contact but that of fingers to its upper surface. The rarity of the case induced me to make a visit to the town in question, where I have had three sittings with the circle and from whence I now write.

The circle is composed of solid citizens of the town and their wives or sisters. They have sat weekly for a couple of years, and impressed me as perfectly sincere and earnest in their quest of facts. They use a four-cornered and four-legged table of wood, thirteen pounds in weight, on the center of which a revolving disk twenty inches in diameter, bearing an alphabet, has been pivoted. The disk revolves with a minimum of friction, and an index hand, pivoted independently, points to the letters and spells messages. The sitters' fingers may be placed on the edges of the table an inch below the disk or on the disk itself. To avoid too much pressure on the rotating disk, a rink or rail of thick brass wire has been adjusted to the corners of the table, surrounding the disk at four inches' distance, on which the wrists of those present may rest while they lay their fingertips on the disk. This ring slides with a moderate

[1] From *The Journal of the American Society for Psychical Research*, Vol. III, No. 2, February 1909.—ED.

friction through four brass collars which sustain it, and which themselves are sustained by brass stems screwed to the angles of the table. The disk and the ring are thus concentric. (I will go into these details about the ring, for reasons which will appear presently.)

For nearly three years nothing happened at this circle but answers to questions by tipping, and messages spelled out by the disk. No one present seemed to be exclusively the medium, though one lady, absent from town at the time of my visit, was considered to have the most "power."

I

Of the first physical phenomenon I got only oral testimony. This was the fact on two occasions, in the autumn of 1907, of explosive sounds as "loud as a pistol shot," seeming to occur each time in the room where the sitting was being held. On one occasion the sound was repeated seven times. On the other, the sitting being held in a house a couple of miles distant from the first one, it occurred but once. It was entirely unexpected and unexplained, seems to have startled everyone very much, and all present believed that it was spiritual.

II

The second physical phenomenon obtained by the circle was the following. I copy the account from the diary of the circle's proceedings, under date of November 24th, 1907.

At this meeting we at first took large center table, placed ordinary finger-bowls on table, one for each person, and partly filled with water. Mrs. M.'s bowl moved with just her fingers in the water, not touching the bowl in any way. Made intelligent movements, moving towards Mr. R. when asked. Other bowls also moved, but fingers had to be in contact with them in some manner.

The five witnesses have signed their names to this record for me. They say that the bowl "waltzed round the edge of the table," that they had tried the experiment on other evenings, but that this was the only attempt that succeeded.

III

The next phenomenon of the kind which happened is given in the following account which I wrote down from the oral testimony of seven of the eight witnesses, and to which all but the absent one have appended their signatures, though they are not willing to have these printed.

On the night of November 19th, 1908, we, the undersigned were having a sitting round the table used for many months in our experiments. [The table I have described above.—W. J.]

On the occasion in question our fingertips were all resting on the top of the disk, so that they could not possibly exert any lifting force whatever on the table. The hands of Mrs. B. alone were in the air, a few inches above the center of the disk. After some of the usual tiltings of the table, with two or three of the legs off the ground, *it rose gently and with all four legs off the ground to the height of six inches or more,* to the great surprise of all of us, and remained in the air two or three seconds, subsiding slowly to the ground.

Some said that the sensation of resistance to their fingers was as if the table were supported by a spiral spring.

Immediately after this a message was spelled out, ordering Mrs. B. to join her hands above the table with those of Mr. D. The same phenomenon was then repeated twice over, the table rising the last time to what seemed to be ten inches from the floor. [Here follow the signatures.]

IV

My own first visit was on Thursday, December 3, 1908. (Thursday is the night on which the circle habitually sits.) Eight persons, counting myself, were present, three women, five men.

We sat at first with our fingers on the solid table beneath the disk, and various tippings came. Then, with our wrists or palms on the ring and our fingers on the disk, various messages were spelt.

Mrs. B., whose fifth sitting it was, had her fingers automatically jerked away whenever she placed them on the disk. This had happened previously; and, during the previous lifting of the table on November 19th, she had held her hands in the air some inches above the disk. She kept them in that situation on this present occasion whenever we made attempts to have the table lifted. Such attempts were several times repeated, but with no success.

On the controls then being asked whether they could not *make the disk rotate* without contact, they spelled "no."

Suddenly, while we were sitting with our wrists on the brass ring and our fingers on the disk, which turned and spelled, *we perceived that the ring or rail itself was moving.* It had never done this on any previous evening. The phenomenon was consequently unexpected, and seemed to strike all present with surprise.

Someone immediately suggested that all wrists should be lifted, and then, in brilliant light, and no one's hands in any way in contact with the rail, our fingers, however, resting on the disk, we all distinctly saw the rail or ring *slide slowly and for several inches through the collars, as if spontaneously.*

We then stuck a mark upon the ring to make its motion more obvious, and repeated five or six times the experiment, the same result ensuing, though more slightly each time. It always took the contact of our wrists to start the rail, but *its motion continued when the contact ceased.* This was not from its acquired momentum, for we ascertained that the friction of the collars which held the rail stopped instantly every motion imparted voluntarily by the hand.

On the succeeding Saturday and Sunday evenings, we sat again (one of the ladies being absent), but nothing but that usual tilting of the table and spelling of messages occurred.

So much for the "record," which all present have signed. It will be observed that all the phenomena reported (save the movements of the finger-bowl) were unexpected and startling to the spectators. The explosions and the table's rising seem to have been eminently so, and to have made a great impression.

On December 3rd, when the ring revolved, the conditions of observation were perfect, the light (from an electric chandelier just overhead) being brilliant, and the phenomena being slow enough, and often enough repeated, to leave my own mind in no doubt at the time as to what was witnessed. I was quite convinced that I saw that no hand was on the ring while it was moving. The maximum length of its path under these circumstances was fully six inches. With this conviction that I saw all there was to see, I have to confess that I am surprised that the phenomenon affected me emotionally so little. I may add, as a psychological fact, that now, after four days' interval, my mind seems strongly inclined not to "count" the observation, as if it were too exceptional to have been probable. I have only once before seen an object moved "paradoxically," and then the conditions were unsatisfactory. But I have supposed that if I could once see the same thing "satisfactorily," the levee by which scientific opinion protects nature would be cracked for me, and I should be as one watching an incipient overflow of the Mississippi of the supernatural into the fields of orthodox culture. I find, however, that I look on nature with unaltered eyes today, and that my orthodox habits tend to extrude this would-be levee-breaker. It forms too much of an exception.

Nevertheless, in the somewhat scandalously divided state of opinion about Eusapia Paladino, I think that every approach to similar phenomena observed anywhere ought to be recorded. It may be that the frequency rather than the quality of the records will establish their "case."

A POSSIBLE CASE OF PROJECTION OF THE DOUBLE [1]

The following case lacks direct personal corroboration from the two witnesses, so that there is only hearsay evidence for the fact of the apparition. But the type of phenomenon is so rare and, if not

[1] From *The Journal of the American Society for Psychical Research,* Vol. II, No. 4, April 1909.—ED.

to be explained by accidental coincidence, so important, that all reported cases of it should be recorded.

In the present case the "agent" is a colleague of mine; an able and respected professor in Harvard University. He originally told me the story shortly after it happened in 18—. The present account, written at my request in 1903, tallies exactly with my memory of that earlier story. "A" at that time was unwilling to give me her version. She is now dead, and of course the narrative is in so far defective.

Cambridge, April 16, 1903

My dear Dr. James:

I recall exactly all the details of the matter which you wish me to write about, but I cannot be sure whether the thing occurred in the latter part of 1883 or the first part of 1884. At this time A and I were seeing each other very frequently, and we were interested, among other things, in that book by Sinett on Esoteric Buddhism. We talked a good deal about it, and about the astral body, but neither ever made any proposal to the other to try any experiments in that line.

One evening, about 9:45 o'clock, or, perhaps, nearer 10, when I had been thinking over that subject as I sat alone in my room, I resolved to try whether I could project my astral body to the presence of A. I did not at all know what the process was, but I opened my window, which looked towards A's house (though that was half a mile away and behind a hill), and sat down in a chair and tried as hard as I could to wish myself into the presence of A. There was no light in my room. I sat there in that state of wishing for about ten minutes. Nothing abnormal in the way of feelings happened to me.

Next day I met A, who said something to this effect. (I mean that I cannot give the exact words.)

"Last night about ten o'clock I was in the dining room at supper with B. Suddenly I thought I saw you looking in thru the crack of the door at the end of the room, towards which I was looking. I said to B.: "There is Blank, looking thru the crack of the door!" B., whose back was towards the door, said: "He can't be there; he would come right in." However, I got up and looked in the outer room, but there was nobody there. Now, what were you doing last night at that time?"

This was what A told me and I then explained what I had been doing.

You see, of course, that the double evidence (I mean, A's and B's) might make this story pretty well founded, but it must be left entirely independent on my account, for there are good reasons why neither A nor B can be appealed to.

IV

———•———

WILLIAM JAMES AND MRS. PIPER

The interest of William James in the Boston medium Mrs. Piper, which began in 1885, persisted up to the time of his death in 1910. Apparently his first published account of the phenomena exhibited in sittings with her was in his "Report of the Committee on Mediumistic Phenomena" published in 1886 in the Proceedings *of the first American Society for Psychical Research, which follows.*

REPORT OF THE COMMITTEE ON MEDIUMISTIC PHENOMENA [1]

The Committee on Mediumistic Phenomena has no definitely concluded piece of work to offer. An account of what has been done during the year, however, with a few reflections, may not be out of place.

My own time was chiefly divided between two mediums—one a trance-medium, whom, at her request, I shall call Mrs. P.; the other, Miss Helen Berry, whose public "materializing" manifestations are reputed to be among the best of their class.

———

[1] *Proceedings of the American Society for Psychical Research*, Vol. I, 1886–1889, pp. 102 ff.—ED.

Concerning Miss Berry, there is little to say. Test conditions against fraud are not habitually offered at her séances. On one occasion it was granted to Mr. Savage to sit behind the cabinet, others being in front, whilst I explored it after the medium's entrance, and found no confederate concealed. A trap-door seemed out of the question. In a minute two forms emerged from the cabinet. But this was our first sitting, and for certain reasons we cannot call the experiment satisfactory until we have an opportunity of taking part in it again. The real test of the Berry's genuineness is supposed to be the resemblance of the forms to deceased friends of the sitters, and the character of what they say. A large amount of testimony can be collected from sitters as to the unmistakable identity of the forms with their dead wives, husbands, brothers, etc.

I visited twelve séances, and took with me, or sent, personal friends enough to have, in all, first-hand reports of thirty-five visits, embracing sixteen or seventeen séances. No spirit form came directly to any one of us, so we offer no opinion regarding the phenomena.

To turn to the much simpler and more satisfactory case of Mrs. P. This lady can at will pass into a trance condition, in which she is "controlled" by a power purporting to be the spirit of a French doctor, who serves as intermediary between the sitter and deceased friends. This is the ordinary type of trance-mediumship at the present day. I have myself witnessed a dozen of her trances, and have testimony at first hand from twenty-five sitters, all but one of whom were virtually introduced to Mrs. P. by myself.

Of five of the sittings we have *verbatim* stenographic reports. Twelve of the sitters, who in most cases sat singly, got nothing from the medium but unknown names or trivial talk. Four of these were members of the society, and of their sittings *verbatim* reports were taken.

Fifteen of the sitters were surprised at the communications they received, names and facts being mentioned at the first interview which it seemed improbable should have been known to the medium in a normal way. The probability that she possessed no clew as to the sitter's identity was, I believe, in each and all of these fifteen cases, sufficient. But of only one of them is there a stenographic report; so that, unfortunately for the medium, the evidence in her favor is, although more abundant, less exact in quality than some of that which will be counted against her.

Of these fifteen sitters, five, all ladies, were blood relatives, and two (I myself being one) were men connected by marriage with the family to which they belonged. Two other connections of this family are included in the twelve who got nothing. The medium showed a most startling intimacy with this family's affairs, talking of many matters known to no one outside, and which *gossip* could not possibly have conveyed to her ears. The details would prove nothing to the reader, unless printed *in extenso,* with full notes by the sitters. It reverts, after all, to personal conviction. My own conviction is not evidence, but it seems fitting to record it. I am persuaded of the medium's honesty, and of the genuineness of her trance; and although at first disposed to think that the "hits" she made were either lucky coincidences, or the result of knowledge on her part of who the sitter was and of his or her family affairs, I now believe her to be in possession of a power as yet unexplained.

The most promising way of investigating phenomena like this seems to be that of learning a great deal about one "subject," who, of course, ought to be a good specimen of the class. Hitherto we have heard a little about a great many subjects. Stenographic reports are expensive, but they seem indispensable for a conclusive discussion of the facts. They do away with doubts about the veracity of the sitter's memory; and they enable us to make a comparison of different sittings, which without them is hardly possible at all. Questions arise as to the irrelevant names and facts which almost every sitting to some extent contains. Are they improvisations of the moment? Are they in themselves right and coherent, but addressed to the wrong sitter? Or are they vestiges of former sittings, now emerging as part of the automatism of the medium's brain? A reading of the stenographic reports already taken makes it probable that, for some of them at least, this last explanation is correct. "Spirits" originally appearing to me have appeared in the sittings of others who knew nothing either of their persons or their names.

What science wants is a *context* to make the trance phenomena continuous with other physiological and psychological facts. Curious to ascertain whether there were continuity between the medium-trance and the ordinary hypnotic trance, I made some observations *ad hoc* upon Mrs. P. My first two attempts to hypnotize her were unsuccessful. Between the second time and the third, I suggested to her "control" in the medium-trance that he should make her a mesmeric subject for me. He agreed. (A suggestion of this sort made by the operator in one hypnotic trance would probably have some effect on the next.) She became partially hypnotized on the third trial; but the effect was so slight that I ascribe it rather to the effect of repetition than to the suggestion made. By the fifth trial she had become a pretty good hypnotic subject, as far as muscular phenomena and automatic imitations of speech and gesture go; but I could not affect her consciousness, or otherwise get her beyond this point. Her condition in this semi-hypnosis is very different from her medium-trance. The latter is characterized by great muscular unrest, even her ears moving vigorously in a way impossible to her in her waking state. But in hypnosis her muscular relaxation and weakness are extreme. She often makes several efforts to speak ere her voice becomes audible; and to get a strong contraction of the hand, for example, express manipulation and suggestion must be practiced. The automatic imitations I spoke of are in the first instance very weak, and only become strong after repetition. Her pupils contract in the medium-trance. Suggestions to the "control" that he should make her recollect after the trance what she had been saying were accepted, but had no result. In the hypnotic trance such a suggestion will often make the patient remember all that has happened.

No sign of thought-transference—as tested by card- and diagram-guessing—has been found in her, either in the hypnotic condition just described, or immediately after it; although her "control" in the medium-trance has said that he would bring them about. So far as tried (only twice), no right guessing of cards in the medium-trance. She was twice tried with epistolary letters in the medium-trance—once indicating the contents in a way rather surprising to the sitter; once failing. In her normal waking state she made one hundred and twenty-seven guesses at playing-cards looked at by me—I sometimes touching her, sometimes not. Suit right (first guess) thirty-eight times—an excess of only six over the "probable" number of thirty-two—obviously affording no distinct evidence of thought-transference. Trials of the "willing game," and attempts at automatic writing, gave similarly negative results. So far as the evidence goes, then, her medium-trance seems an isolated feature in her psychology. This would of itself be an important result if it could be established and generalized, but the record is obviously too imperfect for confident conclusions to be drawn from it in any direction. Being compelled by other work to abandon the subject for the present, these notes are published merely as a suggestion of lines of inquiry which others may be better fitted than myself to carry out.

If a good trance subject could be obtained for the society at the outset of her or his career, and kept from doing miscellaneous work until patiently and thoroughly observed and experimented on, with stenographic reports of trances, and as much attention paid to failures and errors as to successes, I am disposed to think that the results would in any event be of scientific value, and would be worth the somewhat high expense which they necessarily would entail. If the friends of spiritualism would contribute money for the thorough carrying out of any such scheme, they would probably do as much as by any one thing could be done to bring about the "recognition" of trance-mediumship by scientific men.

As for the other kinds of mediumistic phenomena, I have during the past year been very much struck by the volume of evidence which can be collected in their favor. But the mere *volume* of evidence is of no account unless it can be proved that the evidence is likely to be of the ordinary human sort, bad and good mixed together in the usual proportion. If it is possible that it is unusually bad in *quality*, the quantity of it is of little account. Now, that there *are* reasons for believing its quality to be in these matters below the average, no one familiar with the facts can doubt. Only the establishment of one or two absolutely and coercively proven cases —of materialization, for example—will show that the hearsay evidence for *that* phenomenon may be mixed. And only *then* can the volume of evidence already extant on the subject be taken into account by one who has no direct personal experience on which to rely. The ordinary disbeliever rules out all hearsay evidence in advance. The believer accepts far too much of it, because he knows that some of it is good. The committee of the society should first devote itself to the very exact and complete study of a few particular cases. These may consume much labor and time. But if, after studying them, it should reach favorable conclusions, it would do vastly more to make the vaguer testimony already extant influential with the society as a whole than it could do by discussing such testimony now.

In 1890 Frederic Myers asked William James to write a record of his observations of the Piper phenomena to be incorporated in a series of discussions of "Certain Phenomena of Trance" to be published in the Proceedings *of the Society for Psychical Research (London). After Myers had received the report he asked James's brother, Henry, the novelist, who was then in London, to read it before the Society.*

The correspondence between Henry and William James about it, and William James's report to Myers ("My Piper Letter") follow.

LETTERS

From Henry James, London, October 9, 1890 [1]

My dear William,—

. . . Frederic Myers has written to ask *me* to read your letter on Mrs. Piper at a meeting of the Society for Psychical Research

---

[1] All these excerpts are from Ralph Barton Perry, op. cit., Vol. I, pp. 416–17. —ED.

at the Westminster Town Hall on the 31st of this month, and I have said I would, though so alien to the whole business, in order not to seem to withhold from *you* any advantage—though what "advantage" I shall confer remains to be seen. Therefore imagine me at 4 P.M. on that day, performing in your name. . . . Ever your

Henry

To Henry James, Cambridge, October 20, 1890

Dear Harry,—

. . . I think your reading my Piper letter (of which this very morning proof came to me from Myers) is the most comical thing I ever heard of. It shows how first-rate a business man Myers is: he wants to bring variety and *éclat* into the meeting. I will *think of you* on the 31st at about 11 A.M. to make up for the difference of longitude. . . . I wish I could run over and visit you again— your avuncular allusions to our children are very winsome to both Alice's heart and mine! Good night.

W. J.

P.S. I sat up till 4 last night reading Stanley's book. What a jolly book it is. Alice says I have not *melted* enough over your reading of my paper. I *do* melt to perfect liquefaction. 'Tis the most beautiful and devoted brotherly act I ever knew, and I hope it may be the beginning of a new career, on your part, of psychic apostolicism. Heaven bless you for it! Write short and often.

From Henry James, London, November 7, 1890

My dear William,—

. . . It was a week ago today that I read you at the S. P. R. with great *éclat*—enhanced by my being introduced by Pearsall Smith as a Bostonian of Bostonians! You were very easy and interesting to read, and were altogether the "Feature" of the entertainment. It was a full house and Myers was *rayonnant*. . . . Ever your

Henry

CERTAIN PHENOMENA OF TRANCE [1]

Dear Mr. Myers,

You ask for a record of my own experiences with Mrs. Piper, to be incorporated in the account of her to be published in your *Proceedings*. I regret to be unable to furnish you with any direct notes of sittings beyond those which Mr. Hodgson will have already supplied. I admit that in not having taken more notes I was most derelict, and can only cry *peccavi*. The excuse (if it be one) for my negligence was that I wished primarily to satisfy *myself* about Mrs. Piper; and feeling that as evidence for others no notes but stenographic notes would have value, and not being able to get these, I seldom took any. I still think that as far as influencing public opinion goes, the bare fact that So-and-so and So-and-so have been convinced by their personal experience that "there is something in mediumship" is the essential thing. Public opinion follows leaders much more than it follows evidence. Professor Huxley's bare "endorsement" of Mrs. Piper, *e.g.*, would be more effective than volumes of notes by such as I. Practically, however, I ought to have taken them, and the sight of your more scientific methods makes me doubly rue my sins.

Under the circumstances, the only thing I can do is to give you my present state of belief as to Mrs. Piper's powers, with a simple account from memory of the steps which have led me to it.

I made Mrs. Piper's acquaintance in the autumn of 1885. My wife's mother, Mrs. Gibbens, had been told of her by a friend, during the previous summer, and never having seen a medium before, had paid her a visit out of curiosity. She returned with the statement that Mrs. P. had given her a long string of names of members of the family, mostly Christian names, together with facts about the persons mentioned and their relations to each other, the knowledge of which on her part was incomprehensible without supernormal

[1] *Proceedings of the Society for Psychical Research* (London), Vol. II, Part XVII, December 1890.—Ed.

powers. My sister-in-law went the next day, with still better results, as she related them. Amongst other things, the medium had accurately described the circumstances of the writer of a letter which she held against her forehead, after Miss G. had given it to her. The letter was in Italian, and its writer was known to but two persons in this country.

(I may add that on a later occasion my wife and I took another letter from this same person to Mrs. P., who went on to speak of him in a way which identified him unmistakably again. On a third occasion, two years later, my sister-in-law and I being again with Mrs. P., she reverted in her trance to these letters, and then gave us the writer's name, which she said she had not been able to get on the former occasion.)

But to revert to the beginning. I remember playing the *esprit fort* on that occasion before my feminine relatives, and seeking to explain by simple considerations the marvelous character of the facts which they brought back. This did not, however, prevent me from going myself a few days later, in company with my wife, to get a direct personal impression. The names of none of us up to this meeting had been announced to Mrs. P., and Mrs. J. and I were, of course, careful to make no reference to our relatives who had preceded. The medium, however, when entranced, repeated most of the names of "spirits" whom she had announced on the two former occasions and added others. The names came with difficulty, and were only gradually made perfect. My wife's father's name of Gibbens was announced first as Niblin, then as Giblin. A child Herman (whom we had lost the previous year) had his name spelled out as Herrin. I think that in no case were both Christian and surnames given on this visit. But the *facts predicated* of the persons named made it in many instances impossible not to recognize the particular individuals who were talked about. We took particular pains on this occasion to give the Phinuit control no help over his difficulties and to ask no leading questions. In the light of subsequent experience I believe this not to be the best policy. For it often happens, if you give this trance personage a name or some small fact for the lack of which he is brought to a standstill, that he will then start off with a copious flow of additional talk, containing in itself an abundance of "tests."

My impression after this first visit was that Mrs. P. was either possessed of supernormal powers, or knew the members of my wife's family by sight and had by some lucky coincidence become acquainted with such a multitude of their domestic circumstances as to produce the startling impression which she did. My later knowledge of her sittings and personal acquaintance with her has led me absolutely to reject the latter explanation, and to believe that she has supernormal powers.

I visited her a dozen times that winter, sometimes alone, sometimes with my wife, once in company with the Rev. M. J. Savage. I sent a large number of persons to her, wishing to get the results of as many *first* sittings as possible. I made appointments myself for most of these people, whose names were in no instance announced to the medium. In the spring of 1886 I published a brief "Report of the Committee on Mediumistic Phenomena" in the *Proceedings* of the American Society for Psychical Research.[2]

I dropped my inquiries into Mrs. Piper's mediumship for a period of about two years, having satisfied myself that there was a genuine mystery there, but being over-freighted with time-consuming duties, and feeling that any adequate circumnavigation of the phenomena would be too protracted a task for me to aspire just then to undertake. I saw her once, half accidentally, however, during that interval, and in the spring of 1889 saw her four times again. In the fall of 1889 she paid us a visit of a week at our country house in New Hampshire, and I then learned to know her personally better than ever before, and had confirmed in me the belief that she is an absolutely simple and genuine person. No one, when challenged, can give "evidence" to others for such beliefs as this. Yet we all live by them from day to day, and practically I should be willing now to stake as much money on Mrs. Piper's honesty as on that of anyone

---

[2] The report is reprinted in this book. Extracts from it which were included in the letter to Myers are here omitted.—ED.

I know, and am quite satisfied to leave my reputation for wisdom or folly, so far as human nature is concerned, to stand or fall by this declaration.

As for the explanation of her trance phenomena, I have none to offer. The *prima facie* theory, which is that of spirit-control, is hard to reconcile with the extreme triviality of most of the communications. What real spirit, at last able to revisit his wife on this earth, but would find something better to say than that she had changed the place of his photograph? And yet that is the sort of remark to which the spirits introduced by the mysterious Phinuit are apt to confine themselves. I must admit, however, that Phinuit has other moods. He has several times, when my wife and myself were sitting together with him, suddenly started off on long lectures to us about our inward defects and outward shortcomings, which were very earnest, as well as subtle morally and psychologically, and impressive in a high degree. These discourses, though given in Phinuit's own person, were very different in style from his more usual talk, and probably superior to anything that the medium could produce in the same line in her natural state. Phinuit himself, however, bears every appearance of being a fictitious being. His French, so far as he has been able to display it to me, has been limited to a few phrases of salutation, which may easily have had their rise in the medium's "unconscious" memory; he has never been able to understand *my* French; and the crumbs of information which he gives about his earthly career are, as you know, so few, vague, and unlikely sounding as to suggest the romancing of one whose stock of materials for invention is excessively reduced. He is, however, as he actually shows himself, a definite human individual, with immense tact and patience, and great desire to please and be regarded as infallible. With respect to the rough and slangy style which he so often affects, it should be said that the spiritualistic tradition here in America is all in favour of the "spirit-control" being a grotesque and somewhat saucy personage. The *Zeitgeist* has always much to do with shaping trance phenomena, so that a "control" of that temperament is what one would naturally expect. Mr. Hodgson will already have informed you of the similarity between Phinuit's name and that of the "control" of the medium at whose house Mrs. Piper was first entranced. The most remarkable thing about the Phinuit personality seems to me the extraordinary tenacity and minuteness of his memory. The medium has been visited by many hundreds of sitters, half of them, perhaps, being strangers who have come but once. To each Phinuit gives an hourful of disconnected fragments of talk about persons living, dead, or imaginary, and events past, future, or unreal. What normal waking memory could keep this chaotic mass of stuff together? Yet Phinuit does so; for the chances seem to be, that if a sitter should go back after years of interval, the medium, when once entranced, would recall the minutest incidents of the earlier interview, and begin by recapitulating much of what had then been said. So far as I can discover, Mrs. Piper's waking memory is not remarkable, and the whole constitution of her trance memory is something which I am at a loss to understand. But I will say nothing more of Phinuit, because, aided by our friends in France, you are already systematically seeking to establish or disprove him as a former native of this world.

Phinuit is generally the medium of communication between other spirits and the sitter. But two other *soi-disant* spirits have, in my presence, assumed direct "control" of Mrs. Piper. One purported to be the late Mr. E. The other was an aunt of mine who died last year in New York. I have already sent you the only account I can give of my earliest experiences with the "E. control." The first messages came through Phinuit, about a year ago, when, after two years of non intercourse with Mrs. Piper, she lunched one day at our house and gave my wife and myself a sitting afterwards. It was bad enough; and I confess that the human being in me was so much stronger than the man of science that I was too disgusted with Phinuit's tiresome twaddle even to note it down. When later the phenomenon developed into pretended direct speech from E. himself I regretted this, for a complete record would have been useful. I can now merely say that neither then, nor at any other time, was there to my mind the slightest inner verisimilitude in the personation. But the failure to produce a more plausible E. speaks directly in favor of the non-participation of the medium's *conscious* mind in the performance. She could so easily have coached herself to be more effective.

Her trance talk about my own family shows the same innocence. The skeptical theory of her successes is that she keeps a sort of detective bureau open upon the world at large, so that whoever may call is pretty sure to find her prepared with facts about his life. Few things could have been easier, in Boston, than for Mrs. Piper to collect facts about my own father's family for use in my sittings with her. But although my father, my mother, and a deceased brother were repeatedly announced as present, nothing but their bare names ever came out, except a hearty message of thanks from my father that I had "published the book." I *had* published his *Literary Remains;* but when Phinuit was asked "what book?" all he could do was to spell the letters L, I, and say no more. If it be suggested that all this was but a refinement of cunning, for that such skillfully distributed reticences are what bring most credit in to a medium, I must deny the proposition *in toto.* I have seen and heard enough of sittings to be sure that a medium's trump cards are promptitude and completeness in her revelations. It is a mistake in general (however it may occasionally, as now, be cited in her favor) to keep back anything she knows. Phinuit's stumbling, spelling, and otherwise imperfect ways of bringing out his facts is a great drawback with most sitters, and yet it is habitual with him.

The aunt who purported to "take control" directly was a much better personation, having a good deal of the cheery strenuousness of speech of the original. She spoke, by the way, on this occasion, of the condition of health of two members of the family in New York, of which we knew nothing at the time, and which was afterwards corroborated by letter. We have repeatedly heard from Mrs. Piper in trance things of which we were not at the moment aware. If the supernormal element in the phenomenon be thought-transference it is certainly not that of the sitter's *conscious* thought. It is rather the reservoir of his potential knowledge which is tapped;

and not always *that*, but the knowledge of some distant living person, as in the incident last quoted. It has sometimes even seemed to me that too much intentness on the sitter's part to have Phinuit say a certain thing acts as a hindrance.

Mrs. Blodgett, of Holyoke, Massachusetts, and her sister, devised, before the latter died, what would have been a good test of actual spirit return. The sister, Miss H. W., wrote upon her deathbed a letter, sealed it, and gave it to Mrs. B. After her death no one living knew what words it contained. Mrs. B., not then knowing Mrs. Piper, entrusted to me the sealed letter, and asked me to give Mrs. Piper some articles of the deceased sister's personal apparel, to help her to get at its contents. This commission I performed. Mrs. P. gave correctly the full name (which even I did not know) of the writer, and finally, after a delay and ceremony which occupied several weeks on Phinuit's part, dictated what purported to be a copy of the letter. This I compared with the original (of which Mrs. B. permitted me to break the seal); but the two letters had nothing in common, nor were any of the numerous domestic facts alluded to in the medium's letter acknowledged by Mrs. Blodgett to be correct. Mrs. Piper was equally unsuccessful in two later attempts which she made to reproduce the contents of his document, although both times the revelation purported to come direct from its deceased writer. It would be hard to devise a better test than this would have been, had it immediately succeeded, for the exclusion of thought-transference from living minds.

My mother-in-law, on her return from Europe, spent a morning vainly looking for her bankbook. Mrs. Piper, on being shortly afterwards asked where this book was, described the place so exactly that it was instantly found. I was told by her that the spirit of a boy named Robert F. was the companion of my lost infant. The F.'s were cousins of my wife living in a distant city. On my return home I mentioned the incident to my wife, saying, "Your cousin did lose a baby, didn't she? but Mrs. Piper was wrong about its sex, name, and age." I then learned that Mrs. Piper had been quite right in all those particulars, and that mine was the wrong impression. But, obviously, for the source of revelations such as these, one need not go behind the sitter's own storehouse of forgotten or unnoticed experiences. Miss X.'s experiments in crystal-gazing prove how strangely these survive. If thought-transference be the clue to be followed in interpreting Mrs. Piper's trance utterances (and that, as far as my experience goes, is what, far more than any supramundane instillations, the phenomena *seem* on their face to be) we must admit that the "transference" need not be of the conscious or even the unconscious thought of the sitter, but must often be of the thought of some person far away. Thus, on my mother-in-law's second visit to the medium she was told that one of her daughters was suffering from a severe pain in her back on that day. This altogether unusual occurrence, unknown to the sitter, proved to be true. The announcement to my wife and brother of my aunt's death in New York before we had received the telegram (Mr. Hodgson has, I believe, sent you an account of this) may, on the other hand, have been occasioned by the sitters' conscious apprehension of the event. This particular incident is a "test" of the sort which one readily quotes; but to my mind it was far less convincing than the innumerable small domestic matters of which Mrs. Piper incessantly talked in her sittings with members of my family. With the affairs of my wife's maternal kinsfolk in particular her acquaintance in trance was most intimate. Some of them were dead, some in California, some in the State of Maine. She characterized them all, living as well as deceased, spoke of their relations to each other, of their likes and dislikes, of their as yet unpublished practical plans, and hardly ever made a mistake, though, as usual, there was very little system or continuity in anything that came out. A *normal* person, unacquainted with the family, could not possibly have said as much; one acquainted with it could hardly have avoided saying more.

The most convincing things said about my own immediate household were either very intimate or very trivial. Unfortunately the former things cannot well be published. Of the trivial things, I have forgotten the greater number, but the following, *rarae nantes,* may serve as samples of their class: She said that we had lost recently a rug, and I a waistcoat. (She wrongly accused a person of stealing the rug, which was afterwards found in the house.) She told of my killing a gray-and-white cat, with ether, and described how it had "spun round and round" before dying. She told how my New York aunt had written a letter to my wife, warning her against all mediums, and then went off on a most amusing criticism, full of *traits vifs,* of the excellent woman's character. (Of course no one but my wife and I knew the existence of the letter in question.) She was strong on the events in our nursery, and gave striking advice during our first visit to her about the way to deal with certain "tantrums" of our second child, "little Billy-boy," as she called him, reproducing his nursery name. She told how the crib creaked at night, how a certain rocking chair creaked mysteriously, how my wife had heard footsteps on the stairs, etc., etc. Insignificant as these things sound when read, the accumulation of a large number of them has an irresistible effect. And I repeat again what I said before, that, taking everything that I know of Mrs. P. into account, the result is to make me feel as absolutely certain as I am of any personal fact in the world that she knows things in her trances which she cannot possibly have heard in her waking state, and that the definitive philosophy of her trances is yet to be found. The limitations of her trance information, its discontinuity and fitfulness, and its apparent inability to develop beyond a certain point, although they end by rousing one's moral and human impatience with the phenomenon, yet are, from a scientific point of view, amongst its most interesting peculiarities, since where there are limits there are conditions, and the discovery of these is always the beginning of explanation.

This is all that I can tell you of Mrs. Piper. I wish it were more "scientific." But, *valeat quantum!* it is the best I can do.

William James's close friendship with Richard Hodgson, who had been Secretary and Treasurer of the American Society for Psychical Research, made him the logical person to ask, after Hodgson's death

on December 20, 1905, to correlate and report on the long series of
sittings with Mrs. Piper in which Hodgson apparently was Mrs.
Piper's control and seemed desperately to be trying to prove his
identity and substantiate the theories of survival after death which
he himself had voiced before his death.

The difficulties of the task and James's dissatisfaction with the
evidence and his own reporting on it are reflected in the following
extracts from letters written during the three years in which he was
engaged on it. The report itself, slightly abridged, follows them.

LETTERS

To Theodore Flournoy, February 9, 1906 [1]

Yes! [Richard] Hodgson's death was ultra-sudden. He fell dead
while playing a violent game of "hand-ball." He was tremendously
athletic and had said to a friend only a week before that he thought
he could reasonably count on twenty-five years more of life. None
of his work was finished, vast materials amassed, which no one can
ever get acquainted with as he had gradually got acquainted; so
now good-by forever to at least two unusually solid and instructive
books which he would have soon begun to write on "psychic" subjects. As a *man*, Hodgson was splendid, a real man; as an investigator, it is my private impression that he lately got into a sort of
obsession about Mrs. Piper, cared too little for other clues, and continued working with her when all the sides of her mediumship
were amply exhibited. I suspect that our American Branch of the
S. P. R. will have to dissolve this year, for lack of a competent secretary. Hodgson was our only worker, except Hyslop, and *he* is engaged in founding an "Institute" of his own, which will employ
more popular methods. To tell the truth, I'm rather glad of the
prospect of the Branch ending, for the Piper-investigation—and
nothing else—had begun to bore me to extinction. . . .

---

[1] Henry James, ed., op. cit., Vol. II, p. 242.—Ed.

To Theodore Flournoy, 1906 [2]

I have undertaken to coordinate a lot of stuff that is now coming out through Mrs. Piper, purporting to be from Hodgson, in order to make a report. There is a great amount of subliminal automatism involved, but I suspect that the residual doubt will always remain as to whether it may not be a very amnesic extract of the real Hodgson trying to communicate. It will be sad indeed if this undecided verdict will be all that I can reach after so many years. *Ars longa,* indeed!

To James H. Hyslop, October 25, 1906 [3]

Dear Hyslop,—Richard Hodgson at a sitting yesterday said that *he* (not you) had proposed the word *bellum* to be delivered to you at Mrs. Soule's by him, but that he hadn't been able to get it through. Can you send me any definite report of what came?

I proposed a word to him to deliver there yesterday. My wife and Mrs. Pope went in the afternoon to Mrs. Soule, who was ill, and couldn't give a sitting. This A.M. my wife and I went. Immediately "the Piper group" was announced, and Richard Hodgson saying there was a new way being tried of "establishing" his identity —it was "impersonal," a message, but he couldn't bring it out. He alluded to the same result with you recently. He took direct control himself, spoke very slowly and gravely said he feared making mistakes. He called me by my name in full. I have never seen Mrs. S. and I remained outside the house till my wife called me in, and then Mrs. S.'s eyes were shut and remained so. My wife saw her once, some 10 years ago. She was treated by Mrs. S. as a stranger.

To Charles Lewis Slattery, April 21, 1907 [4]

Dear Mr. Slattery—My state of mind is this: Mrs. Piper has supernormal knowledge in her trances; but whether it comes from

[2] Ralph Barton Perry, op. cit. Vol. II, p. 171.—Ed.
[3] Previously unpublished letter in the archives of the American Society for Psychical Research.—Ed.
[4] Ralph Barton Perry, op. cit., Vol. II, p. 287.—Ed.

"tapping the minds" of living people, or from some common cosmic reservoir of memories, or from surviving "spirits" of the departed, is a question impossible for *me* to answer just now to my own satisfaction. The spirit theory is undoubtedly not only the most natural, but the simplest, and I have great respect for Hodgson's and Hyslop's arguments when they adopt it. At the same time the electric current called *belief* has not yet closed in my mind.

Whatever the explanation be, trance mediumship is an excessively complex phenomenon, in which many concurrent factors are engaged. That is why interpretation is so hard.

Make any use, public or private, that you like of this.

To Theodore Flournoy, August 9, 1908 [5]

I have just read Miss Johnson's report in the last S. P. R. *Proceedings,* and a good bit of the proofs of Piddington's on cross-correspondences between Mrs. Piper, Mrs. Verrall, and Mrs. Holland, which is to appear in the next number. You will be much interested, if you can gather the philosophical energy to go through such an amount of tiresome detail. It seems to me that these reports open a new chapter in the history of automatism; and Piddington's and Johnson's ability is of the highest order. Evidently "automatism" is a word that covers an extraordinary variety of fact. I suppose that you have on the whole been gratified by the "vindication" of Eusapia [Paladino] at the hands of Morselli *et al.* in Italy. Physical phenomena also seem to be entering upon a new phase in their history.

To Henry James, December 19, 1908 [6]

My time has been consumed by interruptions almost totally, until a week ago, when I finally got down seriously to work upon my Hodgson report. It means much more labor than one would suppose, and very little result. I wish that I had never undertaken it. I am sending off a preliminary installment of it to be read at the

---

[5] Henry James, ed., op. cit., Vol. II, pp. 311–12.—ED.
[6] Ibid., Vol. II, p. 317.—ED.

S. P. R. meeting in January. That done, the rest will run off easily,
and in a month I expect to actually begin the "Introduction to
Philosophy," which has been postponed so long, and which I hope
will add to income for a number of years to come.

To James H. Hyslop, January 20, 1909 [7]

Dear Hyslop,

Here is a peppercorn for your Journal.

Gottlob, I've finished my Hodgson report, which I expect to fill
nearly 100 pages of the English *Proceedings,* rather less perhaps of
yours. I shall mail the copy to England in a couple of days, but
should like to keep the copy destined for you a little while longer.
I mailed a "preliminary" report some weeks ago, to be read in
London on the 23rd, but not pub. till after the February *Proceedings*
are out, which would make it May, I suppose. Miss Johnson expects
that you will not publish ere she does, so I trust you will not. I wish
they didn't delay so—I like to see a thing quick.

To T. S. Perry, January 29, 1909 [8]

I have just got off my report on the Hodgson control, which has
stuck to my fingers all this time. It is a hedging sort of an affair, and
I don't know what the Perry family will think of it. The truth is
that the "case" is a particularly poor one for testing Mrs. Piper's
claim to bring back spirits. It is *leakier* than any other case, and
intrinsically, I think, no stronger than many of her other good cases,
certainly weaker than the G. P. case. I am also now engaged in
writing a popular article, "the avowals of a psychical researcher,"
for the *American Magazine,* in which I simply state without argument my own convictions, and put myself on record. I think that
public opinion is just now taking a step forward in these matters
—*vide* the Eusapian boom! and possibly both these *Schriften* of
mine will add their influence.

---

[7] Previously unpublished letter in the archives of the American Society for
Psychical Research.—ED.

[8] Henry James, ed., op. cit., Vol. II, pp. 319–20.—ED.

REPORT ON MRS. PIPER'S HODGSON-CONTROL [1]

PART I [2]

SUMMARY OF SPECIAL INCIDENTS

1. Introduction

Richard Hodgson died suddenly upon December 20th, 1905. On December 28th a message purporting to come from him was delivered in a trance of Mrs. Piper's, and she has hardly held a sitting since then without some manifestation of what professed to be Hodgson's spirit taking place. Hodgson had often during his lifetime laughingly said that if he ever passed over and Mrs. Piper was still officiating here below, he would control her better than she had ever yet been controlled in her trances, because he was so thoroughly familiar with the difficulties and conditions on this side. Indeed he was; so that this would seem *prima facie* a particularly happy conjunction of spirit with medium by which to test the question of spirit return.

I have undertaken to collate the various American sittings (75 in number as I write, the latest being that of January 1st, 1908) in which the professed R. H. has appeared, and a few prefatory remarks as to my own relation to the Piper phenomenon would seem to be a needed introduction to what is to follow. I have no space for twice-told tales, so I will assume that my readers are acquainted,

---

[1] Published in the *Proceedings of the American Society for Psychical Research*, Vol. III, 1909, with the following note by William James: "This report is published simultaneously in the English *Proceedings*. I have merely substituted *parentheses* enclosing what the sitters say for initials used in the English Report. As in the English Report, Notes in brackets are distributed throughout the detailed records. Initials connected with Notes indicate the person who made them, usually the sitter."—ED.

[2] This report was prepared to be read at the General Meeting of the Society, on January 28th, 1909. To make a single document by distributing its material through the larger report would cost much labor, so the two parts are printed separately, but readers will understand that they should be read in conjunction.—W. J.

to some degree at any rate, with previously printed accounts of Mrs. Piper's mediumship. I had myself had no sitting with Mrs. Piper and had hardly seen her for some nine years, but for most of that time I had been kept informed of what was going on by reading the typed records, furnished me by my friend Hodgson, of all the trances of which report was taken, and for which the sitters had not asked secrecy to be observed. The "control" most frequently in evidence in these years has been the personage calling himself "Rector." Dr. Hodgson was disposed to admit the claim to reality of Rector and of the whole Imperator Band of which he is a member, while I have rather favored the idea of their all being dream-creations of Mrs. Piper, probably having no existence except when she is in trance, but consolidated by repetition into personalities consistent enough to play their several roles. Such at least is the dramatic impression which my acquaintance with the sittings has left on my mind. I can see no contradiction between Rector's being on the one hand an improvised creature of this sort, and his being on the other hand the extraordinarily impressive personality which he unquestionably is. He has marvelous discernment of the inner states of the sitters whom he addresses, and speaks straight to their troubles as if he knew them all in advance. He addresses you as if he were the most devoted of your friends. He appears like an aged and, when he speaks instead of writing, like a somewhat hollow-voiced clergyman, a little weary of his experience of the world, endlessly patient and sympathetic, and desiring to put all his tenderness and wisdom at your service while you are there. Critical and fastidious sitters have recognized his wisdom, and confess their debt to him as a moral adviser. With all due respect to Mrs. Piper, I feel very sure that her own waking capacity for being a spiritual adviser, if it were compared with Rector's, would fall greatly behind.

As I conceive the matter, it is on this mass of secondary and automatic personality of which of late years Rector has been the center, and which forms the steady background of Mrs. Piper's trances, that the supernormal knowledge which she unquestionably displays is flashed. Flashed, grafted, inserted—use what word you will—the trance automatism is at any rate the intermediating condition, the supernormal knowledge comes as if from beyond, and the automatism uses its own forms in delivering it to the sitter. The most habitual form is to say that it comes from the spirit of a departed friend. The earliest messages from "Hodgson" have been communicated by "Rector," but he soon spoke in his own name, and the only question which I shall consider in this paper is this: Are there any unmistakable indications in the messages in question that something that we may call the "spirit" of Hodgson was probably really there? We need not refine yet upon what the word "spirit" means and on what spirits are and can do. We can leave the meaning of the word provisionally very indeterminate—the vague popular notion of what a spirit is is enough to begin with.

Sources other than R. H.'s surviving spirit for the veridical communications from the Hodgson-control may be enumerated as follows:

(1) Lucky chance-hits.

(2) Common gossip.

(3) Indications unwarily furnished by the sitters.

(4) Information received from R. H., during his lifetime, by the waking Mrs. P. and stored up, either supraliminally or subliminally, in her memory.

(5) Information received from the living R. H., or others, at sittings, and kept in Mrs. Piper's trance-memory, but out of reach of her waking consciousness.

(6) "Telepathy," i.e., the tapping of the sitter's mind, or that of some distant living person, in an inexplicable way.

(7) Access to some cosmic reservoir, where the memory of all mundane facts is stored and grouped around personal centers of association.

Let us call the first five of these explanations "natural," and the last two "supernatural" or "mystical." It is obvious that no mystical explanation ought to be invoked so long as any natural one remains plausible. Only after the first five explanations have been made to appear improbable is it time for the telepathy theory and the cosmic-reservoir theory to be compared with the theory of R. H.'s surviving spirit.

The total amount of truthful information communicated by the R. H.-control to the various sitters is copious. He reminds them, for the most part, of events—usually unimportant ones—which they and the living R. H. had experienced together. Taking any one of these events singly, it is never possible in principle to exclude explanations number 1 and 4. About number 3, a complete record of the sitting ought generally to decide. Number 2 is often excluded either by the trivial or by the intricate nature of the case. Number 5 would be easily settled if the records of the sittings of the living Hodgson with Mrs. Piper were complete and accessible. They are supposed, for the past ten or twelve years at least, to exist in complete form. But parts of them are in Hodgson's private cipher, and they are now so voluminous that it would be rash to say of any recent message from Hodgson, so long as the matter of it might conceivably have been talked of at any previous trance of Mrs. Piper's, that no record of such talk exists. It might exist without having yet been found.

Add, to these several chances that any communication of fact by the Hodgson-control may have had a natural source, the further consideration that Mrs. Piper had known H. well for many years, and one sees that her subliminal powers of personation would have had an unusually large amount of material to draw upon in case they wished to get up a make believe spirit of Hodgson. So far, then, from his particular case being an unusually good one by which to test the claim that Mrs. Piper is possessed during her trances by the spirits of our departed friends, it would seem to be a particularly poor one for that purpose. I have come to the conclusion that it is an exceptionally bad one. Hodgson's familiarity when in the flesh with the difficulties at this end of the line has not made him show any more expertness as a spirit than other communicators have shown; and for his successes there are far more naturalistic explanations available than is the case with the other spirits who have professed to control Mrs. Piper.

So much for generalities, and so much for my own personal equation, for which my various hearers will make their sundry kinds of allowance. But before taking up the messages in detail, a word more about the fourth of the naturalistic explanations which I have instanced (conversations, that is, between Mrs. Piper and Hodgson when alive) is in order. Abstractly, it seems very plausible to suppose that R. H. (who systematically imposed on himself the law of never mentioning the contents of any trance in her waking presence) might have methodically adopted a plan of entertaining her on his visits by reciting all the little happenings of his days, and that it is this chronicle of small beer, stored in her memory, that now comes out for service in simulating his spirit-identity.

In the concrete, however, this is not a highly probable hypothesis. Everyone who knew Hodgson agrees that he was little given to anecdotical small change, unless the incident were comic or otherwise of an impressive order, and that his *souvenirs* of fact were usually of a broad and synthetic type. He had had a "splendid time" at such a place, with a "glorious" landscape, swim, or hill-climb, but no further detail. Gifted with great powers of reserve by nature, he was professionally schooled to secretiveness; and a decidedly incommunicative habit in the way of personal gossip had become a second nature with him—especially towards Mrs. Piper. For many years past he had seen her three times weekly (except during the months of her summer vacation) and had had to transcribe the records afterwards. The work was time-consuming, and he found it excessively fatiguing. He had economized energy upon it by adopting for many years past a purely business tone with the medium, entering, starting the trance, and leaving when it was over, with as few unnecessary words as possible. Great *brusquerie* was among the excellent R. H.'s potentialities, and for a while the amount of it displayed towards Mrs. P. led to a state of feeling on her part of which a *New York Herald* reporter once took advantage to exploit publicly. R. H. was remonstrated with, and was more

considerate afterwards. It may well be that Mrs. Piper had heard
one little incident or another, among those to be discussed in the
following report, from his living lips, but that any large mass of
these incidents are to be traced to this origin, I find incredible.

2. Earlier Communications

The spirit-Hodgson's first manifestation was, as I have said, eight
days after his death. There was something dramatically so like him
in the utterances of those earliest days, gradually gathering
"strength" as they did, that those who had cognizance of them were
much impressed. I will begin by a short account of these earliest
appearances, of which the first was at Miss Pope's sitting on December 28th, 1905. At this sitting "Rector" had been writing, when the
hand dropped the pencil and worked convulsively for several seconds in an excited manner.

(What is the matter?)
[The hand, shaking with apparently great excitement, wrote
the letter H, . . . bearing down so hard on the paper that the
point of the pencil was broken. It then wrote "Hodgson."]
(God bless you!)
[The hand writes "I am"—followed by rapid scrawls, as if
regulator of machine were out of order.]
(Is this my friend?)
[Hand assents by knocking five times on paper-pad.]
[Rector.] Peace, friends, he is here, it was he, but he could
not remain, he was so choked. He is doing all in his power to
return. . . . Better wait for a few moments until he breathes
freer again.
(I will.)
[R.] Presently he will be able to conduct all here.
(That is good news.)
[R.] Listen. Everything is for the best. He holds in his hand a
ring. . . . He is showing it to you. Cannot you see it, friend?
(I cannot see it. Have him tell me about it.)
[R.] Do you understand what it means?
(I know he had a very attractive ring.)
[R.] Margaret.
"All" was then written, with a "B" after it, and Miss P. asked

"What is that?" "A," "B" and "L" followed, but no explanation. [The explanation will be given later.]

The above is the whole of the direct matter from Hodgson at this, the first of the sittings at which he has appeared.

(For the sequel to this ring episode, see pp. 125–30.)

At Miss Pope's next sitting (five days later), after some talk about him from Rector, R. H. appeared for the second time, and in the character, familiar to him, of being a wellspring of poetical lore. Mrs. Piper's hand cramped most awkwardly, first dropped and then broke the pencil. A new one being given, the hand wrote as follows:

RICHARD HODGSON I AM WELL HAPPY GLAD I CAME GOD BLESS POPE
(Many thanks.) [Then the hand wrote:]

> It lies not in her form or face
>   Tho these are passing fair,
> Nor in the woman's tone of grace,
>   Nor in her falling hair;
> It lies not in those wondrous eyes
>   that swiftly light and shine,
> Tho all the stars of all the skies
>   Than these are less divine.

I am only practicing.
(Who wrote it?)
[Rector.] Richard only.
(When?)
Now.
(Doesn't it exist on paper in our world?)
No.
(Did you really make that up?)
Yes.
(Well, you are clever.)
If you ever find this in your world, never believe in this world!
(I shall look for it, you may be sure.)
Good! Think I'm asleep? Not much! My head. I must leave you now.
[Rector.] It is impossible for us to hold him—that is all.
(Rector, did he dictate that poem to you? . . . Do you think he made it up?)
[Rector.] I do positively know he did. . . . Farewell!

At the second sitting after this (January 8th, 1906), Miss Pope again being the sitter, R. H. appeared again, writing as follows:

I am Hodgson. . . . I heard your call—I know you—you are Miss Pope. Piper instrument. I am happy exceedingly difficult to come very. I understand why Myers came seldom. I must leave. I cannot stay. I cannot remain today. . . .

[A tobacco pouch that had belonged to Hodgson was presently given to the medium as an "influence," when the writing went on:]

I am in the witness-box, do you remember?—Do you remember my promise to shake you up?

(I once asked Geo. P[elham] to "shake me up.")

No, I do not mean that.

(What do you mean?)

I said that if I got over here first I would soon learn how to communicate.—I would not make a botch of it.

(I remember—indeed you did.)

I am certainly R. H. I am sure. I have joined dear old G. Pelham, who did so much for me—more than all the rest put together.

[After a few words in Rector's name, a brush that had belonged to Hodgson was put into the medium's hand.]

Remember my theory about objects?

(What was it?)

They carried their own light. I was right.

(Yes, I remember very well.)

I see it now, I was right.

Did you receive my lines to Miss D.? [Referring apparently to the verses at the previous sitting.]

(Good that is most interesting.)

Amen! Miss D—— [This name, correctly given, is that of the cousin of R. H., mentioned as "Q" in previous reports, it must probably well known to the trance-consciousness.—W. J.]

(Miss D——?)

Yes. Ah, ah, ah, (which written words indicate laughter).

(What does that mean?) [referring to the "ah, ah"].

I am amused at you. Yet? found them?

(No, I haven't.)

It will take the remainder of your earthly life, and then you'll fail.

(You are just the same as ever.)
Not quite as full of energy as I wish, but give me time.
[Rector then comes in, and the sitting closes.]

On January 16th and January 17th, R. H. spoke again to Miss Pope, but without anything evidential in matter—or in manner either, unless the following be counted as dramatically like:

I shall never assume control here. Imperator shall lead me. In his care I am safe. I was met by him. There will be no moaning at the bar when I pass out to sea—remember it?

[Miss Pope assents.]

On February 5th, R. H. asks again:

Got any news of my poem?
(No, I give that up.)
I thought you would come to it. I made that up in a moment and composed to Miss D———.

[After some more non-evidential talk, R. H. mentions his living friend, Miss B., and says:]

Give my love to her and tell her I hope to speak with her soon.

It seems as if the wondrous land
    Within her vision lay:
I dimly sense the mystic strand
    Behind the glorious gray.

To Margaret Bancroft. Give her this. She has light.[3] [Correct.—W. J.]
(Yes. Is this your own?)
I just made it for her. . . . Tell her I shall never forget those hills, the water, our talks, and the delightful visit I had with her. [Correct.—W. J.]
(I think she is coming soon to speak with you here.)
Good. I hope so. Will you tell her, give her my message, ask her if she knows anything about my watch being stopped. Do you? I must go out and get a little breath.

[Miss B. writes: "I think the watch means *my* watch. We had a number of jokes about the frequent stopping of my watch."]

---

[3] In spiritist language, this means "she has paranormal powers."—ED.

On January 23rd, 1906, Mrs. Wm. James and W. James, Jr., had a sitting at which R. H. used the medium's voice and gave a very life-like impression of his presence. The record runs as follows: [4]

Why, there's Billy! Is that Mrs. James and Billy? God bless you! Well, well, well, this is good! [Laughs.] I am in the witness-box. [Laughs.] I have found my way, I am here, have patience with me. All is well with me. Don't miss me. Where's William? Give him my love and tell him I shall certainly live to prove all I know. Do you hear me? see me? I am not strong, but have patience with me. I will tell you all. I think I can reach *you*.

Something on my mind. I want Lodge to know everything. I have seen Myers. I must rest.

[After an interval he comes in again:]

Billy, where is Billy? What are you writing, Billy? Are you having any sports? Would you like to take a swim? [R. H.'s chief association with W. J., Jr., had been when fishing or swimming in Chocorua Lake.] Well, come on! Get a good deal of exercise, but don't overdo it! Perhaps I swam too much. [He undoubtedly had done so.] I learned my lesson, but I'm just where I wanted to be.

Do you remember [Q]? [Q] helped me. Then I saw Mother, Rebecca, and Father. I want very much to converse with Annie. [His sister.] She perfectly understood my efforts and was everything to me. I want her to know that I am living, and I am going on to show what I know to the end of all time. Is Ellen well?—that's my sister. I want G. D. [his brother-in-law] to have my watch. [The family names used here are correct, but were known to the trance-consciousness.—W. J.]

Do you play ball?—tennis? Men will theorize—let them do so! I have found out the truth. I said that if I could get over there I would not make a bund of it. If ever R. H. lived in the body, he is talking now. . . . William [James] is too dogmatic. . . . I want George [Dorr] to extricate all those papers and set those marked "private" aside. This has been on my mind. George is

---

[4] In this and in some of my future citations from the records I have condensed the material by leaving out repetitions and digressions, so that what appears is often straighter and more correct than what was originally given. I have, however, scrupulously endeavored to omit nothing that could possibly have determined what was said or influenced its veridicality.—W. J.

to be trusted absolutely with all sincerity and faith. There are some private records which I should not wish to have handled. Let George [Dorr] and Piddington go through them and return them to the sitters. The cipher! I made that cipher, and no one living can read it. [Correct.] I shall explain it later. Let Harry [James] and George keep them till then. [They had been appointed administrators of his estate, a fact probably known to Mrs. Piper.] This is the best I have been able to do yet. I spoke with Miss Pope, but this is the best. Remember, every communication *must* have the human element. I understand better now why I had so little from Myers. [To W. J., Jr.:] What discourages you about your art? [W. J., Jr., was studying painting.] Oh what good times we had, fishing! Believe, Billy, wherever you go, whatever you do, there is a God.

So much for Hodgson's first appearances, which were characteristic enough in manner, however incomplete.

In the space to which this preliminary report is limited one can hardly quote the records *verbatim*, for they are anything but concise. My best plan will be to cull a few of the best veridical communications, and discuss them simply from the point of view of the alternatives of explanation.

I will begin with what I shall call

3. The Ring Incident

On Hodgson's fiftieth birthday, a lady whom I will call Mrs. Lyman, an old friend of his, much interested in the Piper work, had given him a rather massive ring to wear. The source of this ring H. had kept to himself, and after his death Mrs. L. asked the administrator of his estate to return it to her. The ring could not be found.

At the sitting of December 28th (R. H.'s first appearance as a spirit), it will be remembered that the control Rector had said to Miss Pope, the sitter, "He holds in his hand a ring—do you understand what it means?"

(I know he had a very attractive ring.)
[Rector] [writing] Margaret. a ll B, L.

On January 16th, Miss Pope being again the sitter, the R. H.-control suddenly wrote:

> Give ring to Margaret back to Margaret. [Mrs. Lyman's name is not Margaret.]
> (Who is Margaret?)
> I was with her in summer.
> (All right, but the ring has not been found yet. Can you find out where it is?)
> The undertaker got it.
> (Oh, all right.)
> I know. Help me.
> (I shall look it up.)
> It was with me.
> (Yes, I heard so.)
> It was, it was.
> (I will attend to it.)
> Thank you.

On January 24th, Mrs. Lyman herself had her first sitting. As soon as Hodgson appeared he wrote:

> The ring. You gave it me on my fiftieth birthday. When they asked I didn't want to say you gave it me, I didn't want to say that. . . . Two palm-leaves joining each other—Greek. [Here followed an illegible word. The palms truly described the ring, which Mrs. Piper probably had seen; but it bore no Greek inscription, nor was the symbol on it a Greek cross.] You gave it me—
> (Yes, Dick, where is it now?)
> They have got it. They took it off my finger after I was gone.
> (No, they didn't find it on your finger.)
> Pocket, it was in my pocket, I'll find it you shall have it.

On January 29th, Mrs. L. had another sitting. The Hodgson-control wrote:

> I have been trying to make clear about that ring. It is on my mind all the time. I thought if I could get Margaret B. to get it for me, I would get it to you through her, then no one would understand. I could not tell Miss Pope about you.
> (Did you think Margaret B. gave it to you?)

Oh dear no! not at all.

(Then why did you speak of her?)

I could trust her absolutely, and no one could understand. She would never betray it. You gave it to me on my 50th birthday. Palms and R. H. [Then a possible attempt to draw a symbol engraved on the ring.] No one living knows this but myself and yourself.

(That is true, but what was the motto in the ring?)

All will be clear to me in time. Do not ask me test questions now. . . . I wish the ring now to go back to yourself. I thought Margaret would understand and be glad to do it for me. I could not tell Miss Pope about you.

On March 5th R. H. again inquires of Mrs. Lyman about the ring. She then asks him: "Did you have it on that last day when you went to the boat-club?" [R. H. died while playing a game of hand-ball at the boat-club.]

I certainly had it on that day.

(You told Miss P. the undertaker got it.)

Thought he did and I am sure a man took it from my finger. [After a few more words R. H. continues:]

I had that ring on my finger when I started for the club, I recall putting in my pocket. I did so because it hurt my finger when playing ball. I am not dreaming, I am clear. When I get here first I am a little stuffy, but I am as clear now as I ever was, I put it in my waistcoat pocket.

(Why do you think a man stole it?)

I saw it on a finger. . . . I put in my pocket, and the one who took care of my clothes is responsible for it. . . . What did they do with my waistcoat?

On May 16th, on being told that the ring is not yet found, the R. H.-control writes:

I saw it taken by a man from my locker. He was in charge at the time and he has my ring. . . . I shall be able to discover his name so you may be able to find it. I see where he goes and the house where he lives, plainly. . . . Five-story brick house not far from the club and he is on the third story from the street, near the corner of the street, the room is in the rear of the building and I see his face clearly [a description of the man follows]. I see the ring on his finger clearly. The waistcoat was in his room when I entered the light a few moments ago. I am as sure of this as I am that you are Mrs. Lyman.

In point of fact the ring was found a couple of months later in the pocket of Hodgson's waistcoat, which had been too carelessly explored for it, and which had lain during all the interval in a room at the house of Mr. Dorr, with whom the Hodgson-control had all the time been having frequent communications.

The whole incident lends itself easily to a naturalistic interpretation. Mrs. Piper or her trance-consciousness may possibly have suspected the source of the ring. Mrs. Lyman's manner may have confirmed the suspicion. The manner in which the first misleading reference to "Margaret" was afterwards explained away may well have been the cunning of a "control" trying plausibly to cover his tracks and justify his professed identity. The description of the house and of the man to whom he ascribes its present possession sounds like vague groping, characteristic also of control-cunning. The description was but little like that of Mr. Dorr, whose house, moreover, is neither very near a corner nor very near a club.

On the other hand, if the hypothesis be seriously entertained that Hodgson's spirit was there in a confused state, using the permanent Piper automatic machinery to communicate through, the whole record is not only plausible but natural. It presents just that mixture of truth and groping which we ought to expect. Hodgson has the ring "on his mind" just as Mrs. Lyman has. Like her, he wishes its source not to be bruited abroad. He describes it accurately enough, truly tells of his taking it to the fatal boat-club, and of putting into his waistcoat pocket there, of the waistcoat being taken from the locker, and vaguely, but not quite erroneously, indicates its present position.

Mrs. Lyman's own impression of the incident is as follows:

No living person beside myself knew who had given him the ring, and I am quite sure that the living R. H. would have been as desirous as I to keep all mention of me out of the trance-record. Had he had entire control he would never have mentioned the ring until I had come to a sitting, but in his half-dreamy state something slipped out to Miss Pope, the sitter, aided telepathically perhaps by her knowledge that he had lately worn an unusual-looking ring which she knew was missing after his death. I am sure that Miss Pope thought the ring would be a good "test," so that although she was not the first to speak of it, it must certainly have been in her mind. It is characteristic of R. H. that even in his half-conscious state he is able to keep his own counsel so well. The word Margaret and the letters B and L which followed the mention of the ring at the very first sitting seem to refer to Miss Margaret Bancroft and myself. He knew that Miss Bancroft had "light," and he seems to feel that if he can only reach her she will understand what he wants. He was well aware of my own morbid dislike of having my affairs mentioned at the trance outside of my own sittings. You know that curious trait of suspicion in Hodgson's absolutely honest nature—trained in him professionally. When Miss Pope tells him the ring cannot be found, he at once thinks: "There was my body, and my clothes, etc., I believe the undertaker took it." Then I myself, Mrs. Lyman, come and again tell him the ring can't be found. His earthly memories presently become clear and he tells me exactly what he did with it before his death. But his suspicious side has been aroused—you know how anything once registered on the trance-machinery seems to make an impression and tends to recur—and again he thinks that someone took it. Nothing could be more characteristic of H. than his indignant remark about the man who had charge of his clothes being *responsible*. It all seems to me the kind of unpractical thing that a man would do in a dream. There are strong characteristics of R. H. in it, but it is R. H. dreaming and troubled. I am glad I haven't to make myself intelligible to a stranger to the persons involved; but knowing them as I do, I feel my own way straight through the maze, and the explanation is clear.

This incident of the ring seems to me a typical example of the ambiguity of possible interpretation that so constantly haunts us in the Piper phenomenon. If you are willing beforehand to allow that a half-awakened spirit may come and mix its imperfect memories with the habits of the trance automatism, what you get is entirely congenial with your hypothesis—you apperceive the message sympathetically. But if you insist that nothing but knock-down evidence for the spirits shall be counted, since what comes is also compatible with natural causes your hardness of heart remains unbroken, and you continue to explain things by automatic personation and accidental coincidence, with perhaps a dash of thought-transference thrown in. People will interpret this ring episode harmoniously with their prepossessions. Taken by itself its evidential value is weak; but experience shows, I think, that a large number of incidents, hardly stronger than this one, will almost always produce a cumulative effect on the mind of a sitter whose affairs they implicate, and dispose him to the spiritistic view. It grows first possible, then plausible, then natural, and finally probable in a high degree.

The next incident I will recite is one which at a certain moment gave me a little thrill, as if I might be really talking with my old friend. (I have to make the personal confession that this reality-coefficient, as Professor Baldwin calls it, has generally been absent from my mind when dealing with the Piper controls or reading reports of their communications.) I will call the episode "the nigger-talk case."

4. The Nigger-Talk Case

On February 27th, 1906, at a sitting with Professor Hyslop, the following dialogue took place:

[R. H.] I wonder if you recall what I said I would do if I should return first?

(I do not remember exactly.)

Remember that I told Myers that we would talk nigger-talk—Myers—talk nigger-talk?

(No, you must have told that to someone else.)

Ah yes, James. I remember it was James, yes, Will James. He will understand.

Mr. Hyslop immediately wrote to me—I being in California—enclosing the record and soliciting corroboration. I had to reply that the words awakened absolutely no echo in my memory. Three months later, I returned to Cambridge and began to study records of sittings held during my absence. I met this incident again, and again it failed to stir my memory. But the very next day, in a conversation with Messrs. Dorr and Piddington, while I was recalling certain discussions that I had formerly had with Hodgson about the amenability to suggestion of the Piper controls, it suddenly flashed across me that these were probably what the words to Hyslop had meant. I had namely said to Hodgson, more than once, that a little tactful steering on his part would probably change the sacerdotal verbiage of the Imperator group so completely that he would soon find them "talking like nigger minstrels." For a moment I felt sure that this expression of mine, buried so deep in my own mind that it required a peculiar chain of associations to revive it, was what was dimly working in the memory of a surviving Hodgson, and trying to extricate itself. It was so incredible that R. H. would ever have repeated such a remark to either the waking Mrs. Piper or to her controls, that it seemed a good test of his survival. I regret to say, however, that the subsequent developments of the incident have deprived it in my eyes of all test value. Not only did the Hodgson-control, when questioned by me subsequently, fail to recall anything like that discussion of the control's suggestibility which was the setting in which my memory had put the phrase, but Mr. Piddington has found in the Piper records evidence that the Myers-control also had used the words "nigger-talk," so that this expression must be considered as part of the stock of Mrs. P.'s trance vocabulary.[5] Such an incident shows how wary one must be in one's interpretations. A really expert critic of the Piper trances ought to be familiar with the entire mass of material previous to any utterance under consideration. Hodgson was extraordinarily expert in this sense, and one of the weirdest feelings I have had in dealing with the business lately, has been to find the

---

[5] "Feb. 4th, 1902. R. H. (spontaneously to Myers-control): Do you remember about your laughing with me once and your saying that doubtless you would some time be coming back and talking nigger-talk?" A reference to the same incident is also made in the sitting of Feb. 13th, 1901.—W. J.

wish so frequently surging up in me that he were alive beside me to give critical counsel as to how best to treat certain of the communications of his own professed spirit.

5. *The Huldah Episode*

During the voice-sitting of May 2nd, 1906, Mr. Piddington being present, the R. H.-control said:

> Pid, I want very much to give you my private letters concerning a Miss—a Miss—in Chicago [pseudonym]. I do not wish anyone to read them.
> (How shall I know?)
> Look at my letters stamped from Chicago. I wouldn't have them get out for the world.

The name "Densmore" [pseudonym] was then written. Mr. Piddington asked whether the letters would be signed by the surname or the Christian name. The name "Huldah" was then given as that by which the letters would be signed.

On May 14th Piddington reported to the R. H.-control that no such letters could be found, and asked for further information— "Can you tell me at what time this lady wrote letters to you? Was it lately?"

> No, several years previously. I should be much distressed if they fell into other hands. No one living except the lady and myself knows of the correspondence.
> (If I cannot find those letters, should you feel any objection to my writing to the lady to ask if there has been such a correspondence?)
> Yes, I would rather you would do so.

Later (May 29th) Piddington reports unsuccessful search again, and Mr. Dorr, who also is present, asks whether "Huldah" is one of a family of Densmores known to him. "Is she a sister of Mary, Jenny, and Ella [pseudonyms]?"

> Ella is the one. Huldah we used to call her.

[This was emphatically spoken. Then followed a statement (not caught in Mr. Dorr's notes) that the lady's full name was Ella Huldah Densmore.]

No one living could have known it. I hope I have destroyed them—I may have done so and forgotten it. There was a time when I greatly cared for her, and I did not wish it known in the ears of others. I think she can corroborate this. I am getting hazy. I must leave.

On June 5th, Mrs. William James and Mr. Dorr being present, D. asked: "Can you tell us anything more about Huldah Densmore? You said the other day that she was the same person as Ella? Were you clear in saying that?"

Did I say that? That was a mistake. She is a sister. Is one of the three sisters, but not Ella. [She *was* Ella.] I know what I am talking about. I saw Huldah in Chicago. I was very fond of her. I proposed marriage to her, but she refused me.

The statement about proposing marriage was not divulged to me by my wife, until I had already heard from the lady called Ella Densmore in this narrative, who was then in a foreign country, and to whom I had written to ascertain whether she and Hodgson had ever corresponded, or whether she or anyone in her family was christened Huldah. Both Mr. Dorr and I knew her, but I was ignorant that she and Hodgson were acquainted. Great was my surprise when she wrote as follows:

Regarding the utterances of Mrs. Piper, I have no difficulty in telling you the circumstances on which she may have founded her communications. Years ago Mr. H. asked me to marry him, and some letters were exchanged between us which he may have kept. I do not remember how I signed the letters to him. I have sometimes used my middle name, Hannah, instead of Ella. [She knew of no "Huldah" in her family.]

In spite of the confusion that pervades Hodgson's veracious utterances here, it seems improbable that they should merely have been lucky flukes. Two naturalistic explanations offer themselves immediately.

(1) He might have made Mrs. Piper his confidant at the time; but no one who knows Hodgson will regard this explanation for a moment as credible.

(2) Nothing spreads as fast as rumors of this sort; so that if there had been a gossipy rumor, it might very well have spread to Mrs. Piper's ears, although it had skipped over Mr. Dorr's and mine. I accordingly inquired of a dozen of R. H.'s most intimate friends, saying: "Suppose I were to tell you that Hodgson had been in love not long ago, and had offered himself to a certain lady—would any particular person's name arise in your mind in consequence of such a suggestion?" Not a single one of these friends thought of the name of Miss Densmore, although three of them suggested other names very wide of the mark. Evidently no gossip had got into circulation, and R. H. had covered his tracks well. He was indeed the most singular mixture of expansiveness and reticence I have ever known; and the reticence had been increased professionally, as I may say, through his long training in having to guard the private affairs of sitters, and watch himself with Mrs. Piper. I was Hodgson's earliest American friend, and until his death always imagined myself to enjoy an almost perfect intimacy with him. Since his death I have nevertheless found that whole departments of his life were unknown to me. In this "Huldah" matter in particular, not only was I unaware that he and she were acquainted, but if anyone had described him to me as being in love with her, I should have scouted the story as inherently improbable, from the character of the two parties.

Nevertheless the story was true, barring the false name Huldah and a certain vacillation about the real christian name. The sister of the so-called "Huldah" has told me, moreover, that besides herself, she thought that no living person knew from her sister's lips of R. H.'s state of mind. As Hodgson himself had apparently told no one, the incident seemed an excellent one to count in favor of spirit return, unless, indeed, it should turn out that while it was happening, he had been led to consult the Piper controls about it himself, and to use "Huldah's" name as a test of their telepathic or clairvoyant powers. But that even then he could have given them the real name seems unlikely, in view of his habitual methods. The records taken to England have not yet been looked over from this point of view, and no one knows just what they may contain, but fortunately one of the sittings with Mrs. Piper after Hodgson's decease throws decisive light upon the matter. Hodgson *did* consult the Imperator group at the time of his disappointment, and the reasonable conclusion is that the revelation which so surprised Mr. Dorr and myself was thus a product of her trance-memory of previous conversations with the living Hodgson.

The sitting to which I allude was held on January 27th, 1906, by Professor Newbold. In the course of it the Hodgson-control suddenly says:

> Let me ask if you remember anything about a *lady* in [Chicago] to whom I referred.
>
> (Oh Dick, I begin to remember. About eight or nine years ago, was it, Dick?)
>
> Yes.
>
> [Such a lady was frequently mentioned at sittings in 1895, and H. was told he would marry her. I was present when these statements were made, if my memory serves me.—W. R. N.[6]]
>
> (Tell me more, so *I* won't tell *you!*)
>
> And my position regarding her.
>
> (I wasn't sure it was in [Chicago].)
>
> Do you remember . . . Densmore?
>
> (Was it *Jessie* Densmore?)
>
> Yes, good.
>
> [Mr. Dorr, who was present, here interjects:]
>
> "Do you mean the name was *Jessie* Densmore, Hodgson?"
>
> No, no, no, no. [Jessie was the first name of R. H.'s Australian cousin, "Q."—W. J.]
>
> (Dick, you told me years ago about a lady you were interested in, but I have forgotten her name and where she lived.)
>
> She lived in [Chicago].
>
> (Dick, it comes back to me as a cloud.)

---

[6] Professor William Romaine Newbold.—ED.

She was a Miss Densmore; I loved her dearly.

(You used to tell me about her years ago.)

Yes, and she afterwards married. Yes, I told you, and you are the only man I ever told. [Correct, apparently, save for the possibility of his having told Myers. See below.]

(I'm not sure you told me her name.)

Yes, I did.

(The name is the least likely thing for me to remember. . . . What is the married name of Miss Densmore?)

Heaven knows! It has gone from me and I shall soon go myself.

So much for Dr. Newbold's evidence. He has sent me a letter written to him by Hodgson in 1895, from which it would appear that the Piper controls had prophesied that both he and Newbold would ere long be made matrimonially happy, but that whereas the prophecy was being verified in N.'s case, it had been falsified in his own, he having that day received formal announcement of the marriage of Miss Densmore to another. The only other material which I shall quote is the following dialogue, at a sitting of my own, October 24th, 1906. Inquiring about "Huldah," I ask:

(Did you make anyone your confidant?)

No, though I may possibly have given a hint of it to Newbold.

(Did you tell anybody on the other side of the water?)

I may possibly have hinted it to Lodge.

(Her sister tells me she thinks you may have told Myers when he was alive.)

I think not: I may have hinted it to Myers.

(She denies any knowledge of the name Huldah.)

I used that name instead of the right christian name [he here gives the latter correctly] to avoid compromising—it was a very delicate matter, and caused me great disappointment. Have you communicated it to her?

(Yes, and she corroborates. . . .)

[R. H. displays no further curiosity—a living person would probably have asked whether the lady had said nothing about him, etc.]

Do you remember a lady doctor in New York? a member of our Society?

(No, but what about her?)

Her husband's name was Blair, . . . I think.

(Do you mean Mrs. Dr. Blair Thaw?)

Oh yes. Ask Mrs. Thaw if I did not at a dinner party mention something about the lady. I may have done so.

[Mrs. Thaw writes in comment upon this:—"Fifteen years ago, when R. H. was visiting us after his operation for appendicitis he told me that he had just proposed to a young lady and been refused, he gave no name." Mrs. Thaw is the only living person besides Newbold to whom I can certainly find that he ever spoke of this episode, and the clue to Mrs. Thaw comes from the control! —W. J.]

(Do you remember the name of Huldah's present husband?)

[To which R. H. replies by giving his country and title correctly, but fails to give his name.]

The entire incident shows the importance of completeness in the records. Without Professor Newbold's sitting we should have no present assurance that the trance-memory might have furnished the facts which seemed at the first blush to suggest so strongly the return of a "spirit" in a state of confused memory. *Compatible* with the return of such a spirit the facts indeed are. The possibility of the more naturalistic explanation doesn't make the supernatural one impossible; and if spirit return were already made probable by other evidence, this might well be taken as a case of it too. But what I am sifting these records for is *independent* evidence of such return; and so long as the record in this instance lends itself so plausibly to a naturalistic explanation, I think we must refuse to interpret it in the spiritistic way.

A couple of smaller veridical incidents which have seemed to the sitters to make rather strongly for spirit return are connected with R. H.'s financial history. I shall call them

6. The Pecuniary Messages

The American Branch had never fully paid its expenses; and although the Secretary's salary had always been very small, Hodgson had, after the first years, been reluctant to have any part of it charged to the mother country. The result had occasionally been pecuniary embarrassment on his part. During his last visit to England, shortly after Myers's death, this embarrassment had been extreme; but an American friend, divining it in the nick of time, rescued him by an impulsive and wholly unexpected remittance. To this remittance he replied by a letter which contained some banter and, among other things, cited the story of a starving couple who were overheard by an atheist who was passing the house, to pray aloud to God for food. The atheist climbed the roof and dropped some bread down the chimney, and heard them thank God for the miracle. He then went to the door and revealed himself as its author. The old woman replied to him: "Well, the Lord sent it, even if the devil brought it."

At this friend's sitting of January 30th, R. H. suddenly says:

> Do you remember a story I told you and how you laughed, about the man and woman praying?
> (Oh, and the devil was in it. Of course I do.)
> Yes, the devil, they told him it was the Lord who sent it if the devil brought it. . . . About the food that was given to them. . . . I want you to know who is speaking.

The sitter feels quite certain that no one but himself knew of the correspondence, and regards the incident as a good test of R. H.'s continued presence. Others will either favor this interpretation of it, or explain it by reading of the sitter's mind, or treat it as a chance coincidence, according to their several prepossessions. I myself feel morally certain that the waking Mrs. Piper was ignorant of the incident and of the correspondence. Hodgson was as likely to have informed *me*, as anyone, of the affair. He had given me at the time a vivid account of the trouble he had been in, but no hint of the quarter from which relief had come.

Of the other pecuniary message no written record exists, but the sitter has acquainted me with the incident, which ran as follows:

To assure Hodgson a salary, Mr. Dorr had acquainted a certain wealthy friend (who believed in the cause and in the value of the Secretary's work) with the situation of the Branch, and with R. H.'s reasons for not wishing to be indebted to the parent Society. This friend had agreed to pay into the Branch treasury the amount of deficit in the yearly salary account, provided the operation should remain anonymous, and Hodgson should ask no questions. Hodgson agreed to this. But upon the first sitting which this friend had after his death, the "spirit" of R. H. immediately referred to the matter and thanked the sitter warmly for the support given. The donor is of opinion, as I am also, that Hodgson may have suspected the source of the aid while receiving it, and that his "spirit" may therefore naturally have thanked the right person. That Mrs. Piper's waking consciousness should have been acquainted with any part of the transaction is incredible. The donor's name had been kept from me, who was Vice-President of the Society, and had yearly to know the accounts. I had known that the deficit in Hodgson's pay was made up by anonymous American believers in his work, but had supposed that there were several of them. I cannot well understand how Mrs. Piper should have got wind of any part of the financial situation, although her controls may have got wind of it in trance from others who were in the secret.

Few persons will ascribe the affair to chance-coincidence, but with both thought-transference and trance-memory as possible explanations, the incident cannot be deemed to furnish proof of Hodgson's personal survival.

In a later report I shall quote sittings at greater length and discuss briefly some of the control's peculiarities. The conclusions I shall then draw will probably not be different from those which I now draw as follows:

(1) The case is an exceptionally bad one for testing spirit return, owing to the unusual scope it gives to naturalistic explanations.

(2) The phenomena it presents furnish no knock-down proof of the return of Hodgson's spirit.

(3) They are well compatible, however, with such return, provided we assume that the Piper organism not only transmits with great difficulty the influences it receives from beyond the curtain, but mixes its own automatic tendencies most disturbingly there-

with. Hodgson himself used to compare the conditions of spirit communication to those of two distant persons on this earth who should carry on their social intercourse by employing each of them a dead-drunk messenger.

(4) Although this Hodgson case, *taken by itself,* yields thus only a negative, or at the best a baffling conclusion, we have no scientific right to take it by itself, as I have done. It belongs with the whole residual mass of Piper phenomena, and they belong with the whole mass of cognate phenomena elsewhere found. False personation is a ubiquitous feature in this total mass. It certainly exists in the Piper case; and the great question there is as to its limits. If, when lavish allowance has been made for this strange tendency in our subliminal life, there should still appear a balance of probability (which in this case can only mean a balance of simplicity) in the view that certain parts of the Piper communications really emanate from personal centers of memory and will, connected with lives that have passed away; if, I say, this balance of probability should appear decisively anywhere in the mass, then the rest of the mass will have to be interpreted as at least possibly similarly caused. I admire greatly Hodgson's own discussion of the Piper case in Volume XIII of our *Proceedings,* especially in sections 5 and 6, where, taking the whole mass of communication into careful account, he decides for this spiritist interpretation. I know of no more masterly handling anywhere of so unwieldy a mass of material; and in the light of his general conclusions there, I am quite ready to admit that my own denials in this present paper may be the result of the narrowness of my material, and that possibly R. H.'s spirit has been speaking all the time, only my ears were deaf. It is true that I still believe the "Imperator band" to be fictitious entities, while Hodgson ended by accepting them as real; but as to the general probability of there being real communicators somewhere in the mass, I cannot be insensible to Hodgson's able discussion, or fail to feel the authority which his enormous experience gave to his opinion in this particular field.

(5) I therefore repeat that if ever our growing familiarity with these phenomena should tend more and more to corroborate the hypothesis that "spirits" play some part in their production, I shall be quite ready to undeafen my ears, and to revoke the negative conclusions of this limited report. The facts are evidently complicated in the extreme, and we have as yet hardly scratched the surface of them. But methodical exploration has at last seriously begun, and these earlier observations of ours will surely be interpreted one day in the light of future discoveries which it may well take a century to make. I consequently disbelieve in being too "rigorous" with our criticism of anything now in hand, or in our squeezing so evidently vague a material too hard in our technical forceps at the present stage. What we need is more and more observations. Quantity may have to supplement quality in the material. When we have the facts in sufficient number, we may be sure that they will cast plenty of explanatory backward light. We can therefore well afford to play a waiting game.

PART II [7]

SELECTIONS FROM DETAILED RECORDS

1. Introduction

"Believe me, I am not rubbish."—THE HODGSON-CONTROL.

Richard Hodgson had always seemed and felt so robust that the possibility of his death had been thought of by no one, and no provision against it had been made. He had worked the American Branch of our Society practically alone, for many years, and although Professor Hyslop and I were Vice-Presidents, we had no minute acquaintance with details at the office, where Miss Lucy Edmunds, the assistant Secretary, was now left in charge alone.

---

[7] Part I of this report was written to be read at the S. P. R. meeting in London, January 23rd, 1909. I must assume in what follows that my readers are already acquainted with the contents of Part I.—W. J.

What was to be done about the Branch? what was to be done with its mass of records? what with Hodgson's private property? —these were so many problems requiring immediate solution. Last, not least, there was the problem of Mrs. Piper's future.

The question of R. H.'s property was easily answered by the legal appointment of Messrs. Dorr and H. James, Jr., to be administrators of his personal estate, he having left no will. The great mass of members and associates of the Branch being inert and indifferent, the handling of the other questions fell to a small group of more acutely interested persons, of whom Dr. Hyslop and I were the only ones with official authority.

Absent in California for about five months, I found on my return that certain differences of opinions had been developing at home.

Professor Hyslop, who had expended so much labor already on the Piper material, wished, if possible, to secure the records for the new American Society which he was founding. Others, whose sittings had been of a peculiarly intimate nature, claimed that the records of those sittings were their private property. In some quarters an objection was felt to such a mass of American material going to England. One person protested rather vehemently against the prominent part played by a certain other person in the deliberations. There being no one officially empowered to succeed Hodgson in taking charge of Mrs. Piper's sittings, differences of opinion regarding her future relations to the S. P. R. had arisen.

There was, in short, a state of strain, which I have to mention here, for the trance utterances of that period refer to it, and its peculiarities must be taken account of in estimating their significance.

In the end, however, since we all had fair minds and good will, and were united in our common love for Hodgson, everything got settled harmoniously. Mr. Piddington was sent for to represent the English Society; it was decided to extinguish the American Branch, and to carry the Piper reports to England, practically complete, while Hyslop's society should take possession of the other records; workable arrangements were found for Mrs. Piper; the situation, in short, smoothed itself out, leaving nothing but a new system of friendships among persons who before Hodgson's death had for the most part been unacquainted with one another.

The records of the Piper trance show that during all this period the "controls" had cognizance of the main factors of perplexity. There were, however, so many sources of leakage at this epoch that no part of this cognizance can be counted as evidence of supernormal knowledge. Whether in or out of trance, the medium may well have come into possession of what was essential in the facts, and the gaps could be filled by her imagination, either waking or somnambulistic. The result, however, was that those who held sittings at this time had a lively feeling that the control-personality they talked with, whether Rector or Hodgson, was an intelligence which understood the whole situation. It talked appropriately with Dorr about certain records not being made public; with Henry James, Jr., about the disposition of R. H.'s books and other property, and about pecuniary rights connected with Myers's book; with Piddington and Dorr about Hyslop's desires and how best to meet them; with Hyslop about his responsibilities and about mediums in whom he and Hodgson had recently been interested; with Dorr, James, Piddington, and Mrs. Lyman about whom to induce to manage the sittings; with more than one of us about a certain person who was unduly interfering, etc., etc.; the total outcome being that each sitter felt that his or her problems were discriminatingly perceived by the mind that animated the sleeping medium's organism.

More than this—most of us felt during the sittings that we were in some way, more or less remote, conversing with a real Rector or a real Hodgson. And this leads me to make a general remark about the difference between reading the record of a Piper sitting and playing an active part in the conversation recorded.

One who takes part in a good sitting has usually a far livelier sense, both of the reality and of the importance of the communication, than one who merely reads the record. Active relations with a thing are required to bring the reality of it home to us, and in a trance talk the sitter actively cooperates. When you find your questions answered and your allusions understood; when allusions are made that you understand, and your own thoughts are met, either by anticipation, denial, or corroboration; when you have approved, applauded, or exchanged banter, or thankfully listened to advice that you believe in; it is difficult not to take away an impression of having encountered something sincere in the way of a social phenomenon. The whole talk gets warmed with your own warmth, and takes on the reality of your own part in it; its confusions and defects you charge to the imperfect conditions, while you credit the successes to the genuineness of the communicating spirit. Most of us also, when sitters, react more, prick our ears more, to the successful parts of the communication. These consequently *loom* more in our memory, and give the key to our dramatic interpretation of the phenomenon. But a sitting that thus seemed important at the time may greatly shrink in value on a cold rereading, and if read by a non-participant, it may seem thin and almost insignificant.[8]

Somewhat similar fluctuations are noticed in the reality-feeling which the records may awaken at different times in one and the same reader. When I first undertook to collate this series of sittings and make the present report, I supposed that my verdict would be determined by pure logic. Certain minute incidents, I thought, ought to make for spirit return or against it in a "crucial" way. But watching my mind work as it goes over the data, convinces me that exact

---

[8] A striking example of this was furnished me lately by a manuscript which a friend sent me. She had been one of Mrs. Piper's most assiduous clients. Her communications with a certain spirit control had been copious, fluent and veridical, and to herself so comforting and elevating, that she had collomated them in this manuscript which, she thought, ought to be published. Strictly evidential matter was ruled out from it as too minute or private, and what remained was ethical and human matter only. Never having known the communicator, and reading passively and critically, I felt bound to dissuade from publication. I could not believe that readers would find in the communications a twentieth part of the importance which their receivers had found in them. The vital heat was absent, and what remained was ashes. I may well have been wrong in this opinion, but the incident brought vividly home to my own mind the contrast between the inside view of the sitter, and the outside one of the mere critic.—W. J.

logic plays only a preparatory part in shaping our conclusions here; and that the decisive vote, if there be one, has to be cast by what I may call one's general sense of dramatic probability, which sense ebbs and flows from one hypothesis to another—it does so in the present writer at least—in a rather illogical manner. If one sticks to the detail, one may draw an anti-spiritist conclusion; if one thinks more of what the whole mass may signify, one may well incline to spiritist interpretations.

This was the shape in which I myself left the matter in my recent preliminary report. I said that spirit-return was not proved by the Hodgson-control material, taken by itself, but that this adverse conclusion might possibly be reversed if the limited material were read in the light of the total mass of cognate phenomena. To say this is to say that the proof still baffles one. It still baffles me, I have to confess; but whether my subjective insufficiency or the objective insufficiency (as yet) of our evidence be most to blame for this, must be decided by others.

The common-sense rule of presumption in scientific logic is never to assume an unknown agent where there is a known one, and never to choose a rarer cause for a phenomenon when a commoner one will account for it. The usual is always more probable, and exceptional principles should be invoked only when the use of ordinary ones is impossible. Fraud is a form of human agency both known and common though much less common than cynics suppose; "personation" is unquestionably common in the whole realm of our subconscious operations; "telepathy" seems fairly established as a fact, though its frequency is still questionable; accidental coincidences occur, however rarely; but "spirits" of any grade, although they are indeed matters of tradition, seem to have shown themselves (so far as concrete evidence for them goes) nowhere except in the specific phenomena under investigation. Our rule of presumption should lead us then to deny spirits and to explain the Piper phenomena by a mixture of fraud, subconscious personation, lucky accident, and telepathy, whenever such an explanation remains possible. Taking the records in detail, and subjecting their incidents to a piecemeal criticism, such an explanation does seem practically possible everywhere; so, as long as we confine ourselves to the mere logic of presumption, the conclusion against the spirits holds good.

But the logic of presumption, safe in the majority of cases, is bound to leave us in the lurch whenever a real exception confronts us; and there is always a bare possibility that any case before us may be such an exception. In the case at present before us the exceptional possibility is that of "spirits" really having a finger in the pie. The records are fully compatible with this explanation, however explicable they may be without it. Spirits may cooperate with all the other factors, they may indeed find that harnessing the other factors in their service is the only way open to them for communicating their wishes. The lower factors may, in fact, be to a spirit's wishes what the physical laws of a machine are to its maker's and user's aims. A spectator, confining his attention to a machine's parts and their workings, and finding everything there explicable by mechanical push and pull, may be tempted to deny the presence of any higher actuation. Yet the particular pushes and pulls which the form of that machine embodies would not be there at all without a higher meaning which the machine expresses, and which it works out as a human purpose. To understand the parts of the machine fully, we must find the human purpose which uses all this push and pull as its means of realization. Just so the personation, fishing, guessing, using lucky hits, etc., in Mrs. Piper, may be, as it were, the mechanical means by which "spirits" succeed in making her living organism express their thought, however imperfectly.

As soon, therefore, as we drop our routine rule of presumption, and ask straight for truth and nothing but truth, we find that *the whole question is as to whether the exceptional case confronts us.* This is a question of probabilities and improbabilities. Now in every human being who in cases like this makes a decision instead of suspending judgment, the sense of probability depends on the form of dramatic imagination of which his mind is capable. The explanation has *in any event* to be dramatic. Fraud, personation, telepathy, spirits, elementals, are all of them dramatic hypotheses. If your imagination is incapable of conceiving the spirit hypothesis at all, you will just proclaim it "impossible" (as my colleague Munsterberg does, *Psychology and Life,* p. 130), and thus confess yourself incompetent to discuss the alternative seriously.

I myself can perfectly well imagine spirit agency, and find my mind vacillating about it curiously. When I take the phenomena piecemeal, the notion that Mrs. Piper's subliminal self should keep her sitters apart as expertly as it does, remembering its past dealings with each of them so well, not mixing their communications more, and all the while humbugging them so profusely, is quite compatible with what we know of the dream-life of hypnotized subjects. Their consciousness, narrowed to one suggested kind of operation, shows remarkable skill in that operation. If we suppose Mrs. Piper's dream-life once for all to have had the notion suggested to it that it must personate spirits to sitters, the fair degree of virtuosity it shows need not, I think, surprise us. Nor need the exceptional memory shown surprise us, for memory usually seems extraordinarily strong in the subconscious life. But I find that when I ascend from the details to the whole meaning of the phenomenon, and especially when I connect the Piper case with all the other cases I know of automatic writing and mediumship, and with the whole record of spirit-possession in human history, the notion that such an immense current of experience, complex in so many ways, should spell out absolutely nothing but the word "humbug" acquires a character of unlikeliness. The notion that so many men and women, in all other respects honest enough, should have this preposterous monkeying self annexed to their personality seems to me so weird that the spirit theory immediately takes on a more probable appearance. The spirits, if spirits there be, must indeed work under incredible complications and falsifications, but at least if they are present, some honesty is left in a whole department of the universe which otherwise is run by pure deception. The more I realize the quantitative massiveness of the phenomenon and its complexity, the more incredible it seems to me that in a world all of whose vaster features we are in the habit of considering to be *sincere* at least, however brutal, this feature should be wholly constituted of insincerity.

If I yield to a feeling of the dramatic improbability of this, I find myself interpreting the details of the sittings differently. I am able, while still holding to all the lower principles of interpretation, to imagine the process as more complex, and to share the feeling with which Hodgson came at last to regard it after his many years of familiarity, the feeling which Professor Hyslop shares, and which most of those who have good sittings are promptly inspired with. I can imagine the spirit of R. H. talking to me through inconceivable barriers of obstruction, and forcing recalcitrant or only partly consilient processes in the medium to express his thoughts, however dimly.

This is as candid an account of my own personal equation as I can give. I exhibited it in my treatment of special incidents in the preliminary report, and the reader will make allowance for it in what is to follow. In the end he must draw his conclusions for himself; I can only arrange the material.

The best way perhaps to do this will be to begin with certain general characteristics, Hodgson's mannerisms, for example.

Hodgson was distinguished during life by great animal spirits. He was fond of argument, chaff, and repartee, a good deal of a gesticulator, and a great laugher. He had, moreover, an excessive appetite for poetry, I will it excessive, for it was anything but fastidious—he seemed to need sonorous rhyme and meter for his daily food, even if the quality and sentiment were commonplace. All these traits were manifested from the outset in his appearances as a "control"—some examples are given in my preliminary report. Chaff and slang from a spirit have an undignified sound for the reader, but to the interlocutors of the R. H.-control they seem invariably to have been elements of verisimilitude. Thus T. P. writes, *à propos* of a bantering passage in the record of January 16, 1906:

"T. P. and R. H. were such good chums that he was saucy to her, and teasing her most of the time. R. H.'s tone towards T. P. in all his communications is *absolutely characteristic*, and as he was in life." Similarly, Dr. Bayley appends this note to a number of ultra-vivacious remarks from R. H.: "Such expressions and phrases were quaintly characteristic of R. H. in the body, and as they appear, often rapidly and spontaneously, they give the almost irresistible impression that it is really the Hodgson personality, presiding with its own characteristics. To fully appreciate this, of course, one would have had to have known him as intimately as I did."

For these rollicking observations the control chose his sitters well in accordance with his habits during life. This, however, did not exclude very serious talk with the same persons—quite the reverse sometimes, as when one sitter of this class notes: "Then came words of kindness which were too intimate and personal to be recorded, but which left me so deeply moved that shortly afterwards, at the sitting's close, I fainted dead away—it had seemed as though he had in all reality been there and speaking to me."

The extracts given in the earlier report or to be given soon will show what I mean by Hodgson's rollicking manner. The later communications show more of it than the earlier ones; and it quickly manifested the tendency, characteristic in the medium's utterances, to become stereotyped. Whatever they may have been at the outset, they soon fall into what may be called the trance-memory's "stock," and are then repeated automatically. Hodgson quickly acquired a uniform mode of announcing himself: "Well, well, well! I am Hodgson. Delighted to see you. How is everything? First rate? I'm in the witness-box at last," etc., with almost no variety. This habitual use of stock remarks by Mrs. Piper may tempt one to be unjust to the total significance of her mediumship. If the supernormal element in it, whatever it is, be essentially discontinuous and flash-like, an utterance that today belongs to the regular trance stock may have got into that stock at a former moment of supernormal receptivity. Supernormal receptivity of some kind is certainly involved in the total phenomenon, but I believe that information that originally came thus, quickly ceases to be supernormal. The control G. P. at the outset of his appearance gave supernormal information copiously, but within a few years he has degenerated into a shadow of his former self, dashing in and quickly out again, with an almost fixed form of greeting. Whatever he may have been at first, he seems to me at last to have "passed on," leaving that amount of impression on the trance-organism's habits.

I will now cull from the records a number of extracts relative to particular sitters, which show the control's familiarity with their affairs, calling the first of these extracts

2. The Oldfarm Series

Oldfarm is the name of Mr. George B. Dorr's place at Bar Harbor, Maine, where R. H. had often been a summer guest. Mrs. Piper at the time of these sittings had never been at Bar Harbor; and although she had had many interviews, as well with Mr. Dorr as with Mr. Dorr's mother before the latter's death, it is unlikely that many of the small veridical details in what follows had been communicated to her at those interviews. At Mr. Dorr's sitting of June 5th, 1906, he asks the R. H.-control for his reminiscences of Oldfarm: "Do you remember your visits to us there?"

> Certainly I do. One night we stayed out too long and your mother got very nervous, do you remember? Minna was there. . . . We stayed out *much* too long. I felt it was a great breach of etiquette but we couldn't help it! I fear as guests we were bad [laughs].

> [R. H.'s sitting out with "Minna" and others "much too long" and "their being bad as guests" seems excellent. In old days they used often to sit up hopelessly late into the night, when the nights were pleasant, out on the piazza, talking in the dark; and my mother's half-real and half-humorous exasperation over it, expressed in her own vivid way, and R. H.'s boyish delight in doing it and at the scoldings they all used to get for it next day, would naturally be one of the first things he would recall, associated as those evenings were with people whom he cared for.—D.[9]]

---

[9] George B. Dorr.—ED.

And do you remember the discussion I had with Jack, when he got impatient? You were much amused!

[His recollection of his discussion with Jack, who used, together with M., to be at our house with him a great deal in the old days, is characteristic. I do not myself remember the special occasion to which he refers, but the incident, including my own amusement at the heat they used to get into in their talk, falls in most naturally with all my own recollections of that time.—D.]

And I remember your mother's calling me out one Sunday morning to see the servants go to church on a buckboard.

[I cannot now recall my mother taking R. H. out to see the servants off on any special day, but he was with us many Sundays, and I have no doubt that his memory of this is absolutely accurate, nor is it anything of which Mrs. Piper might know—it is not the sort of thing that anyone would have spoken to her of, or mentioned at the trance. The *buckboard* is quite correct. It was a big buckboard that carried six people and was the only wagon which we had big enough to take all the people up, but its use is not sufficiently universal at Bar Harbor to injure the evidential value of his recollection of it. Again, the people used to go off from the kitchen, which is at an end of the house and cannot be seen from the living rooms or piazzas, so that his statement that my mother called him out to see them off, while a small point, seems to me of value; and the event itself, with the arrangements that had to be made to make it possible, was quite enough of a circumstance in our family life to make recollection of it natural.—D.]

I can see the open fireplace in the living room.

[The room is one in which the fireplace, broad and arching, is the central feature and would be first thought of in thinking of the room.—D.]

(Do you remember where you used to sleep?)

Out in the little house just out across the yard, where we used to go and smoke.

[His recollection also of the little house is good. The only mistake in reference to it is in speaking of it as "across the yard," it being in fact across the lawn and garden, upon a hillside opposite the house. We always kept some rooms in it for our guests, overflowing into it when the house was full, and R. H. liked it better than the house itself in the greater freedom that it gave him. We used to close the house itself early in the evening, and R. H. was very apt then to go up to the cottage with some other man or men and sit up and smoke and talk—often until quite late.—D.]

I remember the bathing and the boats and a walk through the woods.

[The bathing was one of the incidents at Oldfarm which R. H. would have best remembered. We used to take long walks over the mountains and go down for a plunge when we returned from them. There were often three or four men or more going in together when the house was full, and it was something in which R. H. delighted especially, so that his recollection of this would be apt to be one of his most vivid ones.—D.]

(Do you remember whether you used to bathe off the beach, or off the rocks?)

We used to bathe off the *rocks;* I'm sure of that. *I can see the whole place.*

[I asked the question as to whether we went in off the rocks or the beach so as to see if he really had a clear remembrance of it, and I asked it in such a way that my companion at the sitting thought R. H.'s answer "off the rocks" was probably wrong. My bath-house was not on the beach, but on a point running far out into the sea, very bold and rocky, and we used to spring off the rocks into deep water, climbing out by a perpendicular ladder fastened to the ledge.—D.]

I can see the little piazza that opened out from your mother's room and the whole beautiful outlook from it, over the water.

[That that piazza and its room should be one of R. H.'s strongest recollections of the place seems to me most natural, while at the same time the piazza itself, which is not a conspicuous object in the house from without, and which was only familiar to my mother's more intimate friends, is not a thing which would occur naturally to anyone not familiar with our life down there.—D.]

Mr. Dorr then asks R. H. if he remembers a walk he once took with a young friend from New York, where R. H. outwalked the other man and was very triumphant about it afterward, and whether he could recall the man's name. He also asks him if he remembers the name of the man who lived in the farmhouse, where R. H. used generally to sleep when staying at Oldfarm. Both of these names would have been quite familiar to R. H. in life. R. H. cannot give them and makes no attempt to do so.

[R. H.] Names are the hardest things to remember; it's extraordinary but it's true. The scenes of my whole life are laid open to me but names go from one's memory like a dream. I remember walking through the woods there and sitting down and lighting my pipe and coming back late to lunch.

On June 20th, 1906, at a sitting of Miss Bancroft's, at which Mr. Dorr was present, the R. H.-control suddenly writes:

Do you remember anything about Celery-root? about Celle root?
[To G. B. D.] (Do *you* remember anything about it?)
[G. B. D. No.]
Or was it at your place, George. [Difficulty in reading this sentence. When read successfully, G. B. D. says "yes."]
Your mother used to have it, and I was surprised to see it there as I thought it the best of it. As I thought it the best part of it. The best part of it. No one would ever think of this thing I know.
(You mean you think you got this at Mr. Dorr's?)
Think! I know. I think so, yes. I think George's mother used to have it and I never got it anywhere but there.

G. B. D., who did not at first recall what is meant, then remembers and says "Good." He appends the following note:

[We used to have a bunch or two of raw celery, when we grew our own, placed on the table as a *hors d'oeuvre,* and served whole, with the upper portion of the root left on it in the French fashion. This part of the root is very good eating, but it is not usually served in America; and though I have no clear remembrance now of special talk about this with R. H., I remember quite well his talking at our table late one fall about these autumn vegetables and think that what is spoken of is this.—D.]

On July 2nd, 1906, Mr. Dorr had a spoken sitting alone, taking the shorthand record himself, and asked again for Oldfarm recollections.

can you give me any names connected with Bar Harbor, or of the mountains there which you used to climb, or of the people to whose houses you used to go with me, or any others that you can recall?)

No, I can't recall any names now. . . . I will think it over and try.

(Can you recall four sisters whom we used to walk with, and be much with, a number of years ago?)

I remember *Minna and Gemma*. [Names known to the medium in former trances, but pertinent as a reply.]

(I will give you the name of the sisters, and see if that recalls anything to you. It was the Minturns.)

Oh! the Minturns! [repeated eagerly and emphatically].

There was Gertrude and Robert, a brother named Robert—and Mary. They lived in New York. I remember them well. [Correct, save that Mary should have been May.]

(There was another sister, who used to walk oftenest with us—can you recall her name?)

[R. H. makes one or two ineffectual attempts, giving wrong names.]

(Now, Hodgson, can't you tell me something about the lady you were interested in, whose letters you asked Piddington to find?)

This was Huldah Densmore.

(But there is no Huldah in the family, that I know, nor can we learn of any. We have asked her sister, and she has never heard the name of Huldah.)

Wait a moment. Let me think. It is most difficult to get earthly memories. They go from one, but I find that they come back to me as I think of things. She married a ——[name of nationality given correctly]. If you will write to her, you will find I am right. Write to her!

(Did you want to marry her?)

Yes, I did. And I remember what a disappointment it was to me.

(Was she out of sympathy with your work?)

She wanted me to give it up—it was a subject she did not care to have to do with. [Correct as to the lady's animus.]

(Was it at our house you met her?)

I met her there, at Bar Harbor. Your mother ought to remember it well. She introduced us to each other. [Correct.—D.]

(But my mother is on your side.)

Oh yes, I had forgotten. It has troubled me over here, thinking I might have left her letters among my papers. So I spoke to Piddington about it.

(I think you must have destroyed them. We didn't find any.)

I think I must have destroyed them—I hope I did.

[This "Huldah" episode is treated in a separate section of Part I of this report, see above, p. 132.—W. J.]

I recall the pansies your mother used to place over the table. I remember that well—delightful to see them! I can see them now.

[My mother used to have pansies spread loosely over the table-cloth, when she had people to dine or sup with us at Bar Harbor, where we had a large bed of them planted near the house so that we could get them freely for this purpose. The custom is not common enough to let H.'s statement pass for a happy guess, nor do I think it likely he would have spoken of it to Mrs. Piper, either awake or in trance. It came out quite suddenly also, and with a positiveness which made me feel that it was a true recollection, something seen at the moment in a mental picture.—D.]

G. B. D., endeavoring to extract Bar Harbor names from R. H., again tries to get that of the man who occupied the farmhouse at which R. H. used generally to sleep when at Oldfarm. He was not able to give that but gave the name of the gardener, Miller. "It is possible," Mr. Dorr writes, "that Mrs. Piper may have heard of Miller's name as that of the manager of my plant-nurseries at Bar Harbor. I remember I once meant to send her some plants from the nurseries for her garden, and think it probable they went. It is also possible that the name may have come up at the trance in my own past sittings."

I remember a beautiful road, a bicycle-road you made, going through the woods.

[A dozen years ago I made a bicycle-road on my own back-land, which ran through the woods beneath a mountain over which we often used to walk. It was a pleasant and familiar feature in our summer life there, and it would naturally be one of the pictures that would come back to R. H. in thinking of the place—like the view from my mother's balcony of which he spoke at the former sitting. But it is not a thing of which either he or I

would have spoken to Mrs. Piper, whether in trance or awake.
—D.]

G. B. D. then tries again to get the name of the man who occupied the farmhouse, describing him to R. H. without mentioning
his name.

Oh yes, I remember him well—I remember going off with him
once fishing—going down the shore in a boat. . . . I remember
one evening, and it impressed me so vividly because your mother
did not like it, and I felt we had done wrong and hurt her—M.
and I were smoking together and we talked too late, and she felt
it was time to retire—

[This would be remarkably good if the incident should prove
not to have come up already in R. H.'s own sittings after M. died.
She used to smoke cigarettes occasionally, and was the only person of the feminine sex whom I now recall as having done so at
our house. Unless in possibly referring to this incident to her
"spirit" at trances, after M. died, Hodgson would have been most
unlikely to speak of it to others—certainly not to Mrs. Piper,
either in trance or awake.—D.]

(Do you remember where you went with John Rich when you
went fishing with him—Oh I forgot! I did not mean to give you
his name!)
John Rich, John, that is his name! But I am sorry you gave
it to me too—it might have come to me. We got a boat and went
over to an island. Coming back we had some difficulty in getting
our fish in. We had poor luck in catching them, and then we lost
them. Ask him, he will remember it, I think.

[R. H.'s recollection of going off with Rich seems to the point,
as I think it over. That he should go off with Rich only and
neither alone nor with me or other guests, is exactly what happened—and yet not what might have been expected to happen.
His going to an island is descriptive also.—D.]

Do you remember what you used to put over your back that
had a cup in it? And there was a little brook where we used to
stop and drink. And then I used to stop and light my pipe—the
whole scene is as vivid to me! If I could only express it to you!

[I used to carry a little canvas bag slung over my shoulder and a cup in it, when we went on long tramps. This may be what R. H. refers to, though I think that he was rather apt to carry a folding leather cup of his own in his pocket. The whole recollection is rather vague in my memory, going back a number of years. The picture is a good one of just what used to happen when we were off on our tramps together, though of course what he describes would be always apt to happen on walks through woods and over mountains. The picture of the little brook we used to stop and drink at is good—I can see it now.—D.]

After some talk about the Tavern Club, Australia, and the state of things in the other world—some of which will be noticed later, R. H. goes on as follows:

Do you remember one summer there was a gentleman at your house who had a violin. I had some interesting talks with him about these things, and I liked to hear him play his violin. A little gentleman—I remember him very well.

[This describes a man named von G., who was an excellent violinist and who also talked interestingly on psychical research matters, in which he professed to have some faculty. As R. H. himself was also fond of the violin, it seems natural that some memory of von G. should stand out now. That Mrs. Piper should have any knowledge of this gentleman seems most improbable. —D.]

My earthly memories come only in fragments. I remember quite well this little gentleman and how interested I was in talking with him about psychics, and in his instrument as well. I remember a man Royce visiting you.

[Professor Royce says that he has been at Oldfarm along with Hodgson, but adds that that might be a natural association in Mrs. Piper's mind, since he thinks that the only time he ever saw her was at the Dorrs' in Boston.]

This is, I think, the whole of the matter relative to Oldfarm which the R. H.-control has given. The number of items mentioned is not great, and some inability to answer questions appears. But there are almost no mistakes of fact, and it is hardly possible that all the veridical points should have been known to Mrs. Piper normally. Some of them indeed were likely *a priori;* others may have been chance hits; but for the mass, it seems to me that either reading of Mr. Dorr's mind, or spirit return, are the least improbable explanations.

The *fewness* of the items may seem strange to some critics. But if we assume a spirit to be actually there, trying to reach us, and if at the same time we imagine that his situation with regard to the transaction is similar to our own, the surprise vanishes. I have been struck over and over again, both when at sittings myself and when reading the records, at the paralyzing effect on one's ready wit and conversational flow, which the strangeness of the conditions brings with it. Constraint and numbness take the place of genial expansiveness. We "don't know what to say," and it may also be so "on the other side." Few persons, I fancy, if suddenly challenged to prove their identity through the telephone, would quickly produce a large number of facts appropriate to the purpose. They would be more perplexed, and waste more time than they imagine.

I next pass to what I will call

3. *The Owl's Head Series*

Owl's Head was the name of the summer place of Miss Margaret Bancroft, overlooking Rockland Harbor, in Maine, where Mrs. Piper had never been. R. H. had very greatly enjoyed visits which he had made there on two successive summers. Miss Bancroft had been a sitter of Mrs. Piper's and was a convert to spiritism, with some degree of "psychic" susceptibility herself. At her first sitting after Hodgson's death, February 19th, 1906, Mr. Dorr also being present, the following dialogue took place: [10]

I am Hodgson! Speak! Well, well, well, I am delighted to see you. How are you?
(I am all right. How are you?)

---

[10] Here, as in all the rest of the records reprinted, I omit repetitions and remarks not connected with the recollections. Nothing is omitted, however, which in my eyes might affect the interpretation of what is printed.—W. J.

First rate.

(I can scarcely speak to you.)

But you must speak to me.

(Will you give me some definite message?)

Surely I will. I have called and called to you. Do you remember what I said to you about coming here if I got a chance?

(Yes, I do.)

I wish you to pay attention to me. [The sitter and Mr. Dorr were together trying to decipher the script.] Do you remember how I used to talk about this subject, evenings? You know what you said about my writing—I think I am getting on first rate.

[Everything accurate so far! Miss B. can herself write automatically, and since R. H.'s departure, has thought that he might have been influencing her subconsciousness in that and other ways. The words "I have called," etc., she interprets in this sense. Rector, however, already knew of her automatic writing.—W. J.]

Do you remember what a good time we had at Head? I am so glad I went. . . . Do you remember a little talk we had about the lights and satellites? Do you remember how interested you were? Do you remember what I used to say about returning if I got over here first?

(Yes, I remember all that.)

[Accurate again. The "Head" must mean Owl's Head, where during two successive summers Hodgson had visited the sitter, and been supremely happy. The "lights" refer to the lights of Rockland, across the bay, of which he greatly admired the effect, and at night on the piazza he had often spoken about the planets and stars, and the question of their habitation.—M. B.[11]]

Well, here I am, now fire away, now fire.

(Can you tell me the names of some who were with you there last summer?)

Remember Miss Wilkinson?

(No.)

You ask me about whom? Not understand. How are the children? [The house had been full of schoolchildren, of whom R. H. was fond.—M. B.]

---

[11] Margaret Bancroft.—ED.

(They are well.)

Good! Do you remember the day I walked across to the Mountain?

(No, I don't remember.)

Ask Putnam if he and I—My watch stopped.

[For this reference to a watch-stopping, compare pages 123 and 205 of this report. I suspect some confused memory of a real incident to be at the bottom of it.—W. J.]

(Can you not recall something you did at the Head?)

That is just what I am trying to do. Don't you remember how I had to laugh at you, laugh on that boat, about that boat?

[This last word being wrongly deciphered as "hat," Miss B. asks:]

(Whose hat blew off?)

My hat, do you not remember the day it blew off? Yes, you are not following me very clearly.

(I am trying to recall about that hat.)

Do you remember fishing?

(Yes, I remember fishing.)

Capital! Remember about my hat? went into the water.

(Yes, I think I do.)

I should say you did. Oh my! but I am not so stupid as some I know. I have not forgotten anything. Get my Poem?

(Yes, and I want to thank you for it.)

Don't bother about that. I want you to know I am really here and recognize you, and the first-rate time I had at Owl's—Thank you very much. How is Bayley? Certainly first-rate time I had at Owl's. Thank you very much. Owl's. Remember the jokes I told you? Jsp. Thank you. Remember what I said about dressing them [or "there"]? Remember our fun well

(How am I getting along?)

Capital! You are doing well, all you need is experience. I would like to take a swim! I would like to take a swim. Plunge.

[Much incoherence hereabouts. The names Bayley and Jessup (Jsp) are correct. Hodgson used to bathe with them off the rocks, and Miss B. recalls jokes between them about dressing there. H. and they went deep-sea fishing almost daily. One day Dr. B. and R. H. went fishing in a gasoline launch, and on their return had much riotous laughter about some happenings in the boat. Miss

B. can remember nothing definite about a hat, but is inclined to interpret the allusion as referring to this incident. The "poem" she conceives to be the verses "It seems as if the wondrous land," etc., written at Miss Pope's sitting of February 5th. See Part I of this report, p. 123.—W. J.]

On the following day Miss B. had a second sitting, and R. H. asked "How is Nellie?" [Nellie is a member of Miss B.'s household, presumably unknown to Mrs. Piper, about whom R. H. always used during his lifetime to inquire.]

On the night of Hodgson's death, Miss B., whom I described above as having "psychic" aptitudes, had received a strong impression of his presence. She now asks:

(Yesterday you said you had "called and called" me. When did you ever call me?)

Just after I passed out I returned to you and saw you resting . . . and came and called to you telling you I was leaving. . . .

(Did I not answer?)

Yes, after a while.

(What did I do?)

You arose and seemed nervous. I felt I was disturbing you. I then left.

(Do you not recall another time when I was sure you were there and I did something? . . . What did I do at one o'clock, Christmas morning?)

I saw you, I heard you speak to me once, yes. I heard you speak to someone, and it looked like a lady. You took something in your hand, and I saw you and heard you talking.

(Yes, that is true.)

I heard you say something about someone being ill, lying in the room. [Nellie was ill in my room.—M. B.]

(Yes, that is true. I also said something else.)

You said it was myself.

(Yes, I said that. Anything else?)

I remember seeing the light, and heard you talking to a lady. [Correct.—M. B.]

(The lady did something after I talked to her.)

You refer to the message, she sat down and wrote a message for me. [I do not understand what is meant by this, unless it be a confused reference to Miss Pope's reception of a message to me

in the sitting of February 5th.—M. B.] [See Part I., p. 123.—
W. J.[12]]

There was nothing more of interest from Hodgson at this sitting.
Dr. Bayley, to whom reference was made in connection with Owl's
Head, at Miss Bancroft's first sitting, had two sittings in April, in
which the hearty and jocose mannerisms of R. H. were vividly reproduced; but there was a good deal of confusion, owing to Dr.
Bayley's lack of familiarity with the handwriting; and the evidential material, so far as the Hodgson-control (whom we are alone
concerned with) went, was comparatively small. One passage was:

[R. H.] Get that book I sent you?
(I received the book, right after your death.)

[Hodgson had addressed some books and some cards to be
sent to friends as Christmas presents. They were mailed after his
death on December 20th. It should be added that Miss Bancroft
had at her sitting of February informed Rector that such a book
had come to *her*, and Rector associated her and Doctor Bayley
as friends.]

Have you seen Billy? [My friend Professor W. R. Newbold.
—B.[13]]

(No, have you any word from him?)
Ask him if he remembers the day we went to the seashore and
we sat on the beach, and I told him how I hoped to come over

---

[12] À *propos* to Miss Bancroft's "psychic" susceptibility, at a sitting on
October 17th, 1906, which Mrs. M. had with Mrs. Piper, the following words
were exchanged:
"(Any other messages, Dick?)
"[R. H.] Not for him [the person last spoken of], but tell Margaret it was
I who produced that light she saw the other night."
The sitter immediately wrote to Miss Margaret Bancroft, with whom she
had recently become acquainted, to ask (not telling her of the message)
whether she had had any special experiences of late. Miss B. answered: "I
had a very curious experience on the morning of the 14th. At four o'clock I
was awakened from a sound sleep, and could feel distinctly the presence of
three people in the room. I sat up and was so attentive that I hardly breathed.
About nine feet from the floor there appeared at intervals curious lights, much
like search-lights, but softer, and there seemed to be a distinct outline of a
figure. . . . This lasted probably from fifteen to twenty minutes . . . when
I went into a sound sleep."—W. J.
[13] Dr. Bayley.—ED.

here any time, only I wanted to finish my work. And ask him if he remembers what I told him about my getting married.

(I don't know anything about it. That's a good test.) [Proves to have been correct.—W. J.]

Also ask him if he remembers what I said about the children of my old friend Pilly.

[W. R. N. remembers R. H. telling him of a certain "Pilly," but forgets about the children.]

No one living could know this but Billy. . . .

I ask if you recall the fishing process.

(Why, Dick, it will be very sad fishing without you.)

[R. H. and I had done much deep-sea fishing together, but my suspicion that this was meant may have deflected him from some explanation of the "fishing" process of controls at sittings.—B.]

I wonder if you remember Miss Nellie.

(Perfectly.)

Give her my kindest regards. . . . Got your feet wet!

(Tell me more about that, Dick.)

Do you remember how I put my pipe in the water? Do you remember my putting my coat on the seat, and my pipe got into the water? Remember ducking?

(Ducking?)

I said plunge.

(Plunge?)

Yes! Let's take a plunge.

(Yes indeed!)

ALL. . . .

(Who was along with us, Dick?)

Jess—. . . I got it in my head. [Dr. Jessup is correct.—B.]

Do you remember the Head? Oh I think it was the best summer I ever had. Best, best, best. . . . Do you remember laugh about Mitchell? Laugh? [This *might* refer to a very distinct incident involving a friend named MacDaniel.—B.] Idiosyncrasies . . . [What immediately followed was illegible.]

On the next day, April 4th, Dr. B. says to Hodgson:

(Give me your password if you can today.)

Password? I had no less than forty. One was shoeing. Yes, yes, do you remember?

(Of course I don't remember about your passwords; but you wrote Mrs. Bayley a charade of your own making, and if you can give the answer to that it will be a splendid test.)

Shoo fly, shoo fly? [It runs in my head that these words were answers to charades propounded last summer, but I can get no confirmation and may be mistaken.—B.]

(I have the letter with the charade here.) [Puts it into the medium's hand.]

Doctor, this is *peacemaker, peacemaker.* I gave this word in my letter. Shoo fly.

[Miss Bancroft writes: "I have a dim recollection about 'peacemaker.' I feel very sure about 'shoo fly.' "]

(I will look it up.) [There were two charades in the letter handed to the medium, but the words given answer neither of them.—B.]

Do you remember anything about that awful *cigar* and my joke about it? [Mrs. Bayley remembers a cigar so huge that neither R. H. nor I would smoke it. He finally broke it up and smoked it in his pipe. This may have been the joke referred to. —B.]

Doc, [This is not R. H.'s usual way of addressing me.—B.] that is peacemaker! And to Mrs. B. I felt I said shoo fly. If you knew the difficulties I am having, you would smile out loud. . . . Can you play ball?

(Well, H., neither of us were very active ball-players in the country.)

Listen, do you remember our late hours?

(Indeed I do.) [R. H. and I used to sit out on the porch smoking to untimely hours.—B.]

Got your sleep made up yet?

(Not quite.)

Next followed some rather unintelligible as well as illegible references to skinning fish and bailing a boat. Then:

Do you remember how we tried to make many words out of one?

(Yes.)

And the fun we had?

(Yes.) [R. H. had enjoyed doing this with some of the ladies at Owl's Head.—B.]

Do you remember reading in the evening?

(Well enough.)

Remember the joke I told you about Blats [Blavatsky] . . . and her tricks? [Correct, but matter of common knowledge.]

(Now, Dick, do you remember some of the words of the song which we all sang so much, and which you brought there last summer?)

Song? awful! song?

(It begins "Come, I will sing you.")

Oh yes!—gone out of my head like a shot!

(Yes, Dick.)

Listen, let me tell you something. Do you remember a little song I sang to the children which went like this: Little Popsey Wopsey . . . Chickey Biddy Chum . . . all. . . . I am tired.

(Dick, that was splendid, I remember it well.) [Known also to Mrs. Piper.—W. J.]

Do you remember my palming trick?

(Yes.) [Known also to Mrs. Piper.—W. J.]

And how you all seemed to enjoy them? . . . I am getting clearer since I have met you here. It helps in recalling many things I had almost forgotten. Listen, do you remember my recitation of a Hindoo?

(No, I don't remember that.)

Which reads like this: "I think till I'm weary of thinking—"

(Yes, I know that well.) [Known also to Mrs. Piper.—W. J.]

Do you remember my letter to Will, in which I told him of the delight of the place [possibly a misreading for "depth of the piece"].

(Who is Will?)

Will James. Or perhaps I didn't read it to you after all.

(No, I didn't hear that letter.) [I recall no letter either about the "place," or about the "piece," but my memory is so bad that that proves nothing. I *have* heard the "piece"; and think I heard it from Hodgson.—W. J.]

. . . Ask Margaret Bancroft if she remembers telling me about you and Mrs. Bayley giving her a watch. I am glad I found her after I came over. I think she is perfectly sincere and a light.

[Miss Bancroft writes: "I felt badly about accepting the watch, and consulted Mr. Hodgson about it. He said a number of things about my sensitiveness, and after that I felt all right about the watch. I don't think I told anybody of this interview with Dr.

Hodgson. As regards my 'sincerity,' the last talk I had with him was on that very subject. . . . He said he would certainly convince Dr. Bayley of my sincerity." The reader knows already that Miss Bancroft is a "light."]

On June 20th, 1906, Miss Bancroft had her third sitting. Some days previous to this Mrs. M., an old friend of Hodgson, had taken to her sitting a cross which remained among his effects, and asked the R. H.-control for directions concerning its disposition. He had ordered it to be sent to Miss Bancroft; and when he appeared to Miss Bancroft at the sitting a few days later almost his first word was:

Get my cross?
(Yes, thank you very much. . . .)
A Mascot I send to you.
(Yes, I know you sent it to me.)
I shall be with you when you are in the cottage.
(Do you know that I have bought the place?)
Of course I do. I understand pretty well what you are about.

[Miss B. had been enabled to buy the land at Owl's Head since her sittings in the previous February.]
. . . There is more help coming to you to enlarge the house.
. . . You remember you thought it necessary to have more room.
(Yes, I remember very well.)
Did you see me in your dream with my trousers rolled up at the bottom?
(I am not sure that I did.)
I spoke to you and you replied.
(I have seen you several times in dreams.)
Remember my knock?
(When did you knock?)
You were sleeping.
(I remember twice when I thought someone knocked my arm.)
But I woke you, I certainly did. [Correct.]
(Can't you do me a favor by knocking now? . . .)
Not while I keep on speaking. You wish me to knock your arm now, eh? I cannot do so and keep on speaking.
Do you remember the evening I told you about my sister Ellen's boy?
(I do not recall it.)

Yes, Ellen's boy and his passing over.

Do you remember—Enid? What I told you about her? And her poems? A scholarship and her poems?

(I remember all that.) [He had told me a great deal about this niece Enid.—M. B. Mrs. Piper denies knowledge of her existence.—W. J.]

Listen. I am in the witness box! I am trying to help you to recognize me. . . .

Do you remember anything about celery root? . . . [See above, p. 153.]

Margaret do you remember the walk through the woods?

(Yes, I remember it.)

Do you remember "Let us sing of—sing you

Let us sing of a"

(Yes, I understand.)

No you do not. No song.

(Yes I do. Try and give it to me.)

I am but you do not understand. You do not understand *at all.* Let us sing the old song.

(You mean the song "Come let us sing"?)

Yes.

(Tell me what it is.)

I am telling you. "Come let us sing the—what would you sing —sing—sing

[He taught us a song last summer, "Come I will sing," and the response was "What will you sing me"; "I will sing you one oh," etc. My idea is that he wanted to have me give him the next line and probably he would have been able to give me the text and perhaps the whole song or part of it, but I did not understand what he wanted to do.—M. B.]

Miss Bancroft had two more sittings, on December 2nd and 3rd, 1907. On December 2nd Hodgson seemed to be cognizant of certain changes in the Owl's Head place, that there was a new wallpaper of yellow color, a new bath-house, a new pier and platform, etc., none of which facts Mrs. Piper was in a way to have known.

He also showed veridical knowledge of a very private affair between two other people, that had come under Miss Bancroft's observation. There was, however, some confusion in this sitting, and R. H. was not "strong." The results were better on December 3rd, but the evidential parts do not lend themselves well to quotation, with one exception, as follows:

(Don't you remember something that happened that you helped us in?)

I remember that one evening—

(What happened that evening?)

We got a little fire and I helped. Yes.

(Yes, that is true.)

Put it out —— the fire —— —— I remember it well.

(What did you tell us to get before the fire occurred?)

Before the fire?

(You told us to get something for the house.)

I said you ought to get a —— in case of fire —— pail, yes.

[Here the hand drew three parallel horizontal lines, which might have meant shelves, and beneath them the outline of a vessel with a cover.]

(What are they for?)

Water pails water pails —— yes, fire buckets —— fire Yes, I did.

[He told us in Maine, when we were experimenting with Mrs. A—— by automatic writing, to get fire buckets and put them up on the shelves, which we did long before the fire occurred. He warned us of this fire many times, but no one seemed to pay much attention to it but myself.—M. B.]

(What did you tell us to put on them?)

Go on you will find that I am not asleep.

(I never thought you were asleep.)

So much for the Owl's Head record, which, as the reader sees, follows a not incoherent thread of associated facts

Few of the items were false, but on the other hand it must be remembered that a mind familiar with Hodgson's tastes and habits might have deduced some of them (swimming and fishing, for example) *a priori* by combining the two abstract ideas "Hodgson" and "seaside." Leakages impossible now to follow might also account for the medium's knowledge of such items as the names Nellie, Jessup, etc., for her connecting Dr. Bayley with "Billy," etc. For the "fire buckets," "watch," "sincerity," and other items, it would seem necessary to invoke either lucky chance or telepathy, unless one be willing to admit spirit return. I should say that I have condensed the record considerably, leaving out some matter irrelevant to Owl's Head memories, some repetitions, and all the talk that grew out of slowness in deciphering the script.

Dr. Bayley himself wrote me after his sittings: "They are pretty good, and have about convinced me (as evidence added to previous experience) that my much loved friend is still about. I had had either four or six sittings, some of them in conjunction with Miss Bancroft, before R. H.'s death. I do not think that Mrs. Piper normally knew me by name, or knew that I was from Philadelphia or that I knew Newbold. I realize that the average reader of these records loses much in the way of little tricks of expression and personality, subtleties impossible to give an account of in language. As I look over the sittings and realize my own blunders in them, I cannot always decide who was the more stupid, the communicator, or myself."

4. Professor Newbold's Sittings

The message given to Dr. Bayley for "Billy" (i.e., Professor William R. Newbold) makes it natural to cite next the experience of this other intimate friend of R. H. Professor Newbold had two written sittings, on June 27th and July 3rd, 1906, respectively, Mr. Dorr being present both times. On June 27th, after a few words with Rector, Hodgson appears, and the dialogue continues as follows:

Well, well, of all things! Are you really here! I am Hodgson. (Hallo, Dick!)
Hello, Billy, God bless you.
(And you, too, though you do not need to have me say it.)
I wonder if you remember the last talk we had together—
(I do remember it, Dick.)
I can recall very well all I said to you that glorious day when we were watching the waves. [Our last talk was on a splendid afternoon of July, 1905, at Nantasket Beach.—N.[14]]

---

[14] Professor Newbold.—ED.

(Yes, Dick, I remember it well.)

I told you of many, many predictions which had been made for me. I told you I hoped to realize them but I would not consent to give up my work.

(First rate, Dick, you told me just that.)

I would give up almost anything else but my work—my work —and my pipe.

(Dick, that sounds like you.)

Don't you remember?

(Do you remember something *I* told *you* on the boat going to Nantasket?)

Yes, of course. Long ago you wrote me of your happiness and I wrote back and asked you if you were trying to make me discontented.

(I don't remember, but I have your letters and will look it up.)

[This allusion to my "happiness" is very characteristic. He often spoke to me of it.—N.] . . .[15]

The Hodgson part of the sitting of July 3rd was as follows:

I am Hodgson.

(Hallo, Dick!)

I am glad to meet you, Billy, old chap! How are you? First rate?

(Yes I am, Dick!)

Capital. Good. So am I. I come to assure you of my continued existence. . . . Do you remember the case of a clergyman—?

(Yes, certainly. I remember a clergyman who lived in Philadelphia and thought he had supernormal experiences, and I told you about them.)

Why didn't you say so before? Yes. I just told you about the case of hysteria—and you were interested in telepathy. [The young clergyman had professed to have telepathic powers; he cheated.—N.]

(Is this the case you were talking about at the last sitting?)

Of course he was. You asked me what experiments we tried with him.

(That is right.)

I said telepathic experiments, and some were pretty poor.

---

[15] There follow in the original James report over twelve pages of dialogue containing trivia and some repetitions which would be of little interest to the contemporary reader, and add only minimally to the evidential value of the report. Much of this section has been omitted.—Ed.

(Right.)

Do you remember, Billy . . . ? [A veridical reference here, which W. R. N. prefers to omit.]

(Yes, Dick.)

I am delighted to recall your telling me you were happy and contented and how pleased you were with your classes—

(Right, Dick.)

And how readily your work was being accepted. You were so happy about it all. It gave me great delight.

(Thank you.)

You certainly did. You also told me of your advancement in a material way.

(Yes, I told you that, that is right.)

Which pleased me greatly.

(Yes, Dick, it did!)

You were my counterpart—counterpart in expressions of delight. You and I were very pleased and I told you I would not give up my work even for a wife.

[I don't recall this remark, but it sounds characteristic.—N.]

(Yes, Dick, you are very clear and easy to understand.)

I am glad to hear it. I am trying my level best to give you facts.

(Very good.)

I said my pipe and my work would not be given up even for a wife. Oh how you have helped me, Billy. Yes, in clearing my mind wonderfully.

[I omit here a few sentences from R. H. in which he credits me with a remark I have often made to him, seldom to others. Important veridically.—N.]

(Dick, I have told you that twenty times.)

You have certainly, but Billy, I used to say it was the most important thing in the world I believed.

[Refers next to psychical research and in particular to the Piper case.]

You said you could not understand why so many mistakes were made, and I talked you blind, trying to explain my ideas of it.

(Dick, this sounds like your own self. Just the way you used to talk to me.)

Well if I am not Hodgson, he never lived.

(But you are so clear.)

Of course I am, I am drawing on all the forces possible for strength to tell you these things.

You laughed about the ungrammatical expressions and said, why in the world do they use bad grammar?

(Yes, Dick, I said that.)

I went into a long explanation and attributed it to the registering of the machine. You were rather amused but were inclined to leave it to my better understanding.

(You mean, I think, that you understood the subject better than I and I took your explanation? You mean that therefore I was inclined to accept your explanation?)

I think I do. I find now difficulties such as a blind man would experience in trying to find his hat. And I am not wholly conscious of my own utterances because they come out automatically, impressed upon the machine.

(Perfectly clear.)

Yes, I am standing beside you.

(Can you see me, Dick?)

Yes, but I feel your presence better. I impress my thoughts on the machine which registers them at random, and which are at times doubtless difficult to understand. I understand so much better the *modus operandi* than I did when I was in your world. . . .

I remember when you were with me I got very much interested in some letters you wrote me after your return home—your saying some things puzzled you very much. [A first-rate veridical statement from R. H. has had to be omitted here. The matter referred to had, however, been mentioned at sittings in 1895. —N.]

(By jingo! that is true, Dick. It was ten years ago.)

Do you remember a woman named Wright? [Name not clearly written.]

(No, not at this moment.)

Did I not tell you about her the day we were at the shore?

(Ah, Dick, I think you did, but I do not remember it well enough to make it a good test.)

Do you remember my remark about the way in which the name was spelled?

(No, I don't remember it, Dick.)

Also about her giving me some very interesting things?

(No, Dick, I do not remember it. Do you remember telling

me that day that when you got on the other side you would make it hot for me?)

I do indeed remember it well. I said I would shake you up—shake you up.

(That is just the word you used Dick.) [I am not now sure the word was "shake you up," but it was some such colloquial expression.—N.]

Yes, I did. Oh—I said, won't I shake you up when I get over there if I go before you do! And here I am, but I find my memory no worse than yours in spite of the fact that I have passed through the transition stage—state. You would be a pretty poor philosopher if you were to forget your subject as you seem to forget some of those little memories which I recall, Billy. Let me ask if you remember anything about a lady in [Chicago] to whom I referred.

(Oh Dick, I begin to remember. About eight or nine years ago was it, Dick?) [Here follows the "Huldah" material already quoted in my Part I of this report. See p. 132.—W. J.] . . .

Don't you remember my old friend?

(No.)

The astronomer? . . . Do you remember my little talk about the satellites?

(Yes, I do.)

And about the inhabitants of Mars?

(I do indeed, I remember very well.) [This was in 1895.—N.]

Do you remember my own talk independent of sittings, and my talks on the subject of canals? [R. H.'s own interest in these things was known to the trance controls, by conversations he had held with them at earlier sittings.—W. J.]

(Yes, indeed, I remember.)

This is what I am reminding you of. I heard you and William—William discussing me, and I stood not one inch behind you.

(William who?)

James.

(What did William James say?) [I recall this talk with W. J. last week.—N.]

He said he was baffled but he felt it was I talking—at one moment—then at another he did not know what to think.

[Perfectly true of my conversation with N. after his sitting with Mrs. P. a week previous.—W. J.]

(Did you hear anything else?)
Yes, he said I was very secretive and careful.
(Did you hear him say that?)
He did. He said I was—I am afraid I am.
(I don't remember his saying so.) [I remember it.—W. J.]
I tell you Billy he said so.
(Did he say anything else?)
He paid me a great compliment, [I recall this.—N.] I fear I did not deserve it. However, I am here to prove or disprove through life. Amen.
Remember my explanations of luminous ether? [A favorite subject of discussion with him, possibly known to Mrs. Piper.—N.]
Good-by. God bless you and your good wife. Remember me to her. Adieu.—R. H.

Some persons seem to make much better "sitters" than others, and Professor Newbold is evidently one of the best. The two sittings of his from which I have quoted are more flowing and contain less waste matter, perhaps, than any others. If the R. H. who appeared therein be only a figment of Mrs. Piper's play-acting subconscious self . . . we must credit that self with a real genius for accumulating the appropriate in the way of items, and not getting out of the right personal key. Not many items were certainly wrong in these sittings, and the great majority were certainly right. If two of the omitted communications could have been printed they would have greatly increased the veridical effect. Professor Newbold gives me his own result and impression in the following words. "The evidence for H.'s identity, as for that of other communicators, seems to me very strong indeed. It is not absolutely conclusive; but the only alternative theory, the telepathic, seems to me to explain the facts not as well as the spiritistic. I find it, however, absolutely impossible to accept the necessary corollaries of the spiritistic theory, especially those connected with the Imperator group, and am therefore compelled to suspend judgment."

After Dr. Newbold's, it would seem natural to cite Dr. Hyslop's sittings, which were six in number during the period which this report covers. But he has himself given an account of them with inferences, so I refrain. It may suffice to say that Hyslop had already been converted, largely by previous experiences with Mrs. Piper, to the spiritist theory of such phenomena, and that he held it in a form similar to that to which Hodgson had been led, supposing namely that at the time of communicating, the communicating spirits are themselves in a dreamy or somnambulic state, and not in full possession of their faculties.[16]

Dr. Hyslop's sittings in the present series, although they seem to me to contain no coercive evidence for a surviving Hodgson, as contrasted with the field of alternatives—I doubt if Hyslop would make any such claim for them—yet lend themselves easily to the notion that Hodgson, in a somewhat amnesic and confused state, was there. They pursued a train of ideas most natural for such a Hodgson to have followed, and they confirmed Dr. Hyslop in the theory which he had already reached as the line of least resistance in these matters: Hodgson was probably communicating as best he might under the available conditions. He led the conversation back to his and Hyslop's earlier experiences, recalled the differences of opinion they had had over the proofs of Hyslop's report on Mrs. Piper in 1901; alluded to a meeting which they were to have had in New York if Hodgson had not "passed over," and to what Hyslop wished to discuss there; reminded Hyslop of some experiments on mediums which they had made together in earlier days, and of messages purporting to be from R. H. which Hyslop was receiving through another medium at present; discussed other mediumistic persons, and especially the aptitudes of a certain young "light" in whom Hyslop was interested; sent a veridical message to Dr. Newbold; recalled a certain "cheese" of which he and Hyslop had partaken on a unique occasion together; gave advice regarding Hyslop's practical perplexities in the crisis of S. P. R. affairs; expressed his sympathy in the most appropriate fashion; etc., etc.— most of all this in an exceedingly scanty way, to be sure, but with

---

[16] Compare with this Mrs. Sidgwick's well-argued theory that they are not *trying* to communicate at all, but that the medium in trances is able telepathically to tap their minds in spots, just as she taps the minds of the sitters. —W. J.

such naturalness of tone, and following such characteristic lines of association with the sitter, that the latter's view was, as I said, only confirmed.

A reader of the records, not having Dr. Hyslop's mental *Apperceptionsmasse* to interpret them by, might fail to find them convincing. My own feeling toward these sittings is what it is towards all the others. The interpretation of them will depend on that of the whole larger mass of material with which they belong.

5. *William James's Sitting* [17]

The evidence is so much the same sort of thing throughout, and makes such insipid reading, that I hesitate to print more of it in full. But I know that many critics insist on having the largest possible amount of *verbatim* material on which to base their conclusions, so I select as a specimen of the R. H.-control's utterances when he was less "strong," one of two voice-sittings which I had with him myself (May 21st, 1906). The reader, I fear, will find it long and tedious, but he can skip.

[R. H. enters, saying:]
Well, well, well, well! Well, well, well, that is . . . here I am. Good morning, good morning, Alice.
[Mrs. J.] (Good morning, Mr. Hodgson.)
I am right here. Well, well, well! I am delighted!
(Hurrah! R. H.! Give us your hand!)
Hurrah, William! God bless you. How are you?
(First rate.)
Well, I am delighted to see you. Well, have you solved those problems yet!
(Which problems do you refer to?)
Did you get my messages?
(I got some messages about your going to convert me.)
Did you hear about that argument that I had? You asked me what I had been doing all those years, and what it amounted to?
[R. H. had already sent me, through other sitters, messages about my little faith.—W. J.]

---

[17] Parts of this section of the report have been omitted.—Ed.

(Yes.)

Well, it has amounted to this—that I have learned by experience that there is more truth than error in what I have been studying.

(Good!)

I am so delighted to see you today that words fail me.

(Well, Hodgson, take your time and don't be nervous.)

No. Well, I think I could ask the same of you! Well, now, tell me—I am very much interested in what is going on in the Society, and Myers and I are also interested in the Society over here. You understand that we have to have a medium on this side while you have a medium on your side, and through the two we communicate with you.

(And your medium is who?)

We have a medium on this side. It is a lady. I don't think she is known to you.

(You don't mean Rector?)

No, not at all. It is . . . do you remember a medium whom we called Prudens?

(Yes.)

Prudens is a great help. Through Prudens we accomplish a great deal. Speak to me, William. Ask me anything. What I want to know first of all is about the Society. I am sorry that it could not go on.

(There was nobody to take your place.)

If it can't go on then it must be—

(Be dissolved. That is what we have concluded. There is nobody competent to take your place. Hyslop is going to—well, perhaps you can find out for yourself what he is going to do.)

I know what he is going to do, and we are all trying to help Hyslop, and trying to make him more conservative, and keener in understanding the necessity of being secretive. . . .

William, can't you see, don't you understand, and don't you remember how I used to walk up and down before that open fireplace trying to convince you of my experiments?

(Certainly, certainly.)

And you would stand with your hands in your trousers pockets. You got very impatient with me sometimes, and you would wonder if I was correct. I think you are very skeptical.

(Since you have been returning I am much more near to feeling as you felt than ever before.)

Good! Well, that is capital.

(Your "personality" is beginning to make me feel as you felt.)

If you can give up to it, William, and feel the influence of it and the reality of it, it will take away the sting of death.

(But, R. H., listen a moment. We are trying to get evidential material as to your identity, and anything that you can recollect in the way of facts is more important than anything else. For instance, do you recollect a Churchill case, Mr. Churchill, who came on from New York or from the West with some materials, and you and I had some discussions? I have just had that worked up in the laboratory. Can you remember anything of that?)

Oh, yes. I had Osler in my mind also and I was preparing some answers for that. [Piddington on May 2nd had told the controls of an MS. reply to Osler found among Hodgson's papers. —W. J.] I think perhaps you have heard about that, have you?

(Yes, I have heard about that.)

Well, Sanger, or Zangler? the clergyman, do you remember him?

(No, I don't remember.) [Impossible to identify.—W. J.]

Don't you remember a young man whom I was going to see? I think I told you about it, William—quite sure I did—who was a clergyman, and who was afraid of his condition, going into the trances. Don't you remember that at all? Ask Alice. Perhaps she remembers.

[Mrs. J.] (No, I don't remember that account of the clergyman. I think perhaps Hyslop may remember it. I remember something about dream-cases and what we called deathbed experiences.) . . .

(Yes, this clergyman had had some of those, had he?)

He had had some experiences in dreams. And then there was a case in Washington that I was anxious to look up. Do you remember my speaking anything about that?

(No, I am not so sure of that. Do you remember a Denver case, a Gower case?)

Oh yes, you recall that to my mind. And do you remember the description of the man whose finger—there was something peculiar about his finger?

(Yes, I do remember that. I remember that incident.)

[I seemed to, at the moment, but the memory has failed to become distinct.—W. J.]

Well, have you found anything more about that?

(No, I have not. If you could recall what kind of a case the Gower case was, it would be interesting.) . . .

Wasn't that a case of hysteria?

(No, not hysteria. He corresponded with you and wanted you to come and see the phenomena. Do you remember?)

I do remember a physical-manifestation case, and I remember an aural case—the voices came. And I think the Gower case was physical manifestation, if I remember. [No voices.—W. J.]

(That is correct. Can you remember what the physical manifestations were?)

Well, I hope I will not get these mixed up in my mind, because I have several that are passing through my thoughts. There was one where they had the table manifestations, and they had also some experiments in knocking about the room after retiring. Do you remember those? [The table had moved without contact, but I fail to remember any "knocking."—W. J.]

(Yes.)

I think I had those correct in my mind, and then I think—do you remember the case where the hands appeared, as though they were in phosphorescent light?

(I don't remember that case.)

I have those two now just on my mind at the moment. I think they will come to you clearly presently. Now tell me a little bit more about the Society. That will help me keep my thoughts clear. I think, William—are you standing?

(Yes, I am standing.)

Well, can't you sit?

(Yes.)

Well, sit. Let's have a nice talk.

(The Society is going to disband. Hyslop and Piddington and George Dorr and I have agreed to that, and we have written a circular, which we have signed, to the members, and I don't think there will be any objection. The American work will have to go on apart from the English work in some way.)

Well, then about Hyslop's society. I think he will succeed in that. I feel very much encouraged in regard to that.

(I certainly hope he will succeed.)

I want to ask you if you have met at all Miss Gaule?

(Maggie Gaule? I have not met her.) [A medium known to R. H. during life, probably also known by name to Mrs. P.—W. J.]

I am very much disappointed in some respects. I have tried to reach her. [In 1908, Hyslop got messages from R. H. through Miss Gaule.—W. J.] I have reached another light and I did succeed in getting a communication through.

(What was your communication?)

I did not believe in her when I was in the body. I thought she was insincere, but I believe her now and know that she has genuine light, and I gave a message recently to a Mrs. M. in the body. I referred to my books and my papers and several other things. Her name is Soule. [R. H. acted as Mrs. Soule's control, and something like incipient cross-correspondences were obtained. —W. J.]

(Soule?)

[The stenographer] (I know her.)

And now, as I go through my rooms [which were still full of R. H.'s effects] I have talked over the matters there very well. Now let me see—tell me more about the Gower case. Are you going to look that up?

(I stopped at Denver on my way from California, and I saw all the witnesses, and I think it is a good case.)

I am inclined to think he is honest and I will investigate and if possible I will give some manifestations there that you will know that it comes from me. I will do everything I can because I am so anxious, and if I cannot prove—wait a moment—will you spell this after me? [Very dramatic change—as if some sudden influence had come upon him.]

(Yes.)

It is Z e i v o r n [spelt out].[18]

[W. J. pronounces each letter after it is spoken by R. H.]

Now put those letters, repeat those backwards, and I have left that word written and I think you will find it among my papers. It is original and nobody saw it, nobody would understand it. [Not found there.—W. J.]

(That is a password?)

Yes.

(Now, Hodgson, do you remember any sealed test that you left with Myers or me or anybody?)

I left one with Lodge.

(Did you leave one with me?)

---

[18] See later reference on page 185 and note on page 204.—ED.

Yes, I left one with you. [I supposed so, but have found none. —W. J.]

(Can you recall anything about that? It is very hard to remember those things.)

It is sealed, if I remember rightly. Now wait a moment. That is one you will find in the office—in my rooms, rather—and I think I left it in a book.

(This one that you just spelt out?)

Yes.

(Did you make that word up?)

I spelt the word, made the word up and spelt it out because I knew no one living could guess at it or hit it.

(It does not mean anything in particular?)

Nothing at all.

(Just a password?)

Yes. And the one I gave to *you,* I shall have to think that over, William.

(Think that over, Hodgson. Think it over carefully. Take your time and see if you can get it, because it is very important.)

I shall do so, and I want to do it in a way to exclude if possible the theory of clairvoyance. Now I want to ask you a question, may I, while it is on my mind? Have you ever asked Harry if he asked Dr. Bayley about that charade? [Reference to a former sitting with H. J., Jr.]

(Yes, there is an answer from Dr. Bayley, about a charade containing the word "peacemaker.") [Dr. Bayley recalls no such charade.—W. J.]

Yes.

(And that is all right.)

The answer?

(Yes.) [I print the record as it stands—it seems incoherent on my part.—W. J.]

Well, about the cheese? Please answer me.

(The cheese is all right. That is a very—) [The "cheese" recalled to me another charade.]

No, no—I want to know if he gave it to Bayley.

(Yes, that was sent to Bayley by Harry, I think, but whether *you* gave it to Bayley originally, I am not sure.) [R. H. did so give it, Dr. Bayley informs me, but Mrs. Piper says she also had heard this charade from R. H.—W. J.]

Well, I wish you would find that out. You see these things are all going through my mind, as though there was a panorama of things going through my vision.

(Hodgson, what are you doing, apart from Mrs. Piper?)

Why, I am working with the Society, William, trying to reach other lights, trying to communicate, trying to get into touch with you all.

(Why can't you tell me more about the other life?)

That is a part of my work. I intend to give you a better idea of this life than has ever been given.

(I hope so.)

It is not a vague fantasy but a reality.

[Mrs. J.] (Hodgson, do you live as we do, as men do?)

What does she say?

(Do you live as men do?)

[Mrs. J.] (Do you wear clothing and live in houses?)

Oh yes, houses, but not clothing. No, that is absurd. [Query: the clothing, or the statement made about it?—W. J.] Just wait a moment. I am going to get out.

(You will come back again?)

Yes.

[Rector.] He has got to go out and get his breath.

[When R. H. comes back he recommences talking about his passwords:]

Philanthropist—That is one of the words, but—wait a moment —that is Lodge's. Now I remember that very well. The other one which I have spelled—you wait a moment—there is something troubling me regarding the—do you remember another case? I want to recall it to your mind. Do you remember a case about a young girl, a young woman that I told you about?

(Yes.)

I have seen her since I came over. Yes, I think Hyslop brought her here to me.

(Yes.)

Well, that is the nearest approach to a case of hysteria of anything I know. Do you remember my telling you about it, William?

(Well, I do remember a case. I don't fully identify it.)

It was about a year before I passed out.

(I do remember a young woman. Have you been influencing her?)

No, I tried to reach her two or three times, one or two messages, but they did not come from me.

(I don't know whether it is the same case. The one I meant had been in an asylum.)

That is the one. I tried to get the message through but I found it was a failure. [Evidently not the person I was thinking of. —W. J.]

[The letter from H——t was here again put into Mrs. Piper's hand.]

I tell you one person, William, who has light, and that is B——g.

(Have you been able to get near Mrs. B——g?)

Yes, I gave her a communication since I passed out. You ask her if she received anything like this: "I have seen the doctor and I put my hands palms to your face facing you." You ask her if she got anything of that kind. [Mrs. B. informs me that she has had no direct impression from Hodgson since his death, but numerous messages from him through mediums on the Pacific Coast.—W. J.]

(How did you get this message to her?)

Appeared to her and thought she saw me. She put her hand up. She had just retired.

(What time of day was it?)

Just retired.

(Gone to bed? Do you remember, Hodgson, anyone by the name of H——t?)

A medium?

(No, not a medium, a friend.)

You mean lived in Providence? [The letter was from a Mr. H——t in England.—W. J.]

(No, I don't think he lived in Providence.)

Oh yes, I remember Mr. H——t who used to live in Providence and from whom I received a great many letters. [Unknown, as yet, to W. J.]

(Have you tried to have any communication with him?)

No, I don't think I have. I think I shall try, though. I have had some communications you know here. I have met several people. But independently I have gone to very few.

[The conversation then goes on about the lost ring (compare Part I. of this report), and about the "cheese" charade. Then I, thinking of a certain pitfall which the children and I had dug for Hodgson, asked:]

(Do you recall any incidents about your playing with the children up in the Adirondacks at the Putnam camp?)

Do you remember—what is that name, Elizabeth Putnam? She came in and I was sitting in a chair before the fire, reading, and she came in and put her hands, crept up behind me, put her hands over my eyes, and said "Who is it?" And do you remember what my answer was?

(Let me see if *you* remember it as I do.)

I said, "Well, it feels like Elizabeth Putnam, but it sounds like—"

(I know who you mean.) [R. H. quite startled me here because what he said reminded me of an incident which I well remembered. One day at breakfast little Martha Putnam (as I recall the fact) had climbed on Hodgson's back, sitting on his shoulders, and clasped her hands over his eyes, saying "Who am I?" To which R. H., laughing, had responded: "It sounds like Martha, but it feels like Henry Bowditch"—the said H. B. weighing nearly 200 lbs. I find that no one but myself, of those who probably were present, remembers this incident.—W. J.]

Do you realize how difficult that is?

(It is evidently; yet you were just on the point of saying it. Is it a man or a woman?)

A man.

(Have you any message for that man now?)

Dr.—not Putnam—Dr. Bowditch!

(That is it, Bowditch.)

"Sounds like Dr. Bowditch."

(It was not Elizabeth Putnam, but it was Charlie Putnam's daughter.)

Charlie Putnam, yes. Now do you remember that?

(But what is the name of Charles Putnam's daughter?)

Of whom? Annie? Oh, she is the youngest. She is the young lady. And there was a Mary—Mamie. [False names!—W. J.] [Names of my wife.—J. H. H.[19]]

(But you *must* remember Charles Putnam's daughter's name.)

I have got it now in my mind. I could not think of it at first. Well it has gone from me at the moment. Never mind. That is less important than the thing itself.

---

[19] Professor James Hervey Hyslop.—Ed.

(Do you remember another thing? We played a rather peculiar game. Possibly you may recall it. Had great fun.)

I remember playing leap-frog with the boys. Do you remember that?

(Yes, that was frequent.)

Yes, that is a very—and then do you remember how I played bear.

(Yes, bear is first rate. I was not there, but I heard them talking about your playing bear. I remember one morning you and I had a very—)

Well, what you remember I might not remember at all.

(Of course not, but you played so often with them that you may have forgotten.) . . .

I wish you would repeat to me those letters, to see if you have got them correct.

(Z e i v o r n.) [20]

That is right. It is written in cipher, the one word, and written by itself, on a large sheet of paper, carefully folded and placed in one of my books, and it is in a book of poems I think, and I think it was Longfellow's, and the book has a scroll up and down the back, and the binding is green in color, and I don't think anyone living knows that but myself.

(Yes, are there any particular things that you would like to have sent to Australia?)

I have talked that over pretty carefully with Piddington and I think those arrangements are already made.

(Yes, that is right.)

I wanted to recall—Alice, perhaps you can help me to recall—what was that balcony where we used to go and smoke?

[Mrs. J.] (Why, yes, it was upstairs, the upper story of the piazza.) [If Chocorua were meant, Mrs. Piper knew of this "balcony."—W. J.]

That is all right. That is perfectly clear. She always did have a clear head. . . . Now I want—William, I want one thing. I want you to get hold of the spiritual side of this thing and not only the physical side. I want you to feel intuitively and instinctively the spiritual truth, and when you do that you will be happy, and you will find that I was not idling and was not spending my time on nonsense; and as I thought over all, as it came to me

---

[20] See earlier reference on page 180 and note on page 204.—ED.

after I entered this life, I thought "What folly! If I could only get hold of him!"

(I wish that what you say could grow more continuous. That would convince me. You are very much like your old self, but you are curiously fragmentary.)

Yes, but you must not expect too much from me, that I could talk over the lines and talk as coherently as in the body. You must not expect too much, but take things little by little as they come and make the best of it, and then you must put the pieces together and make a whole out of it. Before I lose my breath, is there any other question you want to ask me? What do you think of that bust, William? I don't quite approve of it. I think it is all nonsense. [On March 12, Mr. Dorr had told the R. H.-control that Mr. Biela Pratt had begun to model a bust of him for the Tavern Club.]

(I do not know anything about it. I have not seen it. But it is a natural thing for the Tavern Club to want of you, they were so fond of you, all of them.)

I want to know, William, what is that you are writing about me?

(I am not writing anything about you at present.)

Aren't you going to?

(Perhaps so.)

Can I help you out any?

(Yes, I want you to help me out very much. I am going to write about these communications of yours. I want to study them out very carefully, everything that you say to any sitter.)

Well, that is splendid. You could not have said anything to please me more than that.

(I am glad you approve of my taking it in hand.)

Yes, I do. Of all persons you are the one.

(I'll try to glorify you as much as I can!)

Oh, I don't care about that. I would like to have the truth known, and I would like to have you work up these statements as proof that I am not annihilated.

(Precisely so. Well, R. H., you think over that "nigger minstrel" talk. [Compare pp. 130–31.] If you get the whole conversation in which that nigger-minstrel talk was mentioned by me it would be very good proof that it is you talking to me.) [He failed to get it.—W.J.]

Well, I shall do it. I want you to understand one thing, that in the act of communicating it is like trying to give a conversation over the telephone, that the things that you want to say the most slip from you, but when you have ceased to talk they all come back to you. You can understand that.

(I understand that they come back.)

But I shall give that out to someone here, you may be sure, and I hope to see you—this is only the beginning, and I shall be clearer from time to time, but the excitement of seeing you and all has been very beautiful to me. . . .

[Mrs. J.] (Mr. Hodgson, I am so glad to know that you can come at all.)

Well, you were always a great help to me, you always did see me, but poor William was blind. But we shall wholly straighten him out and put him on the right track. . . . I am sorry to be off so soon, but I know there are difficulties in remaining too long. They often told me too frequent communication was not good for anyone. I understand what that means now better than ever. I am going to look up one or two cases and put you on the track of them, William, when I can communicate here—at the same time repeat the messages elsewhere.

(That is first rate.)

I think that is one of the best things I can do. Now I am going to skedaddle. Good-by, William. God bless you. Give my love to the boys.

As I review this somewhat diluted sitting, the only evidential point in it seems to me to be the anecdote about the Putnam child. The incident was very distinct in my own memory, but seems to survive in no one else's. I was hoping for another answer altogether, about a certain "pitfall," namely, and this one was a surprise. Either tapping my subconscious memory, or a surviving R. H. would be possible explanations of it, unless it were more reasonable to assume that someone had told the anecdote to Mrs. Piper at the time, and that her memory was now reproducing it. Obviously the reader's solution will depend on his sense of "dramatic probability," and that will differ with the line of his previous experiences. For myself, considering the possibilities of leakage, impossible to trace, in the whole case, I cannot be positively sure that Mrs. Piper's knowledge of this anecdote was supernormal at all. The rest of the sitting, although quite compatible with the spiritual explanation, seems to me to have no evidential force.

The same is true of the second sitting, which I had a fortnight later. Much of it went over the same matters, with no better results. I vainly tried to make Hodgson remember a certain article he had written for *Mind* in 1885, and to give the name of Thomas Brown, whom he had praised there. Neither could he remember anything about the American Society for Psychical Research, as he found it on arriving in this country. He rightly mentioned his brown dress-suit and his broad-toed boots, when questioned about his costume at that time, but these facts were known to Mrs. Piper. He named a "Grenier" whom my son should have met at Paris but whom we could not identify. He insisted much on my having said of a certain lady "God bless the roof that covers her." I trust I may have said this of many ladies, but R. H. could lead me to no identification.

The only queer thing that happened at this sitting was the following incident. A lady had sent me a pair of gloves as an "influence" to elicit, if possible, a message from her husband, who had recently committed suicide. I put the gloves into Mrs. Piper's hand, naturally without a word of information about the case, when "Hodgson," who had been speaking, said, with a rather startling change of his voice into a serious and confidential tone, that he had just seen the father [known to us both in life] of a young man who a few years before had made away with himself. "I never knew it till I came over here. I think they kept it very quiet, but it is true, and it hastened the father's coming." The apparent suggestion of a suicide, even though it were another one, by the gloves, and the instantaneous change of tone in the communicator, forcibly suggested to me the notion that the gloves were shedding an influence of the kind called "psychometric." The facts given by R. H. about the suicide were veridical; but, with the possibilities of leakage in the case, they cannot count in any way as evidential. . . .

6. *Miss Bergman's Sittings*

I will end my specimens by some extracts from two sittings of Miss R. Bergman [pseudonym]. Miss Bergman had been in previous years an excellent sitter, and was known by name to Mrs. Piper. She dwelt in another state, and her social connections were not in Massachusetts. At her first visit, December 31st, 1907, the communications were in writing and she had much difficulty in deciphering them. At the second sitting, January 1st, 1908, the voice was used and things ran much more smoothly.

At the first sitting R. H. quickly appeared, spoke of having seen two brothers of the sitter in the spirit world [names known to trance personalities, and non-evidential], made a wrong statement about Christmas at the cemetery, and then, being asked to recall his meetings with Miss Bergman on earth, said:

> I will. Do you remember one evening when I came to the hotel where you were staying and I sat and told you of my experiences till it got very late and I asked you if you would not [illegible] I told you so very many jokes, you and Miss Pope were convulsed with laughter over it. [Correct, Hotel Bellevue, Boston, March, 1905.—R. B.[21]]

After a while, Hodgson reappears, saying:

> Do you remember my telling you about my German friends?
> (No.)
> Perhaps Miss Pope remembers.
>
> [I found later that Miss Pope well remembered Dr. Hodgson's telling about his "German friends" and that it was that which "convulsed us with laughter" the evening he had stayed so late when calling at our hotel. At this point I had become so discouraged by the great difficulty of reading the writing and the confusion in making things clear that I felt very indifferent and inert in mind.—R. B.]
>
> Bosh.
> (What do you mean by that?)
> You understand well.

[21] Miss Bergman.—ED.

(Bosh?)
Yes, I say bosh. *B O S H B O S H*
(What do you mean by that?)
Oh I say it is *all bosh.*
(What is bosh?)
Why the way you understand. It is simply awful.
(That sounds like you, Dr. Hodgson.)
I could shake you.
(How can I do better?)
Put all your wits to it, you have plenty of them.
(I will do my best. Go on.)
Do. Do you remember I used to chaff you?
(Indeed I do.)
Well I am still chaffing you a bit just for recognition.
(It helps.)
Amen. Now you are waking up a bit.
(I am.)
Capital. So am I. Don't you remember I told you I would show
you how to manage if I ever came over before you did?
(Indeed I do.) [Sitter had often heard Dr. Hodgson say this.[22]]
Well now I am trying to show you. I used to scold you right
and left and I shall have to keep it up, I think, unless you do better.
(I deserve it.)
If you do not who does?
(You are your old self.)
Oh I am the [two words not deciphered] I was. You'll find it
out before I finish.
(Have you a message for Theo?) [Miss Theodate Pope.]
Yes indeed give her my love and tell her I am not going to for-
sake her. I do not think she has been keeping straight to the mark.
(What do you mean by that?)
I think she has been getting a little mixed up in her thoughts
and ideas of us over here. I am the same old sixpence and I wish
she were the same. I want to see her very much.

["Theo" had had no sitting for a long time, her interest being
lessened by the circumstance that records of sittings were not being kept systematically, as before Dr. Hodgson's death. At this
point the hand wrote comments relating to circumstances which

---

[22] The bracketed comments in the third person are by Miss Bergman herself.
—W. J.

had arisen in Theo's life since Dr. Hodgson's death. These comments were singularly appropriate.—R. B.]

At the second sitting when R. H. appeared, the voice began
speaking very rapidly and heartily.

Well, well, well, this is Miss Bergman; hullo! I felt as though
I could shake you yesterday.

(Well, I was pretty stupid. I think we can do better today.
Please repeat some of the messages you wrote and left sealed to
be opened after your death.)

One message I gave to Will. If I remember correctly it was
"there is no death."

(Who is Will?)

Will James.

(Are you sure you are now giving this quotation correctly as
you wrote it?)

Of course I am. [There followed an outburst spoken so rapidly
that the sitter could not get it down, declaring that the speaker
had not lost his memory any more than had the sitter, etc.]

(Did you leave other messages?)

Yes, another. "Out of life"—how did I quote it—"Out of life,
into life eternal." . . . I know positively what I wrote. I have
promised Piddington to repeat through Mrs. Verrall all the messages that I give through this light. Every message given at this
light must be repeated through Mrs. Verrall before anyone opens
any of my sealed messages. Mrs. Verrall is the clearest light except this which I have found. Moreover she has a beautiful character and is *perfectly honest*. That is saying a great deal. Do
you remember my description of luminiferous ether, and of my
conception of what this life was like? I have found it was not an
erroneous imagination.

[The above words were spoken with great animation and interest. The sitter, although remembering Dr. Hodgson's description of "luminiferous ether," felt that she was not qualified to
enter into a conversation of this character and began to say something else. The voice interrupted her:]

It is never the way to get the best results by peppering with
questions. Intelligences come with minds filled and questions often put everything out of their thought. I am now going to give

you a test. Mention it to no one, not even to Theo. Write down, seal, and give to Alice or to William.

[Directions here followed regarding such a test. After these directions the voice spontaneously took up another subject.]

Your school was—[correct name given], was it not? You are changing, your brother tells me, and he is very pleased. He thinks you are going to broaden out and do a better work. He is very glad. Do not undertake too much. Make use of assistance in the work. [Already known to controls, but probably not to Mrs. Piper when awake.]

(Where were your lodgings in Boston?)

Well, now, that has brought back to my mind Boston— Certainly —there were some doctors in my building—George Street—no— not George—Charles Street—I—I believe. Now let me see, Charles Street. Up three flights, I think I was on the top. [Correct, but known to Mrs. Piper.—W. J.]

(Do you know when I was at your lodgings?]

You were there? Didn't we have tea together? [False.]

(No.)

Did you come and read papers?

(No.)

Did you go there after I passed out?

(Yes. I went to get some articles belonging to you, and did them up in rubber cloth.)

Capital, that is good. Lodge and Piddington consider it good when I can't remember what did not happen! What was the name of that girl who used to work in my office?

(I do not remember.)

Edmund—Edwards—I am thinking of her going to my rooms to read papers. [Her name was Edmunds, known to the medium. —W. J.]

Now I want to ask you if you remember Australia, remember my riding horseback? Remember my telling you of riding through the park in the early morning with the dew on the grass and how beautiful it was.

(Yes, yes, I remember that very well. That is fine.)

I *am* Richard Hodgson. *I am he.* I am telling you what I *remember.* I told you, too, about my preaching. I believed I was in the wrong and I stopped. It hurt some of my people to have me.

(Tell me about your riding.)

I remember telling you about my dismounting and sitting and drinking in the beauty of the morning.

(Tell me any experiences that befell you while riding.)

Oh, I told you about the experience with the fiery horse. You remember he dismounted me. It was the first experience I had in seeing stars. I lost consciousness. I experienced passing into this life. I remember my being unconscious and recovering consciousness. I remember telling you this at the hotel.

[Sitter's mind was filled here with recollections of how Dr. Hodgson had once told her all this when talking with her at the Parker House in Boston, in 1904. He had related just this experience and had said that when he recovered consciousness after being unconscious for some time it seemed to him he had been in a spiritual universe. He also told her at that time of his having given testimony in Methodist meeting as a lad in his teens, and afterwards giving it up because he became skeptical in matters of faith. This, he said, had troubled some of his kinsfolk.—R. B.]

(What did you use to order for luncheon when you lunched with us at the hotel?)

Oh, I have forgotten all about eating—m—m—I was very fond of protose.

[The sitter did not have "protose" in mind but remembers Dr. Hodgson sometimes asking the waiter for one of the prepared breakfast foods, but does not recall its name.—R. B.]

When I found the light it looked like a tremendous window, open window. The canopy—do you remember how they used to talk about the canopy? It is an ethereal veil. If your spiritual eyes were open you could see through this veil and see me here talking to you perfectly.

[The sitter did not care to talk about this, although she remembered perfectly Dr. Hodgson's telling her "how they talked about the canopy," so she asked a question referring to the intimate personal affairs of one of her friends. The replies showed a strange knowledge of the circumstances known only to the sitter and her friend, and were entirely à propos. The voice then went on speaking, and burst out with what follows, in a tone of mingled indignation and amusement.]

Will thinks I ought to walk into the room bodily and shake hands with him. I heard him say "Hodgson isn't so much of a power on the other side." What does he think a man in the ethereal body is going to do with a man in the physical body? [Seems to show some supernormal knowledge of the state of my mind. —W. J.]

(To whom did you speak first from that world?)

Theodate, yes, Theodate, she was the one to whom I first spoke. [Correct.]

[The sitter now asked to talk with another spirit, and reply was made that R. H. would continue talking until he came. R. H. did this by again referring to the accident in the park. He spoke of being seated when he first told us of the incident, and of getting up and walking around the room as he talked. He said it chanced that this incident had been told to few people, and again dwelt upon having seen stars after falling, having been unconscious, having had visions while unconscious, as if the spirit had left the body and passed into another world. All of this corresponded exactly with fact. Dr. Hodgson had commenced the story seated, and had risen and walked about as he talked.—R. B.]

The accurate knowledge thus displayed of R. H.'s conversations at the hotels in Boston where the ladies stayed, seems to me one of the most evidential items in the whole series. It is improbable that such unimportant conversations should have been reported by the living R. H. to Mrs. Piper, either awake or when in trance with other sitters; and to my mind the only plausible explanation is supernormal. Either it spells "spirit return," or telepathic reading of the sitter's mind by the medium in trance.

I now pass to R. H.'s

7. Australian Recollections

R. H. has sent many messages, both of affection and for test purposes, to his sister Annie in Australia. Mrs. M., Mr. Piddington, my wife, myself, Mr. Dorr, Miss Pope, Miss Hillard, all received such messages, which were duly transmitted to the sister, on whose replies what follows is based. Some of these messages were too general to serve as good tests (e.g., "Do you remember my reading

Fenimore Cooper?"); some had been spoken of at previous trances . . . ; some awoke no corresponding memory in Miss Hodgson. There are too many of them to quote in full, so I will go rapidly over the more significant ones, taking them in their time-order.

Melbourne; Latrobe Street; bush in yard with red berries. [Correct, as to town, street, and bush, berries not recalled by Miss H. Had R. H. ever mentioned Latrobe Street and bush to Mrs. Piper? —of course she knew of Melbourne.]

Charley Roberts (or Robertson) at the University. [Not recalled. There was a Roberts at R. H.'s school.]

Little shed where boys used to play. [Correct.]

Sister Rebecca. [Known in previous trances.]

Plums in back yard. [False?]

R. H., ten years old, sat with knees crossed at church, and his mother made him sit straight. Sat on his hat to keep other boys from getting it. A man named Hurley made him stop. [Probably untrue.]

Sister Annie caught him reading in bed and put out the light. [Not remembered.]

Riding horseback. [Correct.]

Holidays spent at the Hydes'. [Correct.]

Kendall. [Name not remembered.]

Great plates of peas raised in our garden. [Not particularly recalled.]

Played fly the garter with Tom [his brother], Jack Munroe, and (?) Roberts. [No reply from Miss Hodgson about Jack Munroe— the rest true.]

Father's mines and losses. [Correct.]

Description of paternal house. [Wrong.]

Sister used to teach him. [False.]

Father nervous over children's noise. Mother used to say "Let them enjoy themselves." [Not remembered.]

Sister helped him to escape punishments. [Possibly, when very young.]

Read Fenimore Cooper. [Possibly true.]

Sunday-school poem about stars. [R. H. wrote juvenile poems—one about "stars" not remembered.]

The account to Miss Bergman of R. H. being thrown from his horse we have already seen. Miss Annie Hodgson writes of the whole collection of messages sent to her: "To my mind there is nothing striking in any of the statements." She propounded in turn three test questions of her own to which no answer was forthcoming; and R. H., questioned by a sitter, couldn't remember the name of his schoolmaster in Melbourne. In interpreting responsibly these Australian messages, tapping the mind of the sitters, and normal acquaintance with the facts on Mrs. Piper's part must probably be excluded as explanations. If a naturalistic interpretation were insisted on, fictitious construction of incidents probable in any boyhood, and accidental coincidence of a certain number of these with fact, would have to be chiefly relied upon. Against fictitious construction is the fact that almost none of the names that had figured in Hodgson's own sittings in 1887 and 1888 were used for reproduction. "Enid," "Ellen," "Eric," were added rightly; and the three names of "Q." [Hodgson had apparently given only the first one to Phinuit] slipped out in full, as it were inadvertently, on May 29th, 1906, Hodgson insisting at the same time that her identity must never be revealed to the outside world.[23] The pos-

---

[23] I wrote to Mrs. Piper for the names of H.'s Australian relatives. Here is her answer, which I take to be sincere:

"Boston, Jan. 11, 1909. Dear Mr. James,—In replying to your letter of this morning I will say I am very sorry I cannot help you in finding Dr. Hodgson's relatives in Australia as I do not know any of them or anything about them except that he had one sister whose name was Annie, and this was unknown to me until some time after Dr. Hodgson's death. Mrs [Lyman] might be able to tell you as it was she who told me, she had some photographs of Dr. H. which I admired, and she said she would give me one later, but those she had she was going to send to his sister Annie in Australia. I was struck by the familiarity with which she used the name and concluded that she must have known her. Dr. Hodgson never talked with me about his relatives or any body else's, on the contrary he most carefully avoided all such subjects when talking with me. I haven't the slightest idea who 'Q' was, I have never heard the name so far as I am aware.

"I am sure my daughters do not know any more than I do about Dr. Hodgson's family.—I am, very sincerely yours, L. E. PIPER."—W. J.

sibility that Hodgson had given "Q's" entire name to later controls than Phinuit cannot be eliminated.

On the whole this series baffles me as much as the rest. It may be spirit return! it may be something else! Leaks of various sorts are so probable that no sharp conclusion can be drawn.

I think that by this time the reader has enough documentary material to gain an adequate impression of the case. Additional citations of sittings would introduce no new factors of solution. The entire lot of reports, read *verbatim*, would, it is true, give a greater relative impression of hesitation, repetition, and boggling generally; and the "rigorously scientific mind" would of course rejoice to find its own explanatory category, "Bosh," greatly confirmed thereby. But the more serious critic of the records will hold his judgment in suspense; or, if he inclines to the spiritistic solution, it will be because an acquaintance with the phenomenon on a much larger scale has altered the balance of presumptions in his mind, and because spirit return has come to seem no unpermissible thing to his sense of the natural dramatic probabilities.

8. Conclusion

Before indulging in some final reflections of my own on nature's possibilities, I will cite a few additional evidential points. I will print them in no order, numbering them as they occur.

(1) First of all, several instances of knowledge that was veridical and seemed unquestionably supernormal. These were confidential remarks, some of which naturally won't bear quotation. One of them, plausible after the fact, could hardly have been thought of by anyone before it. Another would, I think, hardly have been constructed by Mrs. Piper. A third was to the effect that R. H. thought now differently about a certain lady—she was less "selfish" than he had called her in a certain private conversation of which he reminded the sitter.

(2) Again, there was intense solicitude shown about keeping the sittings of a certain former sitter from publicity. It sounded

very natural and Hodgsonian, but the trance-Mrs. Piper might also have deemed it necessary.

(3) The following incident belongs to my wife's and Miss Putnam's sitting of June 12th, 1906:—Mrs. J. said: "Do you remember what happened in our library one night when you were arguing with Margie [Mrs. J.'s sister]?"—"I had hardly said 'remember,'" she notes, "in asking this question, when the medium's arm was stretched out and the fist shaken threateningly," then these words came:

[R. H.] Yes. I did this in her face. I couldn't help it. She was so impossible to move. It was wrong of me, but I couldn't help it.

(I myself well remember this fist-shaking incident, and how we others laughed over it after Hodgson had taken his leave. What had made him so angry was my sister-in-law's defense of some slate-writing she had seen in California.—W. J.) [24]

(4) At a written sitting at which I was present (July 29th, 1907) the following came:

You seem to think I have lost my equilibrium. Nothing of the sort.

---

[24] *Prima facie,* the following incident also sounds evidential:

"[R. H.] Ask Margie if she remembers chaffing me about sitting up late to entertain people."

This happened, as I well remember, at Chocorua, but at this distance of time it is impossible to be sure whether it was not on the occasion when Hodgson and Mrs. Piper were there as visitors together. The evidence is therefore "leaky."

Another case of leaky evidence is the following, which *prima facie* seems striking enough:

In Hodgson's rooms a quantity of MS. was found in a cipher probably invented by himself. In the sitting of Jan. 23rd, this cipher was spontaneously mentioned by the control:

"[R. H.] Is this the Piper case? the Piper phenomenon? . . . There are some private records which I should not wish to have handled. Let George and Piddington go through them and return them. The cipher—let Harry and George take care of them. That was my cipher and no one living can read it. I shall explain it later. [He never has explained it, though it was spoken of later several times.]"

I think it probable here that a question about the cipher from the sitter, preceding the control's reference to it, has been accidentally omitted from the record. If so, there is nothing remarkable in the incident. The record was not stenographic, and neither my wife nor the son who took the notes is now confident that the question was not asked.—W. J.

(You've lost your handwriting, gone from bad to worse.)
I never had any to lose.
[Mrs. M.] (It was a perfectly beautiful handwriting [ironical].)
Ahem! Ahem! William, do you remember my writing you a long letter once when you were ill? You had to get Margaret [my daughter—W. J.] to help you read it and you wrote me it was detestable writing and you hoped I would try and write plainer to a friend who was ill next time. How I laughed over that, but I was really sorry to make you wade through it. Ask Margaret if she remembers it. [Perfectly—it was in London.—Margaret J.]

(5) Another item which seems to mean either telepathy or survival of R. H., came out at a sitting of Miss Pope's on February 7th, 1906.

I am not going to make a botch of anything if I can help it. Not I. Do you remember my telling you what I would do if I got over here first?
(You said several things about it.)
I said if I couldn't do better than some of them I was mistaken. I said some of them were awful. Remember? And if I based my opinion on what they tried to give I should expect to be said to be in the trick. *Remember?*
(Of course I remember.)
Do you remember a story I told you about my old friend Sidgwick? Don't you remember how I imitated him?
(Yes, what word did you say about Sidgwick?) [I had not deciphered the word "imitated."—T. P.[25]]
If I believed in it they would say I was in the trick.
[Still not understanding, T. P. said:]
(What about Sidgwick?)
I imitated him.
(What did you do?)
I said s-s-s-should-be i-n th-e t-r-i-i-c-k.
(I remember perfectly, that's fine.)
No one living could know this but yourself and Mary Bergman.
[It was most interesting to see the hand write these words to imitate stuttering, and then for the first time it flashed over me what he had some time ago told Mary and me about Sidgwick, imitating at the same time Sidgwick's stammer: "H-Hodgson if

---

[25] Miss Theodate Pope.—ED.

you b-b-believe in it, you'll b-be said to be in the t-trick." I cannot quote the exact words but this is very nearly right.

Sidgwick referred to Hodgson's belief that he was actually communicating, through Mrs. Piper, with spirits. He meant that people not only would not believe what Hodgson gave as evidence, but would think he was in collusion with Mrs. Piper.—T. P.]

(6) At a sitting of Miss Pope's and mine, October 24th, 1906, R. H. said of Miss P.—"She goes on and puts on bays and piazzas, changes her piazzas, her house, makes it all over again." As this was literally true, and no one in Boston could well have known about it, it seemed like mind-reading. (R. H.'s saying is possibly explained, however, by a previous sitting [April 16th] of Miss Pope's, in which another of Mrs. Piper's controls had already of his own accord made the same veridical remark, so that the fact had got, however inexplicably, into the trance-consciousness, and could be used by the controls indiscriminately.)

(7) On January 30, 1906, Mrs. M. had a sitting. Mrs. M. said:

(Do you remember our last talk together, at N., and how, in coming home we talked about the work?)
Yes, yes.
(And I said if we had a hundred thousand dollars—)
Buying Billy!!
(Yes, Dick, that was it—"buying Billy.")
Buying only Billy?
(Oh no—I wanted Schiller too. How well you remember.)

Mrs. M., before R. H.'s death, had had dreams of extending the American Branch's operations by getting an endowment, and possibly inducing Professor Newbold (Billy) and Dr. Schiller to co-operate in work. She naturally regards this veridical recall, by the control, of a private conversation she had had with Hodgson as very evidential of his survival.

(8) To the same sitter, on a later occasion (March 5th, 1906), the control showed veridical knowledge of R. H.'s *pipes,* of which two had been presents from herself. She asks him at this sitting about the disposal of some of his effects. He mentions books and photographs in a general way, then says:

I want Tom [his brother] to have my pipes, all except any that my friends wish.

(Do you remember any special ones?)

Yes, I—the one you—[The hand points to me, etc.—Mrs. M.]

(Which?)

Meerschaum. [I gave R. H. a meerschaum pipe some years ago. —M.]

(You do remember! Give it to anyone you would best like to.)

. . . I want Billy James to have it. Will you give it to him? Do you remember, etc.?

(Do you remember any other special pipe?)

You mean with a long stem? Certainly. What about it?

(Can you recall anything special about it?)

What? You mean the one you gave me long ago, some time ago, not the recent one?

(The last one I gave you.)

Last season, last season, yes.

(A year or two ago, I think it was.)

I recall it well. You gave me what I call a briar pipe. [A number of years ago I gave R. H. a briar-root pipe, with rather a long stem, bound round the bowl with silver, but this was not the one of which I was thinking.—M.]

(The one I mean was an odd-looking pipe.)

I know it well, a big large bowl.

(Wasn't that the meerschaum?)

Yes, Billy is to have it. The face one I want Tom to have. I want my brother Tom to have—face on it. The whole thing was a face. I mean the pipe bowl.

[I had seen such a pipe, the whole thing a face, at the Charles Street rooms a short time before. I never remembered seeing Mr. Hodgson use it. The pipe of which I was thinking was a carved Swiss pipe which he evidently does not remember.—M.]

(9) Among my own friends in the Harvard faculty who had "passed over" the most intimate was F. J. Child. Hodgson during life had never met Child. It looks to me like a supernormal reading of my own mental states (for I had often said that the best argument I knew for an immortal life was the existence of a man who deserved one as well as Child did) that a message to me about Professor Child should have been spontaneously produced by the

R. H.-control. I had surely never mentioned C. to Mrs. Piper, had
never before had a message from his spirit, and if I had expressed
my feelings about him to the living R. H., that would make the
matter only more evidential.

The message through R. H. came to Miss Robbins, June 6th, 1906.

> There is a man named Child passed out suddenly, wants to
> send his love to William and his wife in the body.
> (Child's wife?)
> Yes, in the body. He says . . . I hope L. will understand what
> I mean. I [i. e. R. H.] don't know who L. is. [L. is the initial of
> the Christian name of Professor Child's widow.—W. J.]

(10) Miss Putnam had been consulted about the disposition of
certain matters left undone by Hodgson at the date of his death.
At her sitting, much later, these words came out. I copy the
record as it stands:

> Did you get my Christmas present? [A calendar addressed by
> him to me before his death.—A. C. P.[26]] I heard you in the body
> say you didn't want them sent. [Mr. Hodgson had left some Christ-
> mas cards addressed, but unenclosed. I had expressed unwilling-
> ness to mail them unenveloped.—A. C. P.]

(11) Mrs. M., on March 30th, placed a volume in manuscript in
the medium's hands. R. H. immediately wrote:

> Well, well. Isn't that the book I lent you?
> (Yes. You loaned it to me at C———.)
> I remember, but you have it still!
> (I returned it to you.)
> Yes, but isn't it the one I loaned your And the poems I used to
> love so well, I recall. [The book contained poems copied or com-
> posed by Hodgson, and after having been returned to him ere
> he died, had been taken from among his effects and brought to
> the sitting by Mrs. M.]

These eleven incidents sound more like deliberate truth-telling,
whoever the truth-teller be, than like lucky flukes. On the whole
they make on me the impression of being supernormal. I confess

---

that I should at this moment like much to know (although I have no means of knowing) just how all the documents I am exhibiting in this report will strike readers who are either novices in the field, or who consider the subject in general to be as pure "rot" or "bosh." It seems to me not impossible that a bosh-philosopher here or there may get a dramatic impression of there being something genuine behind it all. Most of those who remain faithful to the "bosh" interpretation would, however, find plenty of comfort if they had the entire mass of records given them to read. Not that I have left things out (I certainly have tried not to!) that would, if printed, discredit the detail of what I cite, but I have left out, by not citing the whole mass of records, so much mere mannerism, so much repetition, hesitation, irrelevance, unintelligibility, so much obvious groping and fishing and plausible covering up of false tracks, so much false pretension to power, and real obedience to suggestion, that the stream of veridicality that runs throughout the whole gets lost as it were in a marsh of feebleness, and the total dramatic effect on the mind may be little more than the word "humbug." The really significant items disappear in the total bulk. "Passwords," for example, and sealed messages are given in abundance, but can't be found. [I omit these here, as some of them may prove veridical later.] Preposterous Latin sentences are written, e.g., "Nebus merica este fecrum"—or what reads like that (April 4th, 1906). Poetry gushes out, but how can one be sure that Mrs. Piper never knew it? The weak talk of the Imperator band about *time* is reproduced, as where R. H. pretends that he no longer knows what "seven minutes" mean (May 14th, 1906). Names asked for can't be given, etc., etc.[27] All this mass of diluting material, which can't be reproduced in abridgment, has its inevitable dramatic effect; and if one tends to *hate* the whole phenomenon anyhow

---

[27] For instance, on July 2nd, the sitter asks R. H. to name some of his cronies at the Tavern Club. Hodgson gives six names, only five of which belonged to the Tavern Club, and those five were known to the controls already. None of them, I believe, were those asked for, namely, "names of the men he used to play pool with or go swimming with at Nantasket." Yet, as the sitter (Mr. Dorr) writes, "He failed to realize his failure."—W. J.

(as I confess that I myself sometimes do) one's judicial verdict inclines accordingly.

Nevertheless, I have to confess also that the more familiar I have become with the records, the less *relative significance* for my mind has all this diluting material tended to assume. The active cause of the communications is on any hypothesis a will of some kind, be it the will of R. H.'s spirit, of lower supernatural intelligences, or of Mrs. Piper's subliminal; and although some of the rubbish may be deliberately willed (certain hesitations, misspellings, etc., in the hope that the sitter may give a clue, or certain repetitions, in order to gain time) yet the major part of it is suggestive of something quite different—as if a will were there, but a will to say something which the machinery fails to bring through. Dramatically, most of this "bosh" is more suggestive to me of dreaminess and mind-wandering than it is of humbug. Why should a "will to deceive" prefer to give incorrect names so often, if it can give the true ones to which the incorrect ones so frequently approximate as to suggest that they are meant? True names impress the sitter vastly more. Why should it so multiply false "passwords" ("Zeivorn," for example) and stick to them? [28] It looks to me more

[28] On this remark of William James's J. Fraser Nicol comments: "Nothing more was heard of the case until, after the passing of fourteen years, Hubert Wales, an English novelist and psychical researcher, showed that 'Zeivorn' was an enciphered word, just as the alleged Hodgson had claimed. Wales broke the code, and published it in the A.S.P.R. *Journal*, Volume 14 (1920), 605–614. . . . Write the alphabet twice, as follows:

ABCDEFGHIJ   KLMNOPQ   RSTUVWXYZ
ZYXWVUTSRQ   JKLMNOP   IHGFEDCBA

Now equate the code letters with the required letters and get:

ZEIVORN
AVRENIM

"The result, when reversed, gives 'Minerva,' which was the name of one of Mrs. Piper's daughters. Mrs. Piper could have invented the cipher, though if so she showed a particular lack of subtlety in producing her own daughter's name. But the real point at issue is that the investigator, when presented with a mystery, took no real steps to solve it." [Note that the code as used is a combination of three sub-codes: 1) In the first pair of equated lines, the left and right sections are Reversed Alphabet codes. 2) The central section is obtained like aiming at something definite, and failing of the goal. Sometimes the control gives a message to a distant person quite suddenly, as if for some reason a resistance momentarily gave way, and let pass a definite desire to give such a message. Thus on October 17th, "Give my love to Carl Putnam," a name which neither Mrs. Piper nor the sitter knew, and which popped in quite irrelevantly to what preceded or followed. A definite will is also suggested when R. H. sends a message to James Putnam about his "watch stopping." He sends it through several sitters, and sticks to it in the face of final denial, as if the phrase covered, however erroneously, some distinct "intention to recall," which ought not to be renounced.

That a "will to personate" is a factor in the Piper phenomenon, I fully believe, and I believe with unshakable firmness that this will is able to draw on supernormal sources of information. It can "tap," possibly the sitter's memories, possibly those of distant human beings, possibly some cosmic reservoir in which the memories of earth are stored, whether in the shape of "spirits" or not. If this were the only will concerned in the performance, the phenomenon would be humbug pure and simple, and the minds tapped telepathically in it would play an entirely passive role—that is, the telepathic data would be fished out by the personating will, not forced upon it by desires to communicate, acting externally to itself.

But it is possible to complicate the hypothesis. Extraneous "wills to communicate" may contribute to the results as well as a "will to personate," and the two kinds of will may be distinct in entity, though capable of helping each other out. The will to communicate, in our present instance, would be, on the *prima facie* view of it, the will of Hodgson's surviving spirit; and a natural way of repre-

by equating each letter with its alphabetical *predecessor*. It might be called a Caesarian code since an essentially similar principle of ciphering was used by Julius Caesar and Augustus Caesar (see Suetonius, *The Twelve Caesars*). 3) The third code consists in reversing the order of the letters in the decoded word.] *Proposals for a Research Program Prepared for the President, Board of Trustees, and Research Committee, of The American Society for Psychical Research*, by J. Fraser Nicol, September 1959, pp. 27, 59. See references to "Zeivorn" on pages 180 and 185.—ED.

senting the process would be to suppose the spirit to have found that by pressing, so to speak, against "the light," it can make fragmentary gleams and flashes of what it wishes to say mix with the rubbish of the trance talk on this side. The two wills might thus strike up a sort of partnership and stir each other up. It might even be that the "will to personate" would be inert unless it were aroused to activity by the other will. We might imagine the relation to be analogous to that of two physical bodies, from neither of which, when alone, mechanical, thermal, or electrical effects can proceed, but if the other body be present, and show a difference of "potential," action starts up and goes on apace.

Conceptions such as these seem to connect in schematic form the various elements in the case. Its essential factors are done justice to; and, by changing the relative amounts in which the rubbish-making and the truth-telling wills contribute to the resultant, we can draw up a table in which every type of manifestation, from silly planchet-writing up to Rector's best utterances, finds its proper place. Personally, I must say that, although I have to confess that no crucial proof of the presence of the "will to communicate" seems to me yielded by the Hodgson-control taken alone, and in the sittings to which I have had access, yet the total effect in the way of dramatic probability of the whole mass of similar phenomena on my mind, is to make me believe that a "will to communicate" *is* in some shape there. I cannot demonstrate it, but practically I am inclined to "go in" for it, to bet on it and take the risks.

The question then presents itself: In what shape is it most reasonable to suppose that the will thus postulated is actually there? And here again there are various pneumatological possibilities, which must be considered first in abstract form. Thus the will to communicate may come either from permanent entities, or from an entity that arises for the occasion. R. H.'s spirit would be a permanent entity; and inferior parasitic spirits ("daimons," elementals, or whatever their traditional names might be) would be permanent entities. An improvised entity might be a limited process of consciousness arising in the cosmic reservoir of earth's memories, when certain conditions favoring systematized activity in particular tracts thereof were fulfilled. The conditions in that case might be conceived after the analogy of what happens when two poles of different potential are created in a mass of matter, and cause a current of electricity, or what not, to pass through an intervening tract of space until then the seat of rest.

To consider the case of permanent entities first, there is no *a priori* reason why human spirits and other spiritual beings might not either cooperate at the same time in the same phenomenon, or alternately produce different manifestations. *Prima facie,* and as a matter of "dramatic" probability, other intelligences than our own appear on an enormous scale in the historic mass of material which Myers first brought together under the title of Automatisms. The refusal of modern "enlightenment" to treat "possession" as a hypothesis to be spoken of as even possible, in spite of the massive human tradition based on concrete experience in its favor, has always seemed to me a curious example of the power of fashion in things scientific. That the demon theory will have its innings again is to my mind absolutely certain. One has to be "scientific" indeed, to be blind and ignorant enough to suspect no such possibility. But if the liability to have one's somnambulistic or automatic processes participated in and interfered with by spiritual entities of a different order ever turns out to be a probable fact, then not only what I have called the will to communicate, but also the will to *personate* may fall outside of the medium's own dream-life. The humbugging may not be chargeable to her all alone, centers of consciousness lower than hers may take part in it, just as higher ones may occasion some of the more inexplicable items of the veridical current in the stream.

The plot of possibilities thus thickens; and it thickens still more when we ask how a will which is dormant or relatively dormant during the intervals may become consciously reanimated as a spirit-personality by the occurrence of the medium's trance. A certain theory of Fechner's helps my own imagination here, so I will state it briefly for my reader's benefit.

Fechner in his *Zend-Avesta* and elsewhere [29] assumes that mental and physical life run parallel, all memory processes being, according to him, coordinated with material processes. If an act of yours is to be consciously remembered hereafter, it must leave traces on the material universe such that when the *traced parts of the said universe systematically enter into activity together* the act is consciously recalled. During your life the traces are mainly in your brain; but after your death, since your brain is gone, they exist in the shape of all the records of your actions which the outer world stores up as the effects, immediate or remote, thereof, the cosmos being in some degree, however slight, made structurally different by every act of ours that takes place in it.[30] Now, just as the air of the same room can be simultaneously used by many different voices for communicating with different pairs of ears, or as the ether of space can carry many simultaneous messages to and from mutually attuned Marconi-stations, so the great continuum of material nature can have certain tracts within it thrown into emphasized activity whenever activity begins in any part or parts of a tract in which the potentiality of such systematic activity inheres. The bodies (including, naturally, the brains) of Hodgson's friends who come as sitters, are of course parts of the material universe which carry some of the traces of his ancient acts. They function as receiving stations. Hodgson (at one time of his life at any rate) was inclined to suspect that the sitter himself acts "psychometrically," or by his body being what, in the trance jargon, is called an

---

[29] *Zend Avesta*, and following. Compare also Elwood Worcester, *The Living Word*, New York. Moffatt, Part II, in which a more popular account of Fechner's theory of immortality is given. And Wm. James, *A Pluralistic Universe*, Longmans, Green and Co., 1909, Lecture IV.—W. J.

[30] "It is Händel's work, not the body with which he did the work, that pulls us half over London. There is not an action of a muscle in a horse's leg upon a winter's night as it drags a carriage to the Albert Hall but what is in connection with, and part outcome of, the force generated when Händel sat in his room at Gopsall and wrote the Messiah. . . . This is the true Händel, who is more a living power among us one hundred and twenty-two years after his death than during the time he was amongst us in the body."—Samuel Butler, in the *New Quarterly*, I. 303, March 1908.—W. J.

"influence," in attracting the right spirits and eliciting the right communications from the other side. If, now, the *rest* of the system of physical traces left behind by Hodgson's acts were, by some sort of mutual induction throughout its extent, thrown into gear and made to vibrate all at once, by the presence of such human bodies to the medium, we should have a Hodgson-system active in the cosmos again, and the "conscious aspect" of this vibrating system might be Hodgson's spirit redivivus, and recollecting and willing in a certain momentary way. There seems fair evidence of the reality of psychometry; so that this scheme covers the main phenomena in a vague general way. In particular, it would account for the "confusion" and "weakness" that are such prevalent features: the "system" of physical traces corresponding to the given spirit would then be only imperfectly aroused. It tallies vaguely with the analogy of energy finding its way from higher to lower levels. The sitter, with his desire to receive, forms, so to speak, a drainage opening or sink; the medium, with her desire to personate, yields the nearest lying material to be drained off, while the spirit desiring to communicate is drawn in by the current set up and swells the latter by its own contributions.

It is enough to indicate these various possibilities, which a serious student of this part of nature has to weigh together, and between which his decision must fall. His vote will always be cast (if it ever be cast) by the sense of the dramatic probabilities of nature which the sum total of his experience has begotten in him. *I myself feel as if an external will to communicate were probably there,* that is, I find myself doubting, in consequence of my whole acquaintance with that sphere of phenomena, that Mrs. Piper's dream-life, even equipped with "telepathic" powers, accounts for all the results found. But if asked whether the will to communicate be Hodgson's, or be some mere spirit-counterfeit of Hodgson, I remain uncertain and await more facts, facts which may not point clearly to a conclusion for fifty or a hundred years.

My report has been too rambling in form, and has suffered in cordiality of tone from my having to confine myself to the face value of the Hodgson material taken by itself. The content of that material is no more veridical than is a lot of earlier Piper material, especially in the days of the old Phinuit control. And it is, as I began by saying, vastly more leaky and susceptible of naturalistic explanation than is any body of Piper material recorded before. Had I been reviewing the entire Piper phenomenon, instead of this small section of it, my tone would probably give much less umbrage to some of its spiritistic friends who are also valued friends of mine.

V

---•---

WILLIAM JAMES AND
FREDERIC MYERS

Passionate deep friendships arising out of deep intellectual reso-
nance and spiritual interchange were characteristic of William
James's whole life. He paid what seem today extravagant tributes to
dear friends who are remembered by us largely because of their as-
sociation with him. "Upon thy fame, immortal, graft my love." The
intensely personal quality of this personal interchange might, how-
ever, lead us to overlook the enormous intellectual stimulation
which James actually received from Frederic W. H. Myers, devoted
lover of Greek and Latin literature, who picked up a casual living
as an inspector of schools, but actually gave his mature life to
psychical research. As a young man, overwhelmed, as many a sensi-
tive soul was, by the skepticism engendered by the new world of
impersonal science and of evolutionary biology, Myers struggled in
long, earnest discussions with friends to find philosophical escape
from a deadpan, meaningless universe, in which human personality
was a momentary event devoid of all general significance. We need
to know, said Myers, the answer to the central question: "Is the
universe friendly?" When the new data of psychical research, in
the informal patterns into which they were casting themselves in
the mid-nineteenth century, began to be known to him, he deter-

mined to push the investigations for everything they were worth. Kindred spirits, such as the physicist William Barrett of the University of Dublin, and the clergyman W. Stainton Moses, encouraged the belief in an organized scientific group to probe the new evidence; and when the revered philosopher Henry Sidgwick agreed to become president, a Society for Psychical Research was formed in 1882 in London (compare page 29). Myers shared hugely in the first great investigations by this Society for Psychical Research, having to do with spontaneous telepathy; they received, sifted, and evaluated evidence regarding what appeared to be long-distance telepathic impacts of dying or crisis-threatened persons, and the like, to distant loved ones, and all the material which today has grown up within the vast field of the "spontaneous cases." One of these reported and investigated by William James is described on page 72. Myers shared in this labor with the essentially cautious and acid-minded Frank Podmore and with the eager, vigorous, and highly competent orchestrator of the research, Edmund Gurney. James was, of course, deeply concerned with such studies and gave them a considerable amount of his own precious time.

This is, however, only the surface expression of a much deeper response to Frederic Myers, as will be evident to anyone who studies the letters exchanged between them. Myers was developing over the years from about 1880 to 1900 a theory of the subconscious, a theory of the "subliminal" or below-threshold world of the mind, to which a few, notably the philosopher von Hartmann, had devoted major efforts, and to which a few psychiatrists, such as Pierre Janet, were beginning to direct experimental attention. As we have already seen, William James believed that recognition of this new realm of subliminal mental activity constituted a major breakthrough into the all-important world beyond ordinary volition, a world perhaps fraught with profound implications for the understanding of human nature. It was in the beautiful theory of the subliminal, so persuasively developed in Frederic Myers's great book, Human Personality and Its Survival of Bodily Death, *that the first great source for a psychology of subconscious or subliminal activity became available in the English-speaking world. The book was, on the one hand, an introduction to human subliminal activity and, on the other hand, a manual of the new psychical research. James re-*

*sponded just as vigorously to the vast new architectural structure
of a subliminal mentality as he did to the empirical spirit of Myers's
investigations. He hailed Myers both as a friend who cared about
the same ultimates which meant so much to him and as an original
thinker from whom he could learn with gratitude and devotion.*

*It is surprising to the modern reader to note that, along with this
unstinted enthusiasm and gratitude, James is able to maintain his
usual cautious and critical spirit. As the reader will note, his review
of Myers's book is anything but an efflorescence of admiring acceptance. He feels the great invitation, but on the brink of conviction he holds back. He not only remains unsure as to the meaning
of the phenomena of psychical research; he is unsure whether the
subliminal mind can actually serve at the same time as biological
mainspring of human thought, as key to human evolution and human futures, as wellspring of mystical and paranormal powers; in
short, whether the crudeness or even the satanism of the unconscious and the "trance, possession, and ecstasy" of religious aspira-
tion can all spring from the same central source. Characteristically,
the unlimited devotion to the friend goes hand in hand with the
capacity for refusal to take the final leap. This is, after all, reminiscent of his father's and his family's reaction to the long series of
religious movements of nineteenth-century America: look into them
all; respond to them and with them; welcome all new evidence; but
count all the implications and all the consequences before you leap.*

FREDERIC MYERS'S SERVICE TO PSYCHOLOGY [1]

On this memorial occasion it is from English hearts and tongues
belonging, as I never had the privilege of belonging, to the immediate environment of our lamented President, that discourse of
him as a man and as a friend must come. It is for those who participated in the endless drudgery of his labors for our Society to tell
of the high powers he showed there; and it is for those who have
something of his burning interest in the problem of our human

---

[1] *Proceedings of the Society for Psychical Research* (London), Vol. XVII,
Part XLII, May 1901. Reprinted in *Memories and Studies,* New York: Longmans
Green, 1911.—ED.

destiny to estimate his success in throwing a little more light into its dark recesses. To me it has been deemed best to assign a colder task. Frederic Myers was a psychologist who worked upon lines hardly admitted by the more academic branch of the profession to be legitimate; and as for some years I bore the title of "Professor of Psychology," the suggestion has been made (and by me gladly welcomed) that I should spend my portion of this hour in defining the exact place and rank which we must accord to him as a cultivator and promoter of the science of the Mind.

Brought up entirely upon literature and history, and interested at first in poetry and religion chiefly; never by nature a philosopher in the technical sense of a man forced to pursue consistency among concepts for the mere love of the logical occupation; not crammed with science at college, or trained to scientific method by any passage through a laboratory; Myers had as it were to re-create his personality before he became the wary critic of evidence, the skillful handler of hypothesis, the learned neurologist and omnivorous reader of biological and cosmological matter, with whom in later years we were acquainted. The transformation came about because he needed to be all these things in order to work successfully at the problem that lay near his heart; and the ardor of his will and the richness of his intellect are proved by the success with which he underwent so unusual a transformation.

The problem, as you know, was that of seeking evidence for human immortality. His contributions to psychology were incidental to that research, and would probably never have been made had he not entered on it. But they have a value, for science entirely independent of the light they shed upon that problem; and it is quite apart from it that I shall venture to consider them.

If we look at the history of mental science we are immediately struck by diverse tendencies among its several cultivators, the consequence being a certain opposition of schools and some repugnance among their disciples. Apart from the great contrasts between minds that are teleological or biological and minds that are mechanical, between the animists and the associationists in psychology, there is the entirely different contrast between what I will call the classic-academic and the romantic type of imagination. The former has a fondness for clean pure lines and noble simplicity in its constructions. It explains things by as few principles as possible and is intolerant of either nondescript facts or clumsy formulas. The facts must lie in a neat assemblage, and the psychologist must be enabled to cover them and "tuck them in" as safely under his system as a mother tucks her babe in under the down coverlet on a winter night. Until quite recently all psychology, whether animistic or associationistic, was written on classic-academic lines. The consequence was that the human mind, as it is figured in this literature, was largely an abstraction. Its normal adult traits were recognized. A sort of sunlit terrace was exhibited on which it took its exercise. But where that terrace stopped, the mind stopped; and there was nothing farther left to tell of in this kind of philosophy but the brain and the other physical facts of nature on the one hand, and the absolute metaphysical ground of the universe on the other.

But of late years the terrace has been overrun by romantic improvers, and to pass to their work is like going from classic to Gothic architecture, where few outlines are pure and where uncouth forms lurk in the shadows. A mass of mental phenomena are now seen in the shrubbery beyond the parapet. Fantastic, ignoble, hardly human, or frankly non-human are some of these new candidates for psychological description. The menagerie and the madhouse, the nursery, the prison, and the hospital, have been made to deliver up their material. The world of mind is shown as something infinitely more complex than was suspected; and whatever beauties it may still possess, it has lost at any rate the beauty of academic neatness.

But despite the triumph of romanticism, psychologists as a rule have still some lingering prejudice in favor of the nobler simplicities. Moreover there are social prejudices which scientific men themselves obey. The word "hypnotism" has been trailed about in the newspapers so that even we ourselves rather wince at it, and avoid occasions of its use. "Mesmerism," "clairvoyance," "medium" —*horrescimus referentes!*—and with all these things, infected by their previous mystery-mongering discoverers, even our best friends had rather avoid complicity. For instance, I invite eight of my scientific colleagues severally to come to my house at their own time, and sit with a medium for whom the evidence already published in our *Proceedings* had been most noteworthy. Although it means at worst the waste of the hour for each, five of them decline the adventure. I then beg the "Commission" connected with the chair of a certain learned psychologist in a neighboring university to examine the same medium, whom Mr. Hodgson and I offer at our own expense to send and leave with them. They also have to be excused from any such entanglement. I advise another psychological friend to look into this medium's case, but he replies that it is useless, for if he should get such results as I report, he would (being suggestible) simply believe himself hallucinated. When I propose as a remedy that he should remain in the background and take notes, whilst his wife has the sitting, he explains that he can never consent to his wife's presence at such performances. This friend of mine writes *ex cathedra* on the subject of psychical research, declaring (I need hardly add) that there is nothing in it; the chair of the psychologist with the Commission was founded by a spiritist, partly with a view to investigate mediums; and one of the five colleagues who declined my invitation is widely quoted as an effective critic of our evidence. So runs the world away! I should not indulge in the personality and triviality of such anecdotes, were it not that they paint the temper of our time, a temper which, thanks to Frederic Myers more than to anyone, will certainly be impossible after this generation. Myers was, I think, decidedly exclusive and intolerant by nature. But his keenness for truth carried him into regions where either intellectual or social squeamishness would have been fatal, so he "mortified" his *amour propre*, unclubbed himself completely, and became a model of patience, tact, and humility wherever investigation required it.

Both his example and his body of doctrine will make this temper the only one henceforward scientifically respectable.

If you ask me how his doctrine has this effect, I answer: *By coordinating!* For Myers's great principle of research was that in order to understand any one species of fact we ought to have all the species of the same general class of fact before us. So he took a lot of scattered phenomena, some of them recognized as reputable, others outlawed from science, or treated as isolated curiosities; he made series of them, filled in the transitions by delicate hypotheses or analogies, and bound them together in a system by his bold inclusive conception of the Subliminal Self, so that no one can now touch one part of the fabric without finding the rest entangled with it. Such vague terms of apperception as psychologists have hitherto been satisfied with using for most of these phenomena, as "fraud," "rot," "rubbish," will no more be possible hereafter than "dirt" is possible as a head of classification in chemistry, or "vermin" in zoology. Whatever they are, they are things with a right to definite description and to careful observation.

I cannot but account this as a great service rendered to Psychology. I expect that Myers will ere long distinctly figure in mental science as the radical leader in what I have called the romantic movement. Through him for the first time, psychologists are in possession of their full material, and mental phenomena are set down in an adequate inventory. To bring unlike things thus together by forming series of which the intermediary terms connect the extremes, is a procedure much in use by scientific men. It is a first step made towards securing their interest in the romantic facts, that Myers should have shown how easily this familiar method can be applied to their study.

Myers's conception of the extensiveness of the Subliminal Self quite overturns the classic notion of what the human mind consists in. The supraliminal region, as Myers calls it, the classic-academic consciousness, which was once alone considered either by associationists or animists, figures in his theory as only a small segment of the psychic spectrum. It is a special phase of mentality, teleologically evolved for adaptation to our natural environment, and forms only what he calls a "privileged case" of personality. The outlying subliminal, according to him, represents more fully our central and abiding being.

I think the words subliminal and supraliminal unfortunate, but they were probably unavoidable. I think, too, that Myers's belief in the ubiquity and great extent of the subliminal will demand a far larger number of facts than sufficed to persuade him, before the next generation of psychologists shall become persuaded. He regards the subliminal as the enveloping mother-consciousness in each of us, from which the consciousness we wot of is precipitated like a crystal. But whether this view get confirmed or get over-thrown by future inquiry, the definite way in which Myers has thrown it down is a new and specific challenge to inquiry. For half a century now, psychologists have fully admitted the existence of a subliminal mental region, under the name either of unconscious cerebration or of the involuntary life; but they have never definitely taken up the question of the extent of this region, never sought explicitly to map it out. Myers definitely attacks this problem, which, after him, it will be impossible to ignore.

What is the precise constitution of the subliminal—such is the problem which deserves to figure in our science hereafter as the *problem of Myers;* and willy-nilly, inquiry must follow on the path which it has opened up. But Myers has not only propounded the problem definitely, he has also invented definite methods for its solution. Post-hypnotic suggestion, crystal-gazing, automatic writing and trance speech, the willing game, etc., are now, thanks to him, instruments of research, reagents like litmus paper or the gal-vanometer, for revealing what would otherwise be hidden. These are so many ways of putting the subliminal on tap. Of course without the simultaneous work on hypnotism and hysteria independently begun by others, he could not have pushed his own work so far. But he is so far the only generalizer of the problem and the only user of all the methods; and even though his theory of the extent of the subliminal should have to be subverted in the end, its formulation will, I am sure, figure always as a rather momentous event in the history of our science.

Any psychologist who should wish to read Myers out of the profession—and there are probably still some who would be glad to do so today—is committed to a definite alternative. Either he must say that we knew all about the subliminal region before Myers took it up, or he must say that it is certain that states of supernormal cognition form no part of its content. The first contention would be too absurd. The second one remains more plausible. There are many first-hand investigators into the subliminal who, not having themselves met with anything supernormal, would probably not hesitate to call all the reports of it erroneous, and who would limit the subliminal to dissolutive phenomena of consciousness exclusively, to lapsed memories, subconscious sensations, impulses and *phobias,* and the like. Messrs. Janet and Binet, for aught I know, may hold some such position as this. Against it Myers's thesis would stand sharply out. Of the subliminal, he would say, we can give no ultra-simple account: there are discrete regions in it, levels separated by critical points of transition, and no one formula holds true of them all. And any conscientious psychologist ought, it seems to me, to see that, since these multiple modifications of personality are only beginning to be reported and observed with care, it is obvious that a dogmatically negative treatment of them must be premature, and that the problem of Myers still awaits us as the problem of far the deepest moment for our actual psychology, whether his own tentative solutions of certain parts of it be correct or not.

Meanwhile, descending to detail, one cannot help admiring the great originality with which Myers wove such an extraordinarily detached and discontinuous series of phenomena together. Unconscious cerebration, dreams, hypnotism, hysteria, inspirations of genius, the willing game, planchette, crystal-gazing, hallucinatory voices, apparitions of the dying, medium-trances, demoniacal possession, clairvoyance, thought-transference—even ghosts and other facts more doubtful—these things form a chaos at first sight most discouraging. No wonder that scientists can think of no other principle of unity among them than their common appeal to men's perverse propensity to superstition. Yet Myers has actually made a system of them, stringing them continuously upon a perfectly legitimate objective hypothesis, verified in some cases and extended to others by analogy. Taking the name automatism from the phenomenon of automatic writing—I am not sure that he may not himself have been the first so to baptize this latter phenomenon— he made one great simplification at a stroke by treating hallucinations and active impulses under a common head, as *sensory* and *motor automatisms.* Automatism he then conceived broadly as a message of any kind from the subliminal to the supraliminal. And he went a step farther in his hypothetic interpretation, when he insisted on "symbolism" as one of the ways in which one stratum of our personality will often interpret the influences of another. Obsessive thoughts and delusions, as well as voices, visions, and impulses, thus fall subject to one mode of treatment. To explain them, we must explore the subliminal; to cure them we must practically influence it.

Myers's work on automatism led to his brilliant conception, in 1891, of hysteria. He defined it, with good reasons given, as "a disease of the hypnotic stratum." Hardly had he done so when the wonderfully ingenious observations of Binet, and especially of Janet in France, gave to this view the completest of corroborations. These observations have been extended in Germany, America, and elsewhere; and although Binet and Janet worked independently of Myers, and did work for more objective, he nevertheless will stand as the original announcer of a theory which, in my opinion, makes an epoch, not only in medical, but in psychological science, because it brings in an entirely new conception of our mental possibilities.

Myers's manner of apprehending the problem of the subliminal shows itself fruitful in every possible direction. While official science practically refuses to attend to subliminal phenomena, the circles which do attend to them treat them with a respect altogether too undiscriminating—every subliminal deliverance must be an oracle. The result is that there is no basis of intercourse between those who best know the facts and those who are most competent to discuss them. Myers immediately establishes a basis by his remark that insofar as they have to use the same organism, with its preformed avenues of expression—what may be very different strata of the subliminal are condemned in advance to manifest themselves in similar ways. This might account for the great generic likeness of so many automatic performances, while their different starting-points behind the threshold might account for certain differences in them. Some of them, namely, seem to include elements of supernormal knowledge; others to show a curious subconscious mania for personation and deception; others again to be mere drivel. But Myers's conception of various strata or levels in the subliminal sets us to analyzing them all from a new point of view. The word subliminal for him denotes only a region, with possibly the most heterogeneous contents. Much of the content is certainly rubbish, matter that Myers calls dissolutive, stuff that dreams are made of, fragments of lapsed memory, mechanical effects of habit and ordinary suggestion; some belongs to a middle region where a strange manufacture of inner romances perpetually goes on; finally, some of the content appears superiorly and subtly perceptive. But each has to appeal to us by the same channels and to use organs partly trained to their performance by messages from the other levels. Under these conditions what could be more natural to expect than a confusion, which Myers's suggestion would then have been the first indispensable step towards finally clearing away.

Once more, then, whatever be the upshot of the patient work required here, Myers's resourceful intellect has certainly done a service to psychology.

I said a while ago that his intellect was not by nature philosophic in the narrower sense of being that of a logician. In the broader sense of being a man of wide scientific imagination, Myers was most eminently a philosopher. He has shown this by his unusually daring grasp of the principle of evolution, and by the wonderful way in which he has worked out suggestions of mental evolution by means of biological analogies. These analogies are, if anything, too profuse and dazzling in his pages; but his conception of mental evolution is more radical than anything yet considered by psychologists as possible. It is absolutely original; and, being so radical, it becomes one of those hypotheses which, once propounded, can never be forgotten, but sooner or later have to be worked out and submitted in every way to criticism and verification.

The cornerstone of his conception is the fact that consciousness has no essential unity. It aggregates and dissipates, and what we call normal consciousness—the "human mind" of classic psychology —is not even typical, but only one case out of thousands. Slight organic alterations, intoxications and auto-intoxications, give supraliminal forms completely different, and the subliminal region seems to have laws in many respects peculiar. Myers thereupon makes the suggestion that the whole system of consciousness studied by the classic psychology is only an extract from a larger total, being a part told off, as it were, to do service in the adjustments of our physical organism to the world of nature. This extract, aggregated and personified for this particular purpose, has, like all evolving things, a variety of peculiarities. Having evolved, it may also dissolve, and in dreams, hysteria, and divers forms of degeneration it seems to do so. This is a retrograde process of separation in a consciousness of which the unity was once effected. But again the consciousness may follow the opposite course and integrate still farther, or evolve by growing into yet untried directions. In veridical automatisms it actually seems to do so. It drops some of its usual modes of increase, its ordinary use of the senses, for example, and lays hold of bits of information which, in ways that we cannot even follow conjecturally, leak into it by way of the subliminal. The ulterior source of a certain part of this information (limited and perverted as it always is by the organism's idiosyncrasies in the way of transmission and expression) Myers thought he could reasonably trace to departed human intelligence, or its existing equivalent. I pretend to no opinion on this point, for I have as yet studied the evidence with so little critical care that Myers was always surprised at my negligence. I can therefore speak with detachment from this question and, as a mere empirical psychologist, of Myers's general evolutionary conception. As such a psychologist I feel sure that the latter is a hypothesis of first-rate philosophic importance. It is based, of course, on his conviction of the extent of the subliminal, and will stand or fall as that is verified or not; but whether it stand or fall, it looks to me like one of those sweeping ideas by which the scientific researches of an entire generation are often molded. It would not be surprising if it proved such a leading idea in the investigation of the near future; for in one shape or another, the subliminal has come to stay with us, and the only possible course to take henceforth is radically and thoroughly to explore its significance.

Looking back from Frederic Myers's vision of vastness in the field of psychological research upon the program as most academic psychologists frame it, one must confess that its limitation at their hands seems not only unplausible, but in truth, a little ridiculous. Even with brutes and madmen, even with hysterics and hypnotics admitted as the academic psychologists admit them, the official outlines of the subject are far too neat to stand in the light of analogy with the rest of nature. The ultimates of nature—her simple elements, if there be such—may indeed combine in definite proportions and follow classic laws of architecture; but in her proximates, in her phenomena as we immediately experience them, nature is everywhere Gothic, not classic. She forms a real jungle, where all things are provisional, half-fitted to each other, and untidy. When we add such a complex kind of subliminal region as Myers believed in to the official region, we restore the analogy; and, though we may be mistaken in much detail, in a general way, at least, we become plausible. In comparison with Myers's way of attacking the question of immortality in particular, the official way is certainly so far from the mark as to be almost preposterous. It assumes that when our ordinary consciousness goes out, the only alternative surviving kind of consciousness that could be possible is abstract

mentality, living on spiritual truth, and communicating ideal wisdom—in short, the whole classic platonizing Sunday-school conception. Failing to get that sort of thing when it listens to reports
about mediums, it denies that there can be anything. Myers approaches the subject with no such *a priori* requirement. If he finds
any positive indication of "spirits," he records it, whatever it may be,
and is willing to fit his conception to the facts, however grotesque
the latter may appear, rather than to blot out the facts to suit his
conception. But, as was long ago said by our collaborator, Mr.
Canning Schiller, in words more effective than any I can write, if
any conception should be blotted out by serious lovers of nature,
it surely ought to be the classic academic Sunday-school conception.
If anything is *un*likely in a world like this, it is that the next adjacent
thing to the mere surface-show of our experience should be the
realm of eternal essences, of platonic ideas, of crystal battlements,
of absolute significance. But whether they be animists or associationists, a supposition something like this is still the assumption of our
usual psychologists. It comes from their being for the most part
philosophers in the technical sense, and from their showing the
weakness of that profession for logical abstractions. Myers was
primarily a lover of life and not of abstractions. He loved human
life, human persons, and their peculiarities. So he could easily admit
the possibility of level beyond level of perfectly concrete experience,
all "queer and cactus-like" though it might be, before we touch the
absolute, or reach the eternal essences.

Behind the minute anatomists and the physiologists, with their
metallic instruments, there have always stood the outdoor naturalists
with their eyes and love of concrete nature. The former call the
latter superficial, but there is something wrong about your laboratory biologist who has no sympathy with living animals. In psychology there is a similar distinction. Some psychologists are
fascinated by the varieties of mind in living action, others by the
dissecting out, whether by logical analysis or by brass instruments,
of whatever elementary mental processes may be there. Myers
must decidedly be placed in the former class, though his powerful

use of analogy enabled him also to do work after the fashion of the latter. He loved human nature as Cuvier and Agassiz loved animal nature; in his view, as in their view, the subject formed a vast living picture. Whether his name will have in psychology as honorable a place as their names have gained in the sister science, will depend on whether future inquirers shall adopt or reject his theories; and the rapidity with which their decision shapes itself will depend largely on the vigor with which this Society continues its labor in his absence. It is at any rate a possibility, and I am disposed to think it a probability, that Frederic Myers will always be remembered in psychology as the pioneer who staked out a vast tract of mental wilderness and planted the flag of genuine science upon it. He was an enormous collector. He introduced for the first time comparison, classification, and serial order into the peculiar kind of fact which he collected. He was a genius at perceiving analogies; he was fertile in hypotheses; and as far as conditions allowed it in this meteoric region, he relied on verification. Such advantages are of no avail, however, if one has struck into a false road from the outset. But should it turn out that Frederic Myers has really hit the right road by his divining instinct, it is certain that, like the names of others who have been wise, his name will keep an honorable place in scientific history.

REVIEW OF "HUMAN PERSONALITY AND ITS SURVIVAL OF BODILY DEATH"
(by Frederic W. H. Myers) [1]

Such large portions of the text of these bulky volumes, which are the legacy of Myers's literary life, have already appeared in these *Proceedings*, and their author's general conceptions are so familiar to my readers, that I feel free to omit from this notice all detailed account of the book's contents and composition. For aught I know

[1] *Proceedings of the Society for Psychical Research* (London), Vol. XVIII, Part XLVI, June 1903.—ED.

such an account may be given by my fellow reviewers. The contents are so intricate and the ideas so many that the great danger is that of not seeing the forest for the trees, and of not apprehending with distinctness the steps of Myers's reasoning. It seems to me wisest, therefore, to employ the opportunity accorded me in analyzing his argument into its essential features, following, as I do so, a logical rather than a textual order.

What would entitle Myers, if he were successful in what he attempted, to be regarded as the founder of a new science is that conception of the Subliminal Self, by which he colligated and coordinated a mass of phenomena which had never before been considered together, and thus made a sort of objective continuum of what, before him, had appeared so pure a disconnectedness that the ordinary scientific mind had either disdained to look at it, or pronounced it mostly fictitious. Two years ago I wrote in these *Proceedings* that Myers had endowed psychology with a new problem—*the exploration of the subliminal region* being destined to figure hereafter in that branch of learning as "Myers's problem." Reading these volumes, we gain a definite idea of how far he himself had pushed forward the topographical survey of that region.

Conservatives in anthropologic science will immediately say that Myers used the concept of the "subliminal" far too broadly, and that the only safe demarcation of the term is that of the neuropathologists. These observers for the most part now recognize a subliminal region frankly, but they recognize it only as a dissociated part of the normal personality. Experiences forgotten by the upper consciousness may here still lead a parasitic existence, and in an inferior, dreamlike way may interfere with normal processes. For these critics the subliminal is synonymous with the *forgotten* and forms a region of disintegration exclusively.

Most neurologists either ignore those other "evolutive," "superior," or "supernormal" phenomena, in which Myers's chief interest lay, or scout them wholesale as deceptions. The few who admit them are more likely to see in them another department of experience altogether than to treat them as having continuous connection with the ordinary phenomena of mental dissociation.

Those who simply ignore them (for whatever reason) may themselves be ignored here as belated students. However acutely aware one may be of the sources of fallacy in reports of the marvelous, I fail to see how the records quoted in these volumes, and in vastly greater profusion in Gurney's *Phantasms of the Living* and the other S. P. R. publications, can rightfully be met by a wholesale and indiscriminating *non possumus*. Anyone with a healthy sense for evidence, a sense not methodically blunted by the sectarianism of "science," ought now, it seems to me, to feel that exalted sensibilities and memories, veridical phantasms, haunted houses, trances with supernormal faculty, and even experimental thought-transference, are natural kinds of phenomenon which ought, just like other natural events, to be followed up with scientific curiosity.

Hypnotic phenomena form the center of perspective for Myers's map of the subliminal region. In the first place, the system of faculty of a subject under hypnosis is quite different from his waking system of faculty. While portions of the usual waking system are inhibited, other portions are sometimes supernormally energized in hypnosis, producing not only hallucinations, but after-results in the way of sense-discrimination and control of organic function, to which the waking consciousness is unable to attain. We are thus led to the notion of two different currents of mental life, one deeper, and the other shallower, of which either is best appealed to while the other is in abeyance. That these currents may not only alternate but may co-exist with each other is proved by Gurney's, Binet's, and Janet's discovery of subjects who, receiving suggestions during hypnosis and forgetting them when wakened, nevertheless then wrote them out automatically and unconsciously as soon as a pencil was placed in their hands.

Allying the curative phenomena of hypnosis with the great reparative powers of sleep, and its enhancements of faculty with the enhancements of faculty to which dreaming and natural somnambulism occasionally give rise, Myers postulates a region of sleeping consciousness present at all times in all of us, a region moreover which in certain respects has an advantage over the waking levels of the mind. This subliminal region is usually closed off from the ordinary waking consciousness, but under special conditions of appeal, which vary with the idiosyncrasy of the individual, it may break in with effects which reveal its presence to us. The popular word "suggestion" is only a name for a successful appeal to this subliminal consciousness.

The appeal, in hypnotic subjects, is made through the ordinary consciousness in the first instance; and into that consciousness the effects, when they are "post-hypnotic," return in the form of "automatisms," sensory or motor. In other words, hallucinations or unmotived impulses to act, which in some cases are upheavals from the subliminal into the supraliminal region, may be so in all cases. The two regions thus form environments for each other, with possibilities of interaction, though under ordinary conditions their intercourse is small.

So far Myers would seem to be on perfectly solid ground. There *is* a subliminal region of life which opens fitfully into the supraliminal region. The only doubt is as to whether it be general in human beings, or whether it be not limited to a few hypnotic and hysteric subjects.

The subliminal region being thus established as an actuality, the next question is as to its farther limits, where it exists. My subliminal, for instance, has my ordinary consciousness for one of its environments, but has it additional environments on the remoter side? Has it direct relations of intercourse, for example, with the consciousness, subliminal or supraliminal, of other men?

Some of the phenomena of hypnotism or mesmerism suggest that this is actually the case. I refer to the reports (several of them irreproachably recorded) of hypnotism at a distance, of obedience to unspoken orders, and of "community of sensation" between hypnotizer and subject, of which Sections 568 to 571 of Myers's Volume I give some account. Remote influences, to which the supraliminal region is closed, may thus occasionally pass into the subliminal region, showing that this latter communicates not only with the supraliminal mind of the subject himself, but with the mind of other persons, and possibly with a still wider world.

How wide this world may possibly be is suggested by all the various reports of thought-transference and clairvoyance in the hypnotic state. And if we now pass beyond conditions of artificial hypnosis, and take into account states of abstraction like those produced in some persons by crystal-gazing and by automatic writing, and the "trances" of certain somnambulists and mediums, with the clairvoyant faculty reported to be found therein, we find ourselves obliged (if we credit the reports) to assume that the subliminal life has windows of outlook and doors of ingress which bring it (in some persons at least) into a commerce of which the channels entirely escape our observation, with an indefinitely extended region of the world of truth.

The jump which Myers makes here is that of generalizing his conclusions. The "conservative" critic who does not deny the facts *in toto* would most probably call them pathological freaks of idiosyncrasy. He would protest against their being treated as revelations of the constitution of human nature at large. Myers, on the other hand, regards them as such revelations, and considers that the subjects show their "idiosyncrasy" rather in lying as open as they do to our observation, than in having the kind of human constitution which the observations disclose.

He is thus led to the general conception of a subliminal life belonging to human nature in general, and having its own indefinitely wide environment, distinct from that with which our bodily senses carry on their commerce. Set over against this subliminal life, and in strong contrast with it, we find the normal consciousness, dealing primarily through the senses with the material world, and in possession of faculties of attention, and in particular of memory, which are pitifully small in comparison with those which the subliminal consciousness wields. The normal consciousness is thus only a portion of our nature, adapted primarily to "terrene" conditions. Those more directly intuitive faculties which it lacks, and of which we get glimpses in individuals whose subliminal lies exceptionally open, can hardly be vestiges, degenerations of something which our ancestors once possessed. We should rather regard them as germs of something not yet evolved for methodical use in our natural environment, but possibly even now carrying on a set of active functions in their own wider "cosmic" environment.

The "supernormal" becomes thus for Myers synonymous with the "evolutive" as contrasted with the "dissolutive" with which the ordinary neurologist would prefer to connect it. The supernormal faculties of the subliminal take us into the cosmic environment; and for Myers this cosmic environment takes on more and more, as the volumes proceed, the character of a "spiritual world." From its intercourse with this spiritual world the subliminal self of each of us may draw strength, and communicate it to the supraliminal life. The "energizing of life" seems, in fact, to be one of its functions. The reparativeness of sleep, the curative effects of self-suggestion, the "uprushing" inspirations of genius, the regenerative influences of prayer and of religious self-surrender, the strength of belief which mystical experiences give, are all ascribed by Myers to the "dynamogeny" of the spiritual world, upon which we are enabled to make drafts of power by virtue of our connection with our subliminal. He dreams of a methodical evolution and extension, as our knowledge of the channels shall improve, of our resources in this direction.

Myers's theory, so far, is simple enough. It only postulates an indefinite inward prolongation of our being cut off from common consciousness by a screen or diaphragm not absolutely impervious but liable to leakage and to occasional rupture. The "scientific" critic can only say it is a pity that so vast and vaguely defined a hypothesis should be reared upon a set of facts so few and so imperfectly ascertained.

The vagueness of the hypothesis at this point chiefly consists in the ill-defined relations of the subliminal with its "cosmic" environment. Is this latter the Absolute Soul of the World, with which all our subliminals may be supposed to be substantially continuous? Or are the various subliminals discontinuous?—and is there intercourse transacted across an isolating interval?

As the work proceeds, Myers tends more and more toward the latter conception: the "spiritual world" becomes a "world of spirits" which interact.

This follows naturally from the consideration, to which he next proceeds, of veridical phantasms and mediumistic messages. At first sight "ghosts," etc. (if admitted to be actual phenomena), would seem to require a physical rather than a mental hypothesis for their explanation; and mediumistic messages, if taken at their face value, suggest that the "controlling" spirit intrudes into the very organism of the medium rather than that it merely actuates the medium's subliminal mind. The plot thickens very much hereabouts, and obliges one to ask more definitely whether the environment of the subliminal be mental exclusively or whether it may not also be physical. Myers is shy of putting forth psychophysical hypotheses, but in his conceptions of "phantasmogenetic invasion" of space and of "telergy" and "telekinesis," we find that he is forced to abandon purely mental territory. Subliminal selves, affecting one another in their quality of purely psychic entities, are not the sole factors that need be considered in our explanations. Space and their physical relations to space are also required.

Let me indicate very briefly what are the essential points in Myers's handling of this new range of experiences.

In the first place, take the so-called "veridical phantasms of the living." Assuming them to be established by the evidence, the records show that the mind of the percipient must be at least one of the factors of their production. If they were purely physical or "astral" presences, why should they wear earthly clothes, and carry earthly accessories? and when the percipient is in the midst of companions, why should they so seldom appear to *them?*

Evidently the phantasm, whatever may be its remoter starting-point, involves, as a mere immediate bit of experience, the psycho-physical process called "hallucination" on the part of the percipient himself.

Secondly, since there are well-recorded cases where a living person, A, made his phantasm appear to B by simply willing that it should do so, and since in many of the other cases of phantasms of the living, the person who appeared probably *wished* to appear where he did appear, it seems fair to interpret these appearances generally as hallucinations produced by the action of one mind upon another, somewhat after the pattern of the hallucinations which a hypnotizer makes his subject experience so easily by sug-gesting that he shall have them, either during the hypnosis or after waking up. "Telepathy" is the name which Myers gave to the im-mediate influence of one subliminal upon another. The records seem to prove that telepathy either may or may not be a transfer of ready-made content from one mind to another. Sometimes the influencing mind appears to act only as a suggestive stimulus, and the results on the mind influenced show every variation from a vague emotional mood to an elaborated perception full of acces-sories, or to an automatically impulsive act.

Activity of the influencing mind at a distance from its body is at any rate proved, according to Myers, by these phantasms of the living and by other telepathic phenomena.

It is round this conception of action at a distance, to which Myers applies the term of "psychical invasion," that his theory now turns toward its ulterior developments.

The fact that a phantasm may appear to a whole collection of persons at once, or to an indifferent companion of the person, rather than to the person himself of whom the phantasm's original might reasonably be supposed to be thinking, suggests that our soul's in-vasive powers apply to outer space as well as to other minds. Myers cites examples of these, as of all other special types of case which his argument requires, and considers that the probability of this space-invasion by the subliminal powers of the living is strengthened by two additional kinds of fact. First we have cases of apparent "bilocation" of mind and organism, as when a living person appears to view his own body from a remote position, or to see his own "double" as a phantasm; and second, we have an impressive array of cases which make for "traveling" clairvoyance ("telesthesia," as Myers calls it), whether in dream, in crystal-gazing, or in the mesmeric trance. Myers indulges in no hypothesis whatever as to the *modus operandi* of this space-invasion by our subliminal. At any rate it seems to bring space in as a portion of the subliminal's environment. The subliminal has relations with space as well as with other minds.

So far the powers of living persons have been considered exclusively. But phantasms of the slowly or suddenly dying shade by continuity of time-relation into phantasms of the recently dead, and these in turn shade into phantasms of the long dead, *i.e.* into narratives of the haunted-house type, of which the mass recorded is decidedly imposing.

The order of theoretic construction, if we go back to the beginning, is thus somewhat as follows: From hyperesthesia in the hypnotic state we pass gradually into telepathy between the subject and the operator; from this to phantasmogenetic telepathy between living men at a distance from one another; from this to space-invasions, whether phantasmogenetic or clairvoyant, by the subliminal of living persons; and finally from this to similar invasions (phantasmogenetic, at any rate) by the dead. We thus reach the hypothesis of spirit survival. Primarily, we reach this only in the somewhat idiotic form of "ghosts," for up to this point we have been considering only what Myers calls automatisms of the *sensory* order.

But *motor* automatisms carry us a good deal further toward a "world of spirits." Sensory automatisms seem to be essentially fugacious. Rarely is their content elaborately developed or prolonged. It is quite otherwise with automatic writing and speech, for here the messages are consecutive, and bring explicit professions of origin and purpose along with them. This may obtain when the subject who offers them is awake as well as when he is entranced.

The whole topic of "spirit messages" is thus opened up to our reflection. Although Myers died before he could write out his review of the evidence for spirit messages in detail, he all along shows that he deemed it sufficient: some such messages, at any rate, he held to have been proved authentic. With this our "cosmic" environment, as he believed in it, comes into full view. Our subliminals surround one another and act upon one another, as well as upon space; and spirits of the departed (which may themselves be constituted as we are, and have something like a subliminal condition of their own) may also act upon us and upon space, and receive our action too. When the action is transient, it is probably merely an impact upon our subliminal, of which we need not necessarily suspect the source. When it is more protracted or "invasive," space gets affected, and we either see a ghost or feel a presence; and it is an open question, in such effects as these upon our consciousness, how far our subliminal mind exclusively receives the operation of the invader, and how far he may act directly on our physical nervous system. Prolonged "possession" or "control" of the organism seems to involve the profoundest sort of operation which is possible; and Myers is willing here to admit that the foreign spirit may directly actuate the medium's nervous system.

That spirits of departed men should actuate these living bodies of ours directly, shows a form of physical influence to which Myers gives the name of *telekinesis*, and of which still other instances would be the raps, the table-movings without contact, and the other "physical phenomena of mediumship," as they are commonly termed. Myers discusses these phenomena warily, using delicate methods of gradual approach (see especially the exquisitely ingenious "Scheme of Vital Faculty," which ought to have been prominently printed as the concluding chapter of the whole book, but which appears inconspicuously among the Appendices as Section 926 A, Vol. II., pp. 505–54). On the whole he seems well disposed to treat the evidence for physical phenomena as adequate.

And now his whole theory lies before us. It is a vast synthesis, but a coherent one, notwithstanding the vagueness of some of the terms that figure in it. No one of the dots by which his map is plotted out, no one of the "corners" required by his triangulation, is purely hypothetical. He offers empirical evidence for the concrete existence of every element which his scheme postulates and works with. In logical form the theory is thus a scientific construction of a very high order, against which one can urge only two general kinds of objection. One can say first that the stepping-stones themselves, the corners, are too frail, that the types of fact invoked need much additional corroboration; or one can say, even if the kinds of facts were admitted to be solid where they have been observed, that Myers has ascribed a universality and an extension to them for which he has no warrant, that he has drawn his rules from the exceptional cases, and made his spiritual universe too continuous.

Disregarding these criticisms for the moment, I am impelled to say a word about this matter of Myers's "scientific" ability. Reading him afresh in these two volumes, I find myself filled with an admiration which almost surprises me. The work, whatever weaknesses it may have, strikes me as at least a masterpiece of coordination and unification. The voluminous arsenal of "cases" of which the author's memory disposes might make the most erudite naturalist or historian envy him, and his delicate power of serially assorting his facts, so as to find always just the case he needs to fit into a gap in the scheme, is wholly admirable. He shows indeed a genius not unlike that of Charles Darwin for discovering shadings and transitions, and grading down discontinuities in his argument.

Three circumstances, probably, have worked against the general public recognition of Myers's scientific powers. These have been, first, the nature of the material he worked in; second, his literary fluency; and third, his emotional interest in immortality. The two latter characteristics, combining their effects, have given to certain passages in the present volumes a tone so lyrical that it may well make them distasteful to the ordinary scientific reader. For propagandist purposes the existence of these passages is, I think, to be regretted. Myers could well have afforded (having shown his undisputed lyrical power elsewhere) to be drier in this argument, and by being so he would have doubtless turned certain possible disciples, now lost to him, into respectful listeners. But he so habitually saw the meanest subliminal phenomena in the light of that transterrene world with which they might remotely be connected, that they became glorified in his mind into experiences in themselves majestic. All his materials were objects of love to him, and the richly latinized and hellenized vocabulary in which he spoke of them shows how they affected his imagination.

From this point of view I think we need not regret a feature of these volumes which to some persons may have seemed pathetic. Myers, namely, was cut off by death before he could write his direct discussion of the evidence for spirit return. But that discussion is a matter of dry-as-dust detail which may well be left to the pages of our *Proceedings* and *Journal,* and to workers who are not such universal geniuses. He has fully expressed in this book his general position on the subject; and being so lyrical a fountain in the direction of immortality, he could hardly have embarked on the evidence without alienating still more a class of students whose sympathy may on the whole be precious. Even though the capstone of the work, as he projected it, be lacking, still the essential Myers is in it, for it is as the organizer and coordinator, far more than as the critic of this or that particular set of observations, that posterity will best remember him.

As regards the truth of his theory, as contra-distinguished from its formal merits as a constructive effort, it is certainly too early for anyone to pass dogmatic judgment. Most readers, even those who admire the scheme as a whole, will doubtless shrink from yielding their credence to it unreservedly. It will seem like skating over ice too thin for any intellect less nimble than Myers's to place its feet on boldly. The types of case which he uses as steppingstones are some of them, at present, either in quality or quantity, decidedly weak supports for the weight which the theory would rest upon them, and it remains at least possible that future records may not remedy this frailty.

The reproach that he has over-generalized the exceptional is also one which, in the present state of our knowledge, cannot be decidedly rebutted. He may extend the subliminal too far when he supposes that all of us possess it, and that works of genius generally have their source in it. He may extend "phantasms" too far when he fills a whole cosmic environment with spirits able to engender them. As between the individual subliminal and the cosmic environment, he may also not have drawn the boundary correctly. There may well be more of the "dissolutive" subliminal and less of the "spirit" than he supposes, in some of his palmary phenomena. But however it may have to be contracted in one case, or extended in another, the subliminal region, as Myers conceived it, will remain a *vera causa* in psychology, explanatory, either of the whole or of a part, of the great mass of occult occurrences so far as they are authentic. "Automatisms" are indeed what he first said they were, messages from the subliminal to the supraliminal regions.

The imperfection which I feel most acutely in Myers's survey of the subliminal life is its failure adequately to account for its being so impartially the home both of evolutive and of dissolutive phenomena. The parasitic ideas of psychoneurosis, and the fictitious personations of planchette-writing and mediumship reside there side by side with the inspirations of genius, with the faculties of telepathy and telesthesia, and with the susceptibility of genuine spirit-control. Myers felt the paradoxical character of such cohabitation, and, as usual, was ready with a suggestion for attenuating the difficulty.

"It may be expected," he writes, "that supernormal vital phenomena will manifest themselves as far as possible through the same channels as abnormal or morbid vital phenomena, when the same centers or the same synergies are used. . . . If there be within us a secondary self aiming at manifestation by physiological means, it seems probable that its readiest path of externalization—its

readiest outlet of visible action—may often lie along some track
which has already been shown to be a line of low resistance by the
disintegrating processes of disease, . . . lie along some plane of
cleavage which the morbid dissociations of our psychical synergies
have already shown themselves disposed to follow" (Vol. II, p. 84).

But this conception is deficient in clearness. Are there three
zones of subliminal life, of which the innermost is *dissolutive,* the
middle one *superior* (the zone of genius, telepathy, etc.), and the
outermost *supreme* and receptive directly of the impact of the spirit
world? And can the two latter zones reach the supraliminal consciousness only by passing through the interior and inferior zone,
and consequently using its channels and mixing its morbid effects
with their own? Or is the subliminal superior throughout when
considered in itself, and are the curious parasitisms of hysteria
and alternate personality, and the curious uncritical passivity to
the absurdest suggestions which we observe in hypnosis to be
explained by defective brain-action exclusively, without bringing
in the subliminal mind? Is it the brain, in short, which vitiates
and mixes results, or is it the interior zone of the subliminal mind?
I make no attempt to solve the question. It is practically as well
as theoretically a vital one, for there can be no doubt whatever
that the *great* obstacle to the reception of a *Weltanschauung* like
Myers's is that the superior phenomena which it believes in are
so enveloped and smothered in the mass of their degenerative
congeners and accompaniments that they beget a collective impression of disgust, and that only the strongest of mental stomachs can
pick them over and seek the gold amongst the rubbish.

Meanwhile it must not be forgotten, if one finds Myers's map
unsatisfactory, that no regular psychologist has ever tried his hand
at the problem. Psychologists admit a subliminal life to exist in
hypnosis and in hysteria, and they use a case like that of Janet's
"Adrienne" to explain the manner in which "secondary personalities"
may become organized. But the existence all about us of thousands
and of tens of thousands of persons, not perceptibly hysteric or un-
healthy, who are mediumistic to the degree at any rate of being

automatic writers, and whose mediumism results in these grotesque impersonations, this, I say, is a phenomenon of human life which they do not even attempt to connect with any of the other facts of nature. Add the fact that the mediumship often gives supernormal information, and it becomes evident that the phenomenon cannot consist of pure eccentricity and isolation. There is method in it; it must have a context of some sort and belong to a region where other things can be found also. It cries aloud for serious investigation. Myers's map is the only scientifically serious investigation that has yet been offered. It is to be hoped that those whom it dissatisfies may not merely reject it, but also make some effort to provide something better.

I cannot conclude without paying my tribute to the innumerable felicities of suggestion with which *Human Personality* abounds. Myers's urbanity of style and his genius for analogy were never more profusely displayed, or in so many directions. Bold as his theory is, it is one of its merits that it should be so sober in the way of either physical or metaphysical hypothesis. What "spirits" are, or what their relations are to "space," he never tries to say, but uses the terms like a *Naturforscher*, as mere designations for factors of phenomena. The book on the whole must be considered a worthy monument to his memory.

VI

---•---

RELIGION AND THE PROBLEMS
OF THE SOUL AND IMMORTALITY

William James's oft-repeated arguments in support of, and his long-continued interest in, psychical research rested upon his belief that such carefully controlled and tested investigations as those which were being made by both the American Society for Psychical Research and the Society for Psychical Research (London) had within them the possibility of uncovering hitherto unknown and unsuspected characteristics and powers of the human mind and personality.

This was the hope which spurred him as a psychologist in his own research in the field. In his observations, his testing of evidence, his analyses, he was driven by his never satisfied hunger for facts which could be proclaimed as demonstrated truths.

But his lifelong quarrel with the rigidity of conventional science was based upon his conviction that there were truths for which scientific proof was as yet impossible, but of which there were hints all about us to be perceived and examined seriously by something other than the exact methods of science.

There are here involved two approaches to truth between which James himself distinguished when he spoke of "exact logic" and "a general sense of dramatic probability which sense ebbs and flows

241

*from one hypothesis to another," and pointed out that the two ap-
proaches often led to different conclusions. It was both of these
facets of his own many-sided nature which he brought to psychical
research and to the two related subjects of religion and the question
of human survival of bodily death.*

*In the following expressions of his interest in these subjects, his
discussion of the theory of the soul, from the* Principles of Psychology, *is a precise statement by William James the psychologist,
the man of "exact logic." The personal letters, his answers to the
Pratt questionnaire about his religious beliefs, and the beautiful
Ingersoll lecture on "Human Immortality" are suffused by his "sense
of dramatic probabilities," his warm and immeasurably vast capacity for human feeling, and the depth of a genuinely religious nature
which could not accept the fragile convictions of conventional
dogma, yet which always "knew that there was more" than that
which was yet demonstrable by scientific method.*

*Indeed one may justifiably speculate whether one of the strong
motivating factors in his interest in psychical research was not explained in the statement he made to Henry W. Rankin: "Religion
is the great interest of my life." **

ON THE THEORY OF THE SOUL [1]

The theory of the Soul is the theory of popular philosophy and
of scholasticism, which is only popular philosophy made systematic.
It declares that the principle of individuality within us must be
substantial, for psychic phenomena are activities, and there can be
no activity without a concrete agent. This substantial agent cannot
be the brain but must be something *immaterial;* for its activity,
thought, is both immaterial, and takes cognizance of immaterial
things, and of material things in general and intelligible, as well
as in particular and sensible ways—all which powers are incompatible with the nature of matter, of which the brain is composed.
Thought moreover is simple, whilst the activities of the brain are

---

* Henry James, ed., op. cit., Vol. II, p. 58.—ED.
[1] *Principles of Psychology,* New York: Henry Holt and Company, 1890,
Vol. I, pp. 343 ff.—ED.

compounded of the elementary activities of each of its parts. Furthermore, thought is spontaneous or free, whilst all material activity is determined *ab extra;* and the will can turn itself against all corporeal goods and appetites, which would be impossible were it a corporeal function. For these objective reasons the principle of psychic life must be both immaterial and simple as well as substantial, must be what is called *a Soul.* The same consequence follows from subjective reasons. Our consciousness of personal identity assures us of our essential simplicity: the owner of the various constituents of the self, as we have seen them, the hypothetical Arch-Ego whom we provisionally conceived as possible, is a real entity of whose existence self-consciousness makes us directly aware. No material agent could thus turn round and grasp *itself*—material activities always grasp something else than the agent. And if a brain *could* grasp itself and be self-conscious, it would be conscious of itself *as* a brain and not as something of an altogether different kind. The Soul then exists as a simple spiritual substance in which the various psychic faculties, operations, and affections inhere.

If we ask what a Substance is, the only answer is that it is a self-existent being, or one which needs no other subject in which to inhere. At bottom its only positive determination is Being, and this is something whose meaning we all realize even though we find it hard to explain. The Soul is moreover an *individual* being, and if we ask what that is, we are told to look in upon our Self, and we shall learn by direct intuition better than through any abstract reply. Our direct perception of our own inward being is in fact by many deemed to be the original prototype out of which our notion of simple active substance in general is fashioned. The *consequences* of the simplicity and substantiality of the Soul are its incorruptibility and natural *immortality*—nothing but God's direct *fiat* can annihilate it—and its *responsibility* at all times for whatever it may have ever done.

This substantialist view of the soul was essentially the view of Plato and of Aristotle. It received its completely formal elaboration in the Middle Ages. It was believed in by Hobbes, Descartes, Locke, Leibnitz, Wolf, Berkeley, and is now defended by the entire modern dualistic or spiritualistic or common-sense school. Kant held to it while denying its fruitfulness as a premise for deducing consequences verifiable here below. Kant's successors, the absolute idealists, profess to have discarded it—how that may be we shall inquire ere long. Let us make up our minds what to think of it ourselves.

It is at all events needless for expressing the actual subjective phenomena of consciousness as they appear. We have formulated them all without its aid, by the supposition of a stream of thoughts, each substantially different from the rest, but cognitive of the rest and "appropriative" of each other's content. At least, if I have not already succeeded in making this plausible to the reader, I am hopeless of convincing him by anything I could add now. The unity, the identity, the individuality, and the immateriality that appear in the psychic life are thus accounted for as phenomenal and temporal facts exclusively, and with no need of reference to any more simple or substantial agent than the present thought or "section" of the stream. We have seen it to be single and unique in the sense of having no *separable* parts—perhaps that is the only kind of simplicity meant to be predicated of the soul. The present thought also has being—at least all believers in the Soul believe so—and if there be no other being in which it "inheres," it ought itself to be a "substance." If *this* kind of simplicity and substantiality were all that is predicated of the Soul, then it might appear that we had been talking of the Soul all along, without knowing it, when we treated the present thought as an agent, an owner, and the like. But the thought is a perishing and not an immortal or incorruptible thing. Its successors may continuously succeed to it, resemble it, and appropriate it, but they *are* not it, whereas the Soul-Substance is supposed to be a fixed unchanging thing. By the Soul is always meant something *behind* the present thought, another kind of substance, existing on a non-phenomenal plane.

When we brought in the Soul at the end of Chapter VI, as an

entity which the various brain-processes were supposed to affect simultaneously, and which responded to their combined influence by single pulses of its thought, it was to escape integrated mind-stuff on the one hand, and an improbable cerebral monad on the other. But when (as now, after all we have been through since that earlier passage) we take the two formulations, first of a brain to whose processes pulses of thought *simply* correspond, and second, of one to whose processes pulses of thought *in a Soul* correspond, and compare them together, we see that at bottom the second formulation is only a more roundabout way than the first of expressing the same bald fact. That bald fact is that *where the brain acts, a thought occurs.* The spiritualistic formulation says that the brain-processes knock the thought, so to speak, out of a Soul which stands there to receive their influence. The simpler formulation says that the thought simply *comes.* But what positive meaning has the Soul, when scrutinized, but the *ground of possibility* of the thought? And what is the "knocking" but the *determining of the possibility to actuality?* And what is this after all but giving a sort of concreted form to one's belief that the coming of the thought, when the brain-processes occur, has *some* sort of ground in the nature of things? If the word Soul be understood merely to express that claim, it is a good word to use. But if it be held to do more, to gratify the claim—for instance, to connect rationally the thought which comes with the processes which occur, and to mediate intelligibly between their two disparate natures—then it is an illusory term. It is, in fact, with the word Soul as with the word Substance in general. To say that phenomena inhere in a Substance is at bottom only to record one's protest against the notion that the bare existence of the phenomena is the total truth. A phenomenon would not itself be, we insist, unless there were something *more* than the phenomenon. To the more we give the provisional name of Substance. So, in the present instance, we ought certainly to admit that there is more than the bare fact of coexistence of a passing thought with a passing brain-state. But we do not answer the question "What is that more?" when we say that it is a "Soul" which the brain-state affects. This kind of more *explains* nothing; and when we are once trying metaphysical explanations we are foolish not to go as far as we can. For my own part I confess that the moment I become metaphysical and try to define the more, I find the notion of some sort of an *anima mundi* thinking in all of us to be a more promising hypothesis, in spite of all its difficulties, than that of a lot of absolutely individual souls. Meanwhile, as *psychologists*, we need not be metaphysical at all. The phenomena are enough, the passing thought itself is the only *verifiable* thinker, and its empirical connection with the brain-process is the ultimate known law.

To the other arguments which would prove the need of a Soul, we may also turn a deaf ear. The argument from free will can convince only those who believe in free will; and even they will have to admit that spontaneity is just as possible, to say the least, in a temporary spiritual agent like our "thought" as in a permanent one like the supposed Soul. The same is true of the argument from the kinds of things cognized. Even if the brain could not cognize universals, immaterials, or its "Self," still the "thought" which we have relied upon in our account *is* not the brain, closely as it seems connected with it; and after all, if the brain could cognize at all, one does not well see why it might not cognize one sort of thing as well as another. The great difficulty is in seeing how a thing can cognize *anything*. This difficulty is not in the least removed by giving to the thing that cognizes the name of Soul. The Spiritualists do not deduce any of the properties of the mental life from otherwise known properties of the soul. They simply find various characters ready-made in the mental life, and these they clap into the Soul, saying, "Lo! behold the source from whence they flow!" The merely verbal character of this "explanation" is obvious. The Soul invoked, far from making the phenomena more intelligible, can only be made intelligible itself by borrowing their form—it must be represented, if at all, as a transcendent stream of consciousness duplicating the one we know.

Altogether, the Soul is an outbirth of that sort of philosophizing whose great maxim, according to Dr. Hodgson, is: "Whatever you are *totally* ignorant of, assert to be the explanation of everything else."

Locke and Kant, whilst still believing in the soul, began the work of undermining the notion that we know anything about it. Most modern writers of the mitigated, spiritualistic, or dualistic philosophy—the Scotch school, as it is often called among us—are forward to proclaim this ignorance, and to attend exclusively to the verifiable phenomena of self-consciousness, as we have laid them down. Dr. Wayland, for example, begins his *Elements of Intellectual Philosophy* with the phrase "Of the essence of Mind we know nothing," and goes on: "All that we are able to affirm of it is that it is *something* which perceives, reflects, remembers, imagines, and wills; but what that something *is* which exerts these energies we know not. It is only as we are conscious of the action of these energies that we are conscious of the existence of the mind. It is only by the exertion of its own powers that the mind becomes cognizant of their existence. The cognizance of its powers, however, gives us no knowledge of that essence of which they are predicated. In these respects our knowledge of mind is precisely analogous to our knowledge of matter." This analogy of our two ignorances is a favorite remark in the Scotch school. It is but a step to lump them together into a single ignorance, that of the "unknowable" to which anyone fond of superfluities in philosophy may accord the hospitality of his belief, if it so please him, but which anyone else may as freely ignore and reject.

The Soul theory is, then, a complete superfluity, so far as accounting for the actually verified facts of conscious experience goes. So far, no one can be compelled to subscribe to it for definite scientific reasons. The case would rest here, and the reader be left free to make his choice, were it not for other demands of a more practical kind.

The first of these is *Immortality,* for which the simplicity and substantiality of the Soul seem to offer a solid guarantee. A "stream" of thought, for aught that we see to be contained in its essence, may come to a full stop at any moment; but a simple substance is incorruptible and will, by its own inertia, persist in being so long as the Creator does not by a direct miracle snuff it out. Unquestionably this is the stronghold of the spiritualistic belief—as indeed the popular touchstone for all philosophies is the question, "What is their bearing on a future life?"

The Soul, however, when closely scrutinized, guarantees no immortality of a sort *we care for*. The enjoyment of the atom-like simplicity of their substance *in saecula saeculorum* would not to most people seem a consummation devoutly to be wished. The substance must give rise to a stream of consciousness continuous with the present stream, in order to arouse our hope, but of this the mere persistence of the substance *per se* offers no guarantee. Moreover, in the general advance of our moral ideas, there has come to be something ridiculous in the way our forefathers had of grounding their hopes of immortality on the simplicity of their substance. The demand for immortality is nowadays essentially teleological. We believe ourselves immortal because we believe ourselves *fit* for immortality. A "Substance" ought surely to perish, we think, if not worthy to survive, and an insubstantial "stream" to prolong itself, provided it be worthy, if the nature of things is organized in the rational way in which we trust it is. Substance or no Substance, Soul or "stream," what Lotze says of immortality is about all that human wisdom can say:

> We have no other principle for deciding it than this general idealistic belief that that only created thing will continue whose continuance belongs to the meaning of the world, and so long as it does so belong; whilst every one will pass away whose reality is justified only in a transitory phase of the world's course. That this principle admits of no further application in human hands need hardly be said. We surely know not the merits which may give to one being a claim on eternity, nor the defects which would cut others off.[2]

---

[2] *Metaphysik*, pp. 245 *fin*. This writer, who in his early work, the *Medizinische Psychologie*, was (to my reading) a strong defender of the Soul-Substance the-

A second alleged necessity for a Soul-Substance is our forensic responsibility before God. Locke caused an uproar when he said that the unity of *consciousness* made a man the same *person,* whether supported by the same *Substance* or no, and that God would not, in the great day, make a person answer for what he remembered nothing of. It was supposed scandalous that our forgetfulness might thus deprive God of the chance of certain retributions, which otherwise would have enhanced his "glory." This is certainly a good speculative ground for retaining the Soul—at least for those who demand a plenitude of retribution. The mere stream of consciousness, with its lapses of memory, cannot possibly be as "responsible" as a Soul which *is* at the judgment day all that it ever was. To modern readers, however, who are less insatiate for retribution than their grandfathers, this argument will hardly be as convincing as it seems once to have been.

One great use of the Soul has always been to account for, and at the same time to guarantee, the closed individuality of each personal consciousness. The thoughts of one Soul must unite into one self, it was supposed, and must be eternally insulated from those of every other Soul. But we have already begun to see that, although unity is the rule of each man's consciousness, yet in some individuals, at least, thoughts may split away from the others and form separate selves. As for insulation, it would be rash, in view of the phenomena of thought-transference, mesmeric influence, and spirit-control, which are being alleged nowadays on better authority than ever before, to be too sure about that point either. The definitively closed nature of our personal consciousness is probably an average statistical resultant of many conditions, but not an elementary force or fact; so that, if one wishes to preserve the Soul, the less he draws his arguments from *that* quarter the better. So long as our self, on the whole, makes itself good and practically maintains itself as a closed individual, why, as Lotze says, is not that enough? And why

ory, has written in pp. 243–45 of his *Metaphysik* the most beautiful criticism of this theory which exists.—W. J.

is the *being*-an-individual in some inaccessible metaphysical way so much prouder an achievement?

My final conclusion, then, about the substantial Soul is that it explains nothing and guarantees nothing. Its successive thoughts are the only intelligible and verifiable things about it, and definitely to ascertain the correlations of these with brain-processes is as much as psychology can empirically do. From the metaphysical point of view, it is true that one may claim that the correlations have a rational ground; and if the word Soul could be taken to mean merely some such vague problematic ground, it would be unobjectionable. But the trouble is that it professes to give the ground in positive terms of a very dubiously credible sort. I therefore feel entirely free to discard the word Soul from the rest of this book. If I ever use it, it will be in the vaguest and most popular way. The reader who finds any comfort in the idea of the Soul is, however, perfectly free to continue to believe in it; for our reasonings have not established the non-existence of the Soul; they have only proved its superfluity for scientific purposes.

LETTERS AND MISCELLANY

Nowhere are the richness and warmth of William James's personality, or his capacity for thought and feeling which transcended the limits of "exact logic," more clearly revealed than in his letters to friends and family. This was perhaps especially true when he discussed such matters as religion, God, and the question of immortality, and one has only to read his letters to see that his search for a religious philosophy and the spiritualism which psychical research stimulated were related in his mind.

The letters included here are arranged in chronological order, beginning with one written to his family when he was twenty years old, and ending with a brief extract from a letter to Helen Keller written at the age of sixty-six, two years before his death, and show a definite development in his thought during forty-six years of his life.

Inserted with the letters, in their chronological places, are some comments from an article in The Nation *and a questionnaire concerning his own religious beliefs, and notes for a lecture.*

To His Family, March 1, 1862 [1]

President Felton's death has been the great event of the week, two funerals and I do not know how many prayers and sermons. Today I thought I would go to chapel for the sake of variety, and hear Dr. Peabody's final word on him—and a very long and lugubrious one it was. The prayer was a prolonged moan in which the death (not in its consequences but in itself) was treated of as a great calamity; and the eulogy of the sermon was almost ridiculously overcharged. What was most disagreeable throughout the whole was the wailing tone—not a bit that of simple pagan grief at the *loss* (which would have been honest), but a whine consciously *put on* as if from a sense of duty, and a whine at *nothing* definite either, but a purposeless clothing of all his words in tears. The whole style of the performance was so false and unpleasant that I have concluded to have nothing more to do with funerals till they improve. . . .

To Thomas W. Ward, January 1868 [2]

All I can tell you is the thought that with me outlasts all others, and onto which, like a rock, I find myself washed up when the waves of doubt are weltering over all the rest of the world; and that is the thought of my having a will, and of my belonging to a brotherhood of men possessed of a capacity for pleasure and pain of different kinds. For even at one's lowest ebb of belief, the fact remains empirically certain (and by our will we can, if not *absolutely* refrain from looking beyond that empirical fact, at least practically and *on the whole* accept it and let it suffice us)—that men suffer and enjoy. And if we have to give up all hope of seeing into the purposes of God, or to give up theoretically the idea of final causes, and of God anyhow as vain and leading to nothing

[1] Ralph Barton Perry, op. cit., Vol. I, p. 212.—Ed.
[2] Henry James, ed., op. cit., Vol. I, p. 130 ff.—Ed.

for us, we can, by our will, make the enjoyment of our brothers stand us in the stead of a final cause; and through a knowledge of the fact that that enjoyment on the whole depends on what individuals accomplish, lead a life so active and so sustained by a clean conscience as not to need to fret much. Individuals can add to the welfare of the race in a variety of ways. You may delight its senses or "tastes" by some production of luxury or art, comfort it by discovering some moral truth, relieve its pain by concocting a new patent medicine, save its labor by a bit of machinery, or by some new application of a natural product. You may open a road, help start some social or business institution, contribute your mite in *any* way to the mass of the work which each generation subtracts from the task of the next; and you will come into *real* relations with your brothers—with some of them at least.

I know that in a certain point of view, and the most popular one, this seems a cold activity for our affections, a stone instead of bread. We long for sympathy, for a purely *personal* communication, first with the soul of the world, and then with the soul of our fellows. And happy are they who think, or know, that they have got them! But to those who must confess with bitter anguish that they are perfectly isolated from the soul of the world, and that the closest human love encloses a potential germ of estrangement or hatred, that all *personal* relation is finite, conditional, mixed (*vide* in Dana's *Household Book of Poetry*, stanzas by C. P. Cranch, "Thought is deeper than speech," etc., etc.), it may not prove such an unfruitful substitute. At least, when you have added to the property of the race, even if no one knows your name, yet it is certain that, without what you have done, some individuals must needs be acting now in a somewhat different manner. You have modified their life; you are in *real* relation with them; you have in so far forth entered into their being. And is that such an unworthy stake to set up for our good, after all? Who are these men anyhow? Our predecessors, even apart from the physical link of generation, have made us what we are. Every thought you now have and every act and intention owes its complexion to the acts of your dead and living brothers. *Everything* we know and are is through men. We have no revelation but through man. Every sentiment that warms your gizzard, every brave act that ever made your pulse bound and your nostril open to a confident breath was a man's act. However mean a man may be, man is *the best we know;* and your loathing as you turn from what you probably call the vulgarity of human life—your homesick yearning for a *Better,* somewhere—is furnished by your manhood; your ideal is made up of traits suggested by past men's words and actions. Your manhood shuts you in forever, bounds all your thoughts like an overarching sky—and all the Good and True and High and Dear that you know by virtue of your sharing in it. They are the Natural Product of our Race. So that it seems to me that a sympathy with men as such, and a desire to contribute to the Weal of a species, which, whatever may be said of it, contains All that we acknowledge as good, may very well form an external interest sufficient to keep one's moral pot boiling in a very lively manner to a good old age. The idea, in short, of becoming an accomplice in a sort of "Mankind its own God or Providence" scheme is a *practical* one.

I don't mean, by any means, to affirm that we must come to that, I only say it is *a* mode of envisaging life; which is capable of affording moral support—and may at any rate help to bridge over the despair of skeptical intervals. I confess that, in the lonesome gloom which beset me for a couple of months last summer, the only feeling that kept me from giving up was that by waiting and living, by hook or crook, long enough, I might make my *nick,* however small a one, in the raw stuff the race has got to shape, and so assert my reality. The stoic feeling of being a sentinel obeying orders without knowing the general's plans is a noble one. And so is the divine enthusiasm of moral culture (Channing, etc.), and I think that, successively, they may all help to ballast the same man.

To Henry James, Dresden, April 13, 1868 [3]

My dear Harry,—

I am just in from the theater and feel like dropping you a line to tell you I have got your last *Atlantic* story ("Extraordinary Case"), and read it with much satisfaction. It makes me think I may have partly misunderstood your aim heretofore, and that one of the objects you have had in view has been to give an impression like that we often get of people in life: Their orbits come out of space and lay themselves for a short time along of ours, and then off they whirl again into the unknown, leaving us with little more than an impression of their reality and a feeling of baffled curiosity as to the mystery of the beginning and end of their being, and of the intimate character of that segment of it which we have seen. Am I right in guessing that you had a conscious intention of this sort here? . . . You seem to acknowledge that you can't exhaust any character's feelings or thoughts by an articulate displaying of them. You shrink from the attempt to drag them all reeking and dripping and raw upon the stage, which most writers make and fail in. You expressly restrict yourself, accordingly, to showing a few external acts and speeches, and by the magic of your art making the reader *feel* back of these the existence of a body of being of which these are casual features. You wish to suggest a mysterious fullness which you do not lead the reader through. It seems to me this is a very legitimate method, and has a great effect when it succeeds. . . . Only it must succeed. The gushing system is better to fail in, since that admits of a warmth of feeling and generosity of intention that may reconcile the reader.

To Charles Ritter, January 21, 1869 [4]

Vacherot's book is very interesting. What integrity of mind! What breadth of character and what gentleness! And what an advantage it is for the solution of such problems to have a good little optimistic

---

[3] Ralph Barton Perry, op. cit., Vol. I, p. 271.—ED.
[4] Ibid., Vol. I, p. 292.—ED.

philosophy of one's own! Humanity without religion appears to require either a disinterestedness hitherto unknown in any individual, or a terrestrial paradise. No doubt we are by short steps approaching the latter state as regards material circumstances. And on the other side we can hope for much from education towards the development of cosmic sympathies (so to say) and disinterested sentiments. . . . But all that is only an ideal, the vanishing-point of the perspective, and meanwhile is it not reasonable to expect that the egoism which is ingrained in most of us (and which after all is what enables us to live) will continue to seek beyond the self and in the ground of the universe something that lends it countenance—which authorizes it, in short, as all the gods have done? How does it seem to you on these matters? . . .

From comments in The Nation, *September 21, 1876* [5]

The philosophical teaching, as a rule, in our higher seminaries is in the hands of the president, who is usually a minister of the Gospel, and, as he more often owes his position to general excellence of character and administrative faculty than to any speculative gifts or propensities, it usually follows that "safeness" becomes the main characteristic of his tuition; that his classes are edified rather than awakened, and leave college with the generous youthful impulse, to reflect on the world and our position in it, rather dampened and discouraged than stimulated by the lifeless discussions and flabby formulas they have had to commit to memory. . . .

Let it not be supposed that we are prejudging the question whether the final results of speculation will be friendly or hostile to the formulas of Christian thought. All we contend for is that we, like the Greeks and the Germans, should now attack things as if there were no official answer preoccupying the field. At present we are bribed beforehand by our reverence or dislike for the official answer; and the free-thinking tendency which the *Popular Science Monthly,* for example, represents, is condemned to an even more dismal shallowness than the spiritualistic systems of our textbooks

[5] Henry James, ed., op. cit., Vol. I, pp. 189–91.—ED.

of "Mental Science." We work with one eye on our problem, and with the other on the consequences to our enemy or to our lawgiver, as the case may be; the result in both cases is mediocrity.

If the best use of our colleges is to give young men a wider openness of mind and a more flexible way of thinking than special technical training can generate, then we hold that philosophy (taken in the broad sense in which our correspondent uses the word) is the most important of all college studies. However skeptical one may be of the attainment of universal truths (and to make our position more emphatic, we are willing here to concede the extreme Positivistic position), one can never deny that philosophic study means the habit of always seeing an alternative, of not taking the usual for granted, of making conventionalities fluid again, of imagining foreign states of mind. In a word, it means the possession of mental perspective. Touchstone's question, "Hast any philosophy in thee, shepherd?" will never cease to be one of the tests of a well-born nature. It says, Is there space and air in your mind, or must your companions gasp for breath whenever they talk with you? And if our colleges are to make men, and not machines, they should look, above all things, to this aspect of their influence. . . .

As for philosophy, technically so called, or the reflection of man on his relations with the universe, its educational essence lies in the quickening of the spirit to its *problems*. What doctrines students take from their teachers are of little consequence provided they catch from them the living, philosophic attitude of mind, the independent, personal look at all the data of life, and the eagerness to harmonize them. . . .

In short, philosophy, like Molière, claims her own where she finds it. She finds much of it today in physics and natural history, and must and will educate herself accordingly. . . .

To Thomas Davidson, January 8, 1882 [6]

It is a curious thing, this matter of God! I can sympathize perfectly with the most rabid hater of him and the idea of him, when

---

[6] Ralph Barton Perry, op. cit., Vol. I, pp. 737–38.—Ed.

I think of the use that has been made of him in history and philosophy as a *starting-point*, or premise for grounding deductions. But as an ideal to attain and make probable, I find myself less and less able to do without him. He need not be an *all*-including "subjective unity of the universe," as you suppose. In fact there is nothing I clasp hands with you so heartily in, as in defying the superstition of such a unity. It is only one possible hypothesis amid many and becomes (d——n my eyes, I must call my wife to write for me!) a pure superstition the moment it is treated dogmatically. All I mean is that there must be *some* subjective unity in the universe which has purposes commensurable with my own, and which is at the same time large enough to be, among all the powers that may be there, the strongest. I simply refuse to accept the notion of there being *no* purpose in the objective world. On the other hand, I cannot represent the existence of purpose except as based in a mind. The not-me, therefore, so far as it contains purpose, must spring from a mind; but not necessarily a *one and only* mind. In saying "God exists" all I imply is that my purposes are cared for by a mind so powerful as on the whole to control the drift of the universe. This is as much polytheism as monotheism. As a matter of fact it is neither, for it is hardly a speculative position at all, but a merely practical and emotional faith which I fancy even your Promethean *Gemuth* shares.

The only difficulties of theism are the moral difficulties and meannesses; and they have always seemed to me to flow from the gratuitous dogma of God being the all-exclusive reality. Once think possible a primordial pluralism of which he may be one member and which may have no single subjective synthesis, and piety forthwith ceases to be incompatible with manliness, and religious "faith" with intellectual rectitude. In short, the only theism I defend is that of simple unphilosophic mankind, to which numerical mysteries are added corruptions. If there be a God, how the devil can we know what difficulties he may have had to contend with? (This last remark is from my amanuensis spouse!) *Darauf kommt es an!* Possible difficulties! they save everything. But what are they but limitations to the all-inclusiveness of any single being?

To His Father, Henry James, Sr., December 14, 1882 [7]

We have been so long accustomed to the hypothesis of your being taken away from us, especially during the past ten months, that the thought that this may be your last illness conveys no very sudden shock. You are old enough, you've given your message to the world in many ways and will not be forgotten; you are here left alone, and on the other side, let us hope and pray, dear, dear old Mother is waiting for you to join her. If you go, it will not be an inharmonious thing. . . . As for the other side, and Mother, and our all possibly meeting, I *can't* say anything. More than ever at this moment do I feel that if that *were* true, all would be solved and justified. And it comes strangely over me in bidding you good-by how a life is but a day and expresses mainly but a single note. It is so much like the act of bidding an ordinary good night. Good night, my sacred old Father! If I don't see you again—Farewell! a blessed farewell! Your

William

To Thomas Davidson, March 30, 1884 [8]

I had neither seen your article in the *Unitarian Review* nor heard of it, but ran for it as soon as I got your announcement of its existence. I know not what to think of it practically; though I confess the idea of engrafting the bloodless pallor of Boston Unitarianism on the Roman temperament strikes one at first as rather queer. Unitarianism seems to have a sort of moribund vitality here, because it is a branch of protestantism and the tree keeps the branch sticking out. But whether it could be grafted on a catholic trunk seems to me problematic. I confess I rather despair of any popular religion of a philosophic character; and I sometimes find myself

---

[7] Henry James, ed., op. cit., Vol. I, pp. 219–20. This letter was written during the final illness of Henry James, Sr.—ED.

[8] Ibid., Vol. I, pp. 236–37.—ED.

wondering whether there can be any popular religion raised on the ruins of the old Christianity without the presence of that element which in the past has presided over the origin of all religions, namely, a belief in new *physical* facts and possibilities. Abstract considerations about the soul and the reality of a moral order will not do in a year what the glimpse into a world of new phenomenal possibilities enveloping those of the present life, afforded by an extension of our insight into the order of nature, would do in an instant. Are the much despised "Spiritualism" and the "Society for Psychical Research" to be the chosen instruments for a new era of faith? It would surely be strange if they were; but if they are not, I see no other agency that can do the work.

To His Sister, Alice James, July 6, 1891 [9]

Dearest Alice,— . . . Of course [this medical verdict on your case may mean] as all men know, a finite length of days; and then, good-by to neurasthenia and neuralgia and headache, and weariness and palpitation and disgust all at one stroke—I should think you would be reconciled to the prospect with all its pluses and minuses! I know you've never cared for life, and to me, now at the age of nearly fifty, life and death seem singularly close together in all of us—and life a mere farce of frustration in all, so far as the realization of the innermost ideals go to which we are made respectively capable of feeling an affinity and responding. Your frustrations are only rather more flagrant than the rule; and you've been saved many forms of self-dissatisfaction and misery which appertain to such a multiplication of responsible relations to different people as I, for instance, have got into. Your fortitude, good spirits and unsentimentality have been simply unexampled in the midst of your physical woes; and when you're relieved from your post, just *that* bright note will remain behind, together with the inscrutable and mysterious character of the doom of nervous weakness which has chained you down for all these years. As for that, there's more in it than has ever been told to so-called science. These

---

[9] Ibid., Vol. I, pp. 309–11.—ED.

inhibitions, these split-up selves, all these new facts that are gradually coming to light about our organization, these enlargements of
the self in trance, etc., are bringing me to turn for light in the direction of all sorts of despised spiritualistic and unscientific ideas.
Father would find in me today a much more receptive listener—all
that philosophy has got to be brought in. And what a queer contradiction comes to the ordinary scientific argument against immortality (based on body being mind's condition and mind going
out when body is gone), when one must believe (as now, in these
neurotic cases) that some infernality in the body *prevents* really
existing parts of the mind from coming to their effective rights at
all, suppresses them, and blots them out from participation in this
world's experiences, although they are *there* all the time. When
that which is *you* passes out of the body, I am sure that there will
be an explosion of liberated force and life till then eclipsed and
kept down. I can hardly imagine *your* transition without a great
oscillation of both "worlds" as they regain their new equilibrium
after the change! Everyone will feel the shock, but you yourself
will be more surprised than anybody else.

It may seem odd for me to talk to you in this cool way about
your end; but, my dear little sister, if one has things present to
one's mind, and I know they are present enough to *your* mind, why
not speak them out? I am sure you appreciate that best. How many
times I have thought, in the past year, when my days were so full
of strong and varied impression and activities, of the long unchanging hours in bed which those days stood for with you, and won-
dered how you bore the slow-paced monotony at all, as you did!
You can't tell how I've pitied you. But you *shall* come to your
rights erelong. Meanwhile take things gently. Look for the little
good in each day as if life were to last a hundred years. Above
all things, save yourself from bodily pain, if it can be done. You've
had too much of that. Take all the morphia (or other forms of
opium if that disagrees) you want, and don't be afraid of becoming an opium-drunkard. What was opium created for except for
such times as this? Beg the good Katharine (to whom *our* debt can

never be extinguished) to write me a line every week, just to keep
the currents flowing, and so farewell until I write again. Your ever
loving,

W. J.

To Henry W. Rankin, February 1, 1897 [10]

One of my lectures in New York is at the Academy of Medicine
before the Neurological Society, the subject being "Demoniacal
Possession." I shall of course duly advertise the Nevius book.[11] I
am not as positive as you are in the belief that the obsessing agency
is really demonic individuals. I am perfectly willing to adopt that
theory if the facts lend themselves best to it; for who can trace
limits to the hierarchies of personal existence in the world? But
the lower stages of mere automatism shade off so continuously
into the highest supernormal manifestations, through the intermediary ones of imitative hysteria and "suggestibility," that I feel
as if no *general theory* as yet would cover all the facts. So that the
most I shall plead for before the neurologists is the recognition of
demon possession as a regular "morbid-entity" whose commonest
homologue today is the "spirit-control" observed in test-mediumship, and which tends to become the more benignant and less alarm-
ing, the less pessimistically it is regarded. This last remark seems
certainly to be true. Of course I shall not ignore the sporadic cases
of old-fashioned malignant possession which still occur today. I
am convinced that we stand with all these things at the threshold
of a long inquiry, of which the end appears as yet to no one, least
of all to myself. And I believe that the best theoretic work yet done
in the subject is the beginning made by F. W. H. Myers in his
papers in the S. P. R. *Proceedings.* The first thing is to start the
medical profession out of its idiotically *conceited ignorance* of all
such matters—matters which have everywhere and at all times
played a vital part in human history.

You have written me at different times about conversion, and

---

[10] Ibid., Vol. II, pp. 56–58.—ED.
[11] *Demon Possession and Allied Themes,* by John C. Nevius.—ED.

about miracles, getting as usual no reply, but not because I failed to heed your words, which come from a deep life-experience of your own evidently, and from a deep acquaintance with the experiences of others. In the matter of conversion I am quite willing to believe that a new truth may be supernaturally revealed to a subject when he really *asks.* But I am sure that in many cases of conversion it is less a new truth than a new power gained over life by a truth always known. It is a case of the conflict of two *self-systems* in a personality up to that time heterogeneously divided, but in which, after the conversion crisis, the higher loves and powers come definitively to gain the upper hand and expel the forces which up to that time had kept them down in the position of mere grumblers and protesters and agents of remorse and discontent. This broader view will cover an enormous number of cases *psychologically,* and leaves all the *religious importance* to the result which it has on any other theory.

As to true and false miracles, I don't know that I can follow you so well, for in any case the notion of a miracle as a mere attestation of superior power is one that I cannot espouse. A miracle must in any case be an expression of personal purpose, but the demon purpose of antagonizing God and winning away his adherents has never yet taken hold of my imagination. I prefer an open mind of inquiry, first *about the facts,* in all these matters; and I believe that the S. P. R. methods, if pertinaciously stuck to, will eventually do much to clear things up. You see that, although religion is the great interest of my life, I am rather hopelessly non-evangelical, and take the whole thing too impersonally.

To His Wife, Alice Gibbens James, July 9, 1898 [12]

The temperature was perfect either inside or outside the cabin, the moon rose and hung above the scene before midnight, leaving only a few of the larger stars visible, and I got into a state of spiritual alertness of the most vital description. The influences of nature, the wholesomeness of the people round me, especially the

[12] Henry James, ed., op. cit., Vol. I, pp. 76–77.—Ed.

good Pauline, the thought of you and the children, dear Harry on the wave, the problem of the Edinburgh lectures, all fermented within me till it became a regular Walpurgis Nacht. I spent a good deal of it in the woods, where the streaming moonlight lit up things in a magical checkered play, and it seemed as if the Gods of all the nature-mythologies were holding an indescribable meeting in my breast with the moral Gods of the inner life. The two kinds of Gods have nothing in common—the Edinburgh lectures made quite a hitch ahead. The intense significance of some sort, of the whole scene, if one could only *tell* the significance; the intense inhuman remoteness of its inner life, and yet the intense *appeal* of it; its everlasting freshness and its immemorial antiquity and decay; its utter Americanism, and every sort of patriotic suggestiveness, and you, and my relation to you part and parcel of it all, and beaten up with it, so that memory and sensation all whirled inexplicably together; it was indeed worth coming for, and worth repeating year by year, if repetition could only procure what in its nature I suppose must be all unplanned for and unexpected. It was one of the happiest lonesome nights of my existence, and I understand now what a poet is. He is a person who can feel the immense complexity of influences that I felt, and make some partial tracks in them for verbal statement. In point of fact, I can't find a single word for all that significance, and don't know what it was significant of, so there it remains, a mere boulder of *impression*. Doubtless in more ways than one, though, things in the Edinburgh lectures will be traceable to it.

To Frances Morse, April 13, 1900 [13]

I scribble a little in bed every morning, and have reached page 48 of my third Gifford lecture—though Lecture II, alas! must be rewritten entirely. The conditions don't conduce to an energetic grip of the subject, and I am afraid that what I write is pretty slack and not what it would be if my vital tone were different. The problem I have set myself is a hard one: *first,* to defend (against all the

[13] Ibid., Vol. II, pp. 126–27.—ED.

prejudices of my "class") "experience" against "philosophy" as being the real backbone of the world's religious life—I mean prayer, guidance, and all that sort of thing immediately and privately felt, as against high and noble general views of our destiny and the world's meaning; and *second,* to make the hearer or reader believe, what I myself invincibly do believe, that, although all the special manifestations of religion may have been absurd (I mean its creeds and theories), yet the life of it as a whole is mankind's most important function. A task well-nigh impossible, I fear, and in which I shall fail; but to attempt it is *my* religious act.

To Henry W. Rankin, June 16, 1901 [14]

I have given nine of my lectures and am to give the tenth to-morrow. They have been a success, to judge by the numbers of the audience (300-odd) and their non-diminution towards the end. No previous "Giffords" have drawn near so many. It will please you to know that I am stronger and tougher than when I began, too; so a great load is off my mind. You have been so extraordinarily brotherly to me in writing of your convictions and in furnishing me ideas, that I feel ashamed of my churlish and chary replies. You, however, have forgiven me. Now, at the end of this first course, I feel my "matter" taking firmer shape, and it will please you less to hear me say that I believe myself to be (probably) permanently incapable of believing the Christian scheme of vicarious salvation, and wedded to a more continuously evolutionary mode of thought. The reasons you from time to time have given me, never better expressed than in your letter before the last, have somehow failed to convince. In these lectures the ground I am taking is this: The mother sea and fountainhead of all religions lie in the mystical experiences of the individual, taking the word mystical in a very wide sense. All theologies and all ecclesiasticisms are secondary growths superimposed; and the experiences make such flexible combinations with the intellectual prepossessions of their subjects,

[14] Ibid., Vol. II, pp. 149–50.—ED.

that one may almost say that they have no proper *intellectual* deliverance of their own, but belong to a region deeper, and more vital and practical, than that which the intellect inhabits. For this they are also indestructible by intellectual arguments and criticisms. I attach the mystical or religious consciousness to the possession of an extended subliminal self, with a thin partition through which messages make irruption. We are thus made convincingly aware of the presence of a sphere of life larger and more powerful than our usual consciousness, with which the latter is nevertheless continuous. The impressions and impulsions and emotions and excitements which we thence receive help us to live, they found invincible assurance of a world beyond the sense, they melt our hearts and communicate significance and value to everything and make us happy. They do this for the individual who has them, and other individuals follow him. Religion in this way is absolutely indestructible. Philosophy and theology give their conceptual interpretations of this experiential life. The farther margin of the subliminal field being unknown, it can be treated as by Transcendental idealism, as an Absolute mind with a part of which we coalesce, or by Christian theology, as a distinct deity acting on us. Something, not our immediate self, does act on our life! So I seem doubtless to my audience to be blowing hot and cold, explaining away Christianity, yet defending the more general basis from which I say it proceeds. I fear that these brief words may be misleading, but let them go! When the book comes out, you will get a truer idea.

Believe me, with profound regards, your always truly,

WM. JAMES

To James Ward, July 29, 1902 [15]

I don't accept all Myers's opinions as "gospel truth," quite the reverse. But I think Myers's *problem*, the "exploration of the subliminal," to be the most important definite investigation opened of late in psychology, and I think Myers's way of going at it on the

[15] Ralph Barton Perry, op. cit., Vol. II, pp. 649–50.—ED.

whole admirable. Who has brought together and simplified as much as he? Have you seen an obituary article on his relation to psychology by me in the S. P. R. *Proceedings* of last year?

As for the derivative nature of the subliminal, it *certainly* in my view is not entire. The existence of supernormal memory (*vide* Fluornoy's case) and supernormal cognitions (*vide* Piper) proves that there *is* a region for exploration, and that Myers's problem is genuinely important. The relation of it all to religion is through mysticism. I *can't* ignore the vital prominence of that sort of experience in the religious life. I have fully admitted the necessary cooperation of intellect in elaborating results, and think you misapprehend me as saying "all feeling and no reason."

But I feel sure that contemplative reason would produce no religion (even with desire to prompt results) unless there were in addition some of these other non-rational intuitive processes to clinch persuasion. The persuasion gets *form* from the *Zeitgeist,* etc. But form depends on where quickening emphasis falls, this gives the perspective and fixes the center, and those non-rational feelings of reality, and automatic promptings towards certain kinds of life, play the same part in our spiritual experience which sensations do in ordinary affairs. They determine the distribution of our energies, and our reason cooperates in the resultant. I may maximize unduly the non-derivative character of these forces, which you minimize. But if one is on a hunt, it is better not to assume at the start that there is no game, or you won't get what little there is.

To Grace Norton, August 29, 1902 [16]

The scourge of life is *responsibility*—always there with its scowling face, and when it ceases to someone else, it begins to yourself, or to your God, if you have one. Consider the lilies, how free they are from it, and yet how beautiful the expression of their face. Especially should those emerging from "nervous prostration" be suffered to be without it—they have trouble enough in any case.

---

[16] Henry James, ed., op. cit., Vol. II, p. 174.—Ed.

To Henry W. Rankin, June 10, 1903 [17]

I do not (and I fear cannot) follow the gospel scheme as you do, and that the Bible itself, in both its testaments (omitting parts of John and the Apocalypse), seems to me, by its intense naturalness and humanness, the most fatal document that one can read against the orthodox theology, in so far as the latter claims the words of the Bible to be its basis. I myself believe that the orthodox theology contains elements that are permanently true, and that such writers as Emerson, by reason of their extraordinary healthy-mindedness and "once-born"-ness, are incapable of appreciating. I believe that they will have to be expressed in any ultimately valid religious philosophy; and I see in the temper of friendliness of such a man as you for such writings as Emerson's and mine (*magnus comp. parvo*) a foretaste of the day when the abstract essentials of belief will be the basis of communion more than the particular forms and concrete doctrines in which they articulate themselves.

From Notes for a Metaphysical Seminary, 1903–1904 [18]

Man is too helpless against the cosmic forces, unless there be a wider Ally. Religion, the belief in this Ally, has thus the simplest of motives. Its arguments for me lie in the conviction that our normal experience is only a fraction, and in the mystical phenomena. But by this extension of experience only possibilities are opened, and what most men want are certainties. They are not *bare* possibilities, however. To make a live possibility, more than an existent stock for a graft is required. The stock must, by idealizing the graft, exert tractive force upon it. . . . How to formulate it? I don't know. . . . If we cling to pure experience, it is in part experience of activity . . . a kind of experienced transition, a part of the content. . . . It involves sense of *direction*. . . . If present experiences cannot only welcome, but introduce, then there are live possibilities. Leave as problem!

---

[17] Ibid., Vol. II, pp. 196–97.—Ed.
[18] Ralph Barton Perry, op. cit., Vol. II, pp. 383–84.—Ed.

Meanwhile I ask whether a world of hypothetical perfection conditional on each part doing its duty be not as much as can firmly be demanded.

Unidentified Comment, 1904 [19]

I came down to Sarah Whitman's funeral, and being here, have stayed till Commencement, but return today. I can't go without an overflow to you, Sarah Whitman's death was so abrupt and bewildering. Pathetic, inscrutable, lover of life, outreacher to the good, spreader of friendliness—where is she now? And what does it all mean? I never had the pathos or the mystery brought so sharply home, and one's thought of her now is all one tenderness. How much more real are people's lives than all our criticisms of them! It is a lesson to cultivate each other, all of us, while we yet have each other. . . .

Everything in this beautiful world is good except old age and death if one supposes no "behind the veil" of any kind. Mrs. Whitman's funeral was wonderful for beauty. The crowd of friends at the grave were all swayed by one pathetic emotion. And now she seems in retrospect like a little slender, lonely, trustful, blind creature, passionately curving and twisting her naïf little life to that black coffin as its terminus. It's queer!

Poor [Richard] Hodgson's death was the event, before I left. Absolutely sudden, dropt dead while playing violent handball. Had said to a friend, a week before, that he thought he could count reasonably on twenty-five more years of life. All his work unfinished. No one can over learn those records as he knew them—he would have written certainly two or three solid books. Too bad, too bad! And the manliest, unworldliest, kindliest of human beings. May he still be *energizing* somewhere—it's not a case for *requiescat*.

To James H. Leuba, April 17, 1904 [20]

You hide your own religious cards, so that one does [not] know exactly how to reply to you. You may think there is no God, nothing but Nature, and that all these vague experiences are "poppy-cock" and nerves. Or you may think there is a God, but that the evidence for him must always be indirect—induction from sensations, or "philosophic" reasoning. Most readers, from your evident anti-"pathological" bias, would infer the former; and if that be your state of mind, reply to you is harder. If, however, you do concede the possibility of a God, and your final sentence is not merely diplomatic, argument grows easier. For then, just as the foundation of "natural" knowledge is sensation, due to immediate non-rational influence of either body on body (or, if you are an idealist, of mental fact), so there might be a similar direct influence from God, and our knowledge might be partly at least founded thereon. So far as the feelings of influence harmonized with the rational evidence, the hypothesis that God was the source of influence would be corroborated. Otherwise not. They are bound to harmonize in part, because the mystical and the rational spheres of life are not absolutely discontinuous. It is evident that our intellectual stock in trade plays a suggestive part in our mystical life, and that this suggestive part changes with the progress of our thoughts, so that Vedantic and Christian mysticism have slightly different forms.

If mystical states with all their differences have a common nucleus, then this nucleus should be reckoned a coordinate factor with reason in the building of religious belief. The intellect is interpretative, and critical of its own interpretation, but there must have been a thesis to interpret, and that thesis seems to me the non-rational sense of a "higher" power. Religious men largely agree that this sense has been that of their "best" moments—best not only in passing, but when looked back upon. The notion of it has leaked into mankind from their authority, the rest of us being imitative, just

---

[20] Ibid., Vol. II, pp. 349–51. Also (in part) Henry James, ed., op. cit., Vol. II, pp. 311–12.—ED.

as we are of scientific men's opinions. Now may not this mystical
testimony that there is a God be true, even though his precise
determinations, being so largely "suggestive" contributions of our
rational factor, should widely differ? It seems to me that to throw
out, as you do, the whole mystical life from a hearing, because of
the facility with which it combines with discrepant interpretations,
would be like throwing out the senses, for a similar reason, from
recognition as factors of our "rational" knowledge. . . . It is evident
that our data are complex, however we confine them, and that *sifting* is necessary, be the mystical door left open or kept closed. The
truth is what will survive the sifting—sifting by successive genera-
tions, and "on the whole." Your critical method sifts out everything,
lets nothing survive of mystical authority in God's favor, even
though (let me suppose) you admit the possibility of a God.

I find it preposterous to suppose that if there be a feeling of unseen reality shared by large numbers of best men in their best
moments, responded to by other men in their "deep" moments, good
to live by, strength-giving—I find it preposterous, I say, to suppose
that the goodness of that feeling for living purposes should be held
to carry no objective significance, and especially preposterous if it
combines harmoniously with our otherwise grounded philosophy of
objective truth. *You* say we must consider it a purely subjective
affection. But this opens the whole subject of what the word
"truth" means, and I cannot enter that except to say that if inferences from "good for life" to "true" were on principle forbidden,
not religion but the whole notion of truth would probably have to
be the thing overhauled and revised.

My personal position is simple. I have no living sense of commerce with a God. I envy those who have, for I know that the
addition of such a sense would help me greatly. The Divine, for
my active life, is limited to impersonal and abstract concepts which,
as ideals, interest and determine me, but do so but faintly in comparison with what a feeling of God might effect, if I had one. This,
to be sure, is largely a matter of intensity, but a shade of intensity

may make one's whole center of moral energy shift. Now, although I am so devoid of *Gottesbewusstsein* in the directer and stronger sense, yet there is *something in me* which *makes response* when I hear utterances from that quarter made by others. I recognize the deeper voice. Something tells me:—*"thither lies truth"*—and I am sure it is not old theistic prejudices of infancy. Those in my case were Christian, but I have grown so out of Christianity that entanglement therewith on the part of a mystical utterance has to be abstracted from and overcome, before I can listen. Call this, if you like, my mystical *germ*. It is a very common germ. It creates the rank and file of believers. As it withstands in my case, so it will withstand in most cases, all purely atheistic criticism, but *interpretative* criticism (not of the mere "hysteria" and "nerves" order) it can energetically combine with.

To Carl Stumpf, July 17, 1904 [21]

Your own confidences as to your religious state of mind interest me deeply. I agree that a God of the *totality* must be an unacceptable religious object. But I do not see why there may not be superhuman consciousness of *ideals* of ours, and *that* would be *our* God. It is all very dark. I never felt the *rational* need of immortality as you seem to feel it; but as I grow older I confess that I feel the practical need of it much more than I ever did before; and that combines with reasons, not exactly the same as your own, to give me a growing faith in its reality. I wish that you, some day, anonymously or over your name, would expand and publish these reflections. I think that these states of mind, which are what people live by, are thoroughly normal; but the artificial rationalistic conscience of professional *Gelehrten*, makes them so often ashamed of the public expression of these inner faiths, that the literature of the world is getting too much weighted the other way; and, lacking examples of faith in minds whose intellects they respect, common people grow ashamed to have any faith of their own.

---

[21] Ralph Barton Perry, op. cit., Vol. II, p. 345.—ED.

QUESTIONNAIRE [22]

It is being realized as never before that religion, as one of the most important things in the life both of the community and of the individual, deserves close and extended study. Such study can be of value only if based upon the personal experiences of many individuals. If you are in sympathy with such study and are willing to assist in it, will you kindly write out the answers to the following questions and return them with this questionnaire, as soon as you conveniently can, to James B. Pratt, 20 Shepard Street, Cambridge, Mass.

Please answer the questions at length and in detail. Do not give philosophical generalizations, but your own personal experience.

1. What does religion mean to you personally? Is it
   (1) A belief that something exists? *Yes.*
   (2) An emotional experience? *Not powerfully so, yet a social reality.*
   (3) A general attitude of the will toward God or toward righteousness? *It involves these.*
   (4) Or something else?

If it has several elements, which is for you the most important? *The social appeal for corroboration, consolation, etc., when things are going wrong with my causes (my truth denied), etc.*

2. What do you mean by God? *A combination of Ideality and (final) efficacity*
   (1) Is He a person—if so, what do you mean by His being a person? *He must be cognizant and responsive in some way.*
   (2) Or is He only a Force? *He must do.*
   (3) Or is God an attitude of the Universe toward you? *Yes, but more conscious. "God," to me, is not the only spiritual real-*

---

[22] Sent to James and others in 1904 by Professor James B. Pratt of Williams College. James's answers are printed in italics. Henry James, ed., op. cit., Vol .II, pp. 212–15.—ED.

*ity to believe in. Religion means primarily a universe of
spiritual relations surrounding the earthly practical ones,
not merely relations of "value," but agencies and their activities. I suppose that the chief premise for my hospitality
towards the religious testimony of others is my conviction
that "normal" or "sane" consciousness is so small a part of
actual experience. What e'er be true, it is not true exclusively, as philistine scientific opinion assumes. The other
kinds of consciousness bear witness to a much wider universe of experiences, from which our belief selects and em-
phasizes such parts as best satisfy our needs.*

How do you apprehend His relation to mankind and to
you personally?
If your position on any of these matters is uncertain,
please state the fact.
                                    Uncertain

3. Why do you believe in God? Is it
  (1) From some argument? *Emphatically, no.*
Or (2) Because you have experienced His presence? *No, but
rather because I need it so that it "must" be true.*
Or (3) From authority, such as that of the Bible or of some prophetic person? *Only the whole tradition of religious people, to which something in me makes admiring response.*
Or (4) From any other reason? *Only for the social reasons.*
If from several of these reasons, please indicate carefully
the order of their importance.

4. Or do you not so much *believe* in God as want to *use* Him?
I can't use him very definitely, yet I believe. Do you accept
Him not so much as a real existent Being, but rather as an
ideal to live by? *More as a more powerful ally of my own ideals.*
If you should become thoroughly convinced that there was no
God, would it make any great difference in your life—either
happiness, morality, or in other respects? *Hard to say. It would
surely make some difference.*

5. Is God very real to you, as real as an earthly friend, though
different? *Dimly [real]; not [as an earthly friend].*

Do you feel that you have experienced His presence? If so, please describe what you mean by such an experience. *Never.*

How vague or how distinct is it? How does it affect you mentally and physically?

If you have had no such experience, do you accept the testimony of others who claim to have felt God's presence directly? Please answer this question with special care and in as great detail as possible. *Yes! The whole line of testimony on this point is so strong that I am unable to pooh-pooh it away. No doubt there is a germ in me of something similar that makes response.*

6. Do you pray, and if so, why? That is, is it purely from habit, and social custom, or do you really believe that God hears your prayers? *I can't possibly pray—I feel foolish and artificial.*

Is prayer with you one-sided or two-sided—i.e., do you sometimes feel that in prayer you receive something—such as strength or the divine spirit—from God? Is it a real communion?

7. What do you mean by "spirituality"? *Susceptibility to ideals, but with a certain freedom to indulge in imagination about them. A certain amount of "other worldly" fancy. Otherwise you have mere morality, or "taste."*

Describe a typical spiritual person. *Phillips Brooks.*

8. Do you believe in personal immortality? *Never keenly; but more strongly as I grow older.* If so, why? *Because I am just getting fit to live.*

9. Do you accept the Bible as *authority* in religious matters? Are your religious faith and your religious life based on it? If so, how would your belief in God and your life toward Him and your fellow men be affected by loss of faith in the authority of the Bible? *No. No. No. It is so human a book that I don't see how belief in its divine authorship can survive the reading of it.*

10. What do you mean by a "religious experience"? *Any moment of life that brings the reality of spiritual things more "home" to one.*

To W. Lutoslawski, May 6, 1906 [23]

. . . Your long and beautiful letter about Yoga, etc., greets me on my return from California. It is a most precious human document, and some day, along with that sketch of your religious evolution and other shorter letters of yours, it must see the light of day. What strikes me first in it is the evidence of improved moral "tone"—a calm, firm, sustained joyousness, hard to describe, and striking a new note in your epistles—which is already a convincing argument of the genuineness of the improvement wrought in you by Yoga practices. . . .

You are mistaken about my having tried Yoga discipline—I never meant to suggest that. I have read several books (A.B., by the way, used to be a student of mine, but in spite of many noble qualities, he always had an unbalanced mind—obsessed by certain morbid ideas, etc.), and in the slightest possible way tried breathing exercises. These go terribly against the grain with me, are extremely disagreeable, and even when tried this winter (somewhat perseveringly), to put myself asleep, after lying awake at night, failed to have any soporific effect. What impresses me most in your narrative is the obstinate strength of will shown by yourself and your chela in your methodical abstentions and exercises. When could I hope for such will-power? I find, when my general energy is *in Anspruch genommen* by hard lecturing and other professional work, that then particularly what little *ascetic* energy I have has to be remitted, because the exertion of inhibitory and stimulative will required increases my general fatigue instead of "tonifying" me.

But your sober experience gives me new hopes. Your whole narrative suggests in me the wonder whether the Yoga discipline may not be, after all, in all its phases, simply a methodical way of *waking up deeper levels of will-power than are habitually used,* and thereby increasing the individual's vital tone and energy. I have no doubt whatever that most people live, whether physically, intellectually or morally, in a very restricted circle of their potential

---

[23] Ibid., Vol. II, pp. 252–55.—ED.

being. They *make use* of a very small portion of their possible consciousness, and of their soul's resources in general, much like a
man who, out of his whole bodily organism, should get into a habit
of using and moving only his little finger. Great emergencies and
crises show us how much greater our vital resources are than we
had supposed. Pierre Janet discussed lately some cases of pathological impulsion or obsession in what he has called the "psychasthenic"
type of individual, bulimia, exaggerated walking, morbid love of
feeling pain, and explains the phenomenon as based on the under-
lying *sentiment d'incomplétude,* as he calls it, or *sentiment de
l'irréel* with which these patients are habitually afflicted, and which
they find is abolished by the violent appeal to some exaggerated
activity or other, discovered accidentally perhaps, and then used
habitually. I was reminded of his article in reading your descriptions and prescriptions. May the Yoga practices not be, after all,
methods of getting at our deeper functional levels? And thus only
be substitutes for entirely different crises that may occur in other
individuals, religious crises, indignation-crises, love-crises, etc.?

What you say of diet is in striking accordance with the views
lately made popular by Horace Fletcher—I dare say you have
heard of them. You see I am trying to generalize the Yoga idea,
and redeem it from the pretension that, for example, there is something intrinsically holy in the various grotesque postures of Hatha
Yoya. I have spoken with various Hindus, particularly with three
last winter, one a Yogi and apostle of Vedanta; one a "Christian"
of scientific training; one a Bramo-Somaj professor. The former
made great claims of increase of "power," but admitted that those
who had it could in no way demonstrate it *ad oculos,* to outsiders.
The other two both said that Yoga was less and less frequently
practiced by the more intellectual, and that the old-fashioned *Guru*
was becoming quite a rarity.

I believe with you, fully, that the so-called "normal man" of
commerce, so to speak, the healthy philistine, is a mere extract
from the potentially realizable individual whom he represents, and
that we all have reservoirs of life to draw upon, of which we do

not dream. The practical problem is "how to get at them." And the answer varies with the individual. Most of us never can, or never do get at them. *You* have indubitably got at your own deeper levels by the Yoga methods. I hope that what you have gained will never again be lost to you. You must keep there! *My* deeper levels seem very hard to find—I am so rebellious at all formal and prescriptive methods—a dry and bony *individual*, repelling fusion, and avoiding voluntary exertion. No matter, art is long! and *qui vivra verra*. I shall try fasting and again try breathing—discovering perhaps some individual rhythm that is more tolerable. . . .

To Charles A. Strong, April 9, 1907 [24]

Your warnings against my superstitious tendencies, for such I suppose they are—this is the second heavy one I remember— touch me, but not in the prophetic way, for they don't weaken my trust in the healthiness of my own attitude, which in part (I fancy) is less remote from your own than you suppose. For instance, my "God of things as they are," being part of a pluralistic system, is responsible for only such of them as he knows enough and has enough power to have accomplished. For the rest he is identical with your "ideal" God. The "omniscient" and "omnipotent" God of theology I regard as a disease of the philosophy-shop. But, having thrown away so much of the philosophy-shop, you may ask me why I don't throw away the whole? That would mean too strong a negative will-to-believe for me. It would mean a dogmatic disbelief in any extant consciousness higher than that of the "normal" human mind; and this in the teeth of the extraordinary vivacity of man's psychological commerce with something ideal that *feels as if it* were also actual (I have no such commerce—I wish I had, but I can't close my eyes to its vitality in others); and in the teeth of such analogies as Fechner uses to show that there may be other consciousness than man's. If other, then why not higher and bigger? Why *may* we not be in the universe as our dogs and cats are in our drawingrooms and libraries? It's a will-to-believe on both sides: I

---
[24] Ibid., Vol. II, pp. 269–70.—Ed.

am perfectly willing that others should disbelieve: why should you not be tolerantly interested in the spectacle of my belief? What harm does the little residuum or germ of actuality that I leave in God do? If ideal, why (except on epiphenomenist principles) may he not have got himself at least partly real by this time? I do not believe it to be healthy-minded to nurse the notion that ideals are self-sufficient and require no actualization to make us content. It is a quite unnecessarily heroic form of resignation and sour grapes. Ideals ought to aim at *transformation of reality*—no less! When you defer to what you suppose a certain authority in scientists as confirming these negations, I am surprised. Of all insufficient authorities as to the total nature of reality, give me the "scientists," from Münsterberg up, or down. Their interests are most incomplete and their professional conceit and bigotry immense. I know no narrower sect or club, in spite of their excellent authority in the lines of fact they have explored, and their splendid achievement there. Their only authority *at large* is for *method*—and the pragmatic method completes and enlarges them there. When you shall have read my whole set of lectures (now with the printer, to be out by June 1st) I doubt whether you will find any great harm in the God I patronize—the poor thing is so largely an ideal possibility. Meanwhile I take delight, or shall take delight, in any efforts you may make to negate all superhuman consciousness, for only by these counter-attempts can a finally satisfactory modus vivendi be reached.

To Helen Keller, December 9, 1908 [25]

The great world, *the background*, in all of us, is the world of our *beliefs*. This is the world of the permanencies and the immensities.

---

[25] Ralph Barton Perry, op. cit., Vol. II, p. 455.—ED.

HUMAN IMMORTALITY:
TWO SUPPOSED OBJECTIONS TO THE DOCTRINE [1]

PREFACE TO SECOND EDITION

So many critics have made one and the same objection to the doorway to immortality which my lecture claims to be left open by the "transmission theory" of cerebral action, that I feel tempted, as the book is again going to press, to add a word of explanation.

If our finite personality here below, the objectors say, be due to the transmission through the brain of portions of a pre-existing larger consciousness, all that can remain after the brain expires is the larger consciousness itself as such, with which we should thenceforth be perforce reconfounded, the only means of our existence in finite personal form having ceased.

But this, the critics continue, is the pantheistic idea of immortality, survival, namely, in the soul of the world; not the Christian idea of immortality, which means survival in strictly personal form.

In showing the possibility of a mental life after the brain's death, they conclude, the lecture has thus at the same time shown the impossibility of its identity with the personal life, which is the brain's function.

Now I am myself anything but a pantheist of the monistic pattern; yet for simplicity's sake I did in the lecture speak of the "mother-sea" in terms that must have sounded pantheistic, and suggested that I thought of it myself as a unit. On page 30 [page 302], I even added that future lecturers might prove the loss of some of our personal limitations after death not to be matter for absolute regret. The interpretation of my critics was therefore not un-

---

[1] This was originally delivered as a lecture by William James at Harvard University in 1898 as one of the annual Ingersoll Lectures on Immortality established in 1893 by the will of Miss Caroline Haskell Ingersoll. It was later published as a small book. It is here reprinted with the Preface to the Second Edition, in which James expands somewhat upon concepts expressed in the original lecture, from *The Will to Believe and Other Essays* (New York: Dover Publications, 1956).—ED.

natural; and I ought to have been more careful to guard against its being made.

In note 5 on page 58 [note 7, page 295] I partially guarded against it by saying that the "mother-sea" from which the finite mind is supposed to be strained by the brain, need not be conceived of in pantheistic terms exclusively. There might be, I said, many minds behind the scenes as well as one. The plain truth is that *one may conceive the mental world behind the veil in as individualistic a form as one pleases, without any detriment to the general scheme by which the brain is represented as a transmissive organ.*

If the extreme individualistic view were taken, one's finite mundane consciousness would be an extract from one's larger, truer personality, the latter having even now some sort of reality behind the scenes. And in transmitting it—to keep to our extremely mechanical metaphor, which confessedly throws no light on the actual *modus operandi*—one's brain would also leave effects upon the part remaining behind the veil; for when a thing is torn, both fragments feel the operation.

And just as (to use a very coarse figure) the stubs remain in a check-book whenever a check is used, to register the transaction, so these impressions on the transcendent self might constitute so many vouchers of the finite experiences of which the brain had been the mediator; and ultimately they might form that collection within the larger self of memories of our earthly passage, which is all that, since Locke's day, the continuance of our personal identity beyond the grave has by psychology been recognized to mean.

It is true that all this would seem to have affinities rather with pre-existence and with possible reincarnations than with the Christian notion of immortality. But my concern in the lecture was not to discuss immortality in general. It was confined to showing it to be *not incompatible* with the brain-function theory of our present mundane consciousness. I hold that it is so compatible, and compatible moreover in fully individualized form. The reader would be in accord with everything that the text of my lecture intended to say, were he to assert that every memory and affection of his present life is to be preserved, and that he shall never *in saecula saeculorum* cease to be able to say to himself: "I am the same personal being who in old times upon the earth had those experiences."

HUMAN IMMORTALITY

It is a matter unfortunately too often seen in history to call for much remark, that when a living want of mankind has got itself officially protected and organized in an institution, one of the things which the institution most surely tends to do is to stand in the way of the natural gratification of the want itself. We see this in laws and courts of justice; we see it in ecclesiasticisms; we see it in academies of the fine arts, in the medical and other professions, and we even see it in the universities themselves.

Too often do the place-holders of such institutions frustrate the spiritual purpose to which they were appointed to minister, by the technical light which soon becomes the only light in which they seem able to see the purpose, and the narrow way which is the only way in which they can work in its service.

I confess that I thought of this for a moment when the Corporation of our University invited me last spring to give this Ingersoll lecture. Immortality is one of the great spiritual needs of man. The churches have constituted themselves the official guardians of the need, with the result that some of them actually pretend to accord or to withhold it from the individual by their conventional sacraments—withhold it at least in the only shape in which it can be an object of desire. And now comes the Ingersoll lectureship. Its high-minded founder evidently thought that our University might serve the cause he [2] had at heart more liberally than the churches do, because a university is a body so much less trammeled by traditions and by impossibilities in regard to choice of persons. And yet one of the first things which the University does is to appoint a man like him who stands before you, certainly not

---

[2] William James was, of course, in error in the gender of the pronoun. See footnote on page 279.—ED.

because he is known as an enthusiastic messenger of the future
life, burning to publish the good tidings to his fellow men, but
apparently because he is a University official.

Thinking in this way, I felt at first as if I ought to decline the
appointment. The whole subject of immortal life has its prime
roots in personal feeling. I have to confess that my own personal
feeling about immortality has never been of the keenest order, and
that, among the problems that give my mind solicitude, this one
does not take the very foremost place. Yet there are individuals
with a real passion for the matter, men and women for whom a life
hereafter is a pungent craving, and the thought of it an obsession; and in whom keenness of interest has bred an insight into the
relations of the subject that no one less penetrated with the mystery
of it can attain. Some of these people are known to me. They are
not official personages; they do not speak as the scribes, but as
having direct authority. And surely, if anywhere a prophet clad in
goatskins, and not a uniformed official, should be called to give
inspiration, assurance, and instruction, it would seem to be here,
on such a theme. Office, at any rate, ought not to displace spiritual
calling.

And yet, in spite of these reflections, which I could not avoid
making, I am here tonight, all uninspired and official as I am. I am
sure that prophets clad in goatskins, or, to speak less figuratively,
laymen inspired with emotional messages on the subject, will often
enough be invited by our Corporation to give the Ingersoll lecture
hereafter. Meanwhile, all negative and deadening as the remarks
of a mere professional psychologist like myself may be in comparison with the vital lessons they will give, I am sure, upon mature reflection, that those who have the responsibility of administer-
ing the Ingersoll foundation are in duty bound to let the most
various kinds of official personages take their turn as well. The
subject is really an enormous subject. At the back of Mr. Alger's
"Critical History of the Doctrine of a Future Life," there is a
bibliography of more than five thousand titles of books in which
it is treated. Our Corporation cannot think only of the single lec-

ture: it must think of the whole series of lectures *in futuro*. Single lectures, however emotionally inspired and inspiring they may be, will not be enough. The lectures must remedy each other, so that out of the series there shall emerge a collective literature worthy of the importance of the theme. This unquestionably was what the founder had in mind. He wished the subject to be turned over in all possible aspects, so that at last results might ponderate harmoniously in the true direction. Seen in this long perspective, the Ingersoll foundation calls for nothing so much as for minute division of labor. Orators must take their turn, and prophets; but narrow specialists as well. Theologians of every creed, metaphysicians, anthropologists, and psychologists must alternate with biologists and physicists and psychical researchers—even with mathematicians. If any one of them presents a grain of truth, seen from his point of view, that will remain and accrete with truths brought by the others, his will have been a good appointment.

In the hour that lies before us, then, I shall seek to justify my appointment by offering what seem to me two such grains of truth, two points well fitted, if I am not mistaken, to combine with anything that other lecturers may bring.

These points are both of them in the nature of replies to objections, to difficulties which our modern culture finds in the old notion of a life hereafter—difficulties that I am sure rob the notion of much of its old power to draw belief, in the scientifically cultivated circles to which this audience belong.

The first of these difficulties is relative to the absolute dependence of our spiritual life, as we know it here, upon the brain. One hears not only physiologists, but numbers of laymen who read the popular science books and magazines, saying all about us, How can we believe in life hereafter when science has once for all attained to proving, beyond possibility of escape, that our inner life is a function of that famous material, the so-called "gray matter" of our cerebral convolutions? How can the function possibly persist after its organ has undergone decay?

Thus physiological psychology is what is supposed to bar the way to the old faith. And it is now as a physiological psychologist that I ask you to look at the question with me a little more closely.

It is indeed true that physiological science has come to the conclusion cited; and we must confess that in so doing she has only carried out a little farther the common belief of mankind. Everyone knows that arrests of brain development occasion imbecility, that blows on the head abolish memory or consciousness, and that brain-stimulants and poisons change the quality of our ideas. The anatomists, physiologists, and pathologists have only shown this generally admitted fact of a dependence to be detailed and minute. What the laboratories and hospitals have lately been teaching us is not only that thought in general is one of the brain's functions, but that the various special forms of thinking are functions of special portions of the brain. When we are thinking of things seen, it is our occipital convolutions that are active; when of things heard, it is a certain portion of our temporal lobes; when of things to be spoken, it is one of our frontal convolutions. Professor Flechsig of Leipzig (who perhaps more than anyone may claim to have made the subject his own) considers that in other special convolutions those processes of association go on which permit the more abstract processes of thought to take place. I could easily show you these regions if I had here a picture of the brain.[3] Moreover, the diminished or exaggerated associations of

---

[3] The gaps between the centers first recognized as motor and sensory—gaps which form in man two-thirds of the surface of the hemispheres—are thus positively interpreted by Flechsig as intellectual centers strictly so called. (Compare his *Gehirn und Seele*, the *Ausgabe*, 1896, p. 23.) They have, he considers, a common type of microscopic structure, and the fibers connected with them are a month later in gaining their medullary sheath than are the fibers connected with the other centers. When disordered, they are the starting-point of the insanities, properly so called. Already Wernicke had defined insanity as disease of the organ of association, without so definitely pretending to circumscribe the latter—compare his *Grundriss der Psychiatrie*, 1894, p. 7. Flechsig goes so far as to say that he finds a difference of symptoms in general paralytics according as their frontal or their more posterior association centers are diseased. Where it is the frontal centers, the patient's consciousness of self is more deranged than is his perception of purely objective relations. Where the posterior associative regions suffer, it is rather the patient's system of objective ideas that undergoes disintegration (loc. cit., pp. 89–91). In rodents Flechsig thinks there is a com-

what this author calls the *Körperfühlsphäre* with the other regions accounts, according to him, for the complexion of our emotional life, and eventually decides whether one shall be a callous brute or criminal, an unbalanced sentimentalist, or a character accessible to feeling, and yet well poised. Such special opinions may have to be corrected; yet so firmly established do the main positions worked out by the anatomists, physiologists, and pathologists of the brain appear, that the youth of our medical schools are everywhere taught unhesitatingly to believe them. The assurance that observation will go on to establish them ever more and more minutely is the inspirer of all contemporary research. And almost any of our young psychologists will tell you that only a few belated scholastics, or possibly some crack-brained theosophist or psychical researcher, can be found holding back, and still talking as if mental phenomena might exist as independent variables in the world.

For the purposes of my argument, now, I wish to adopt this general doctrine as if it were established absolutely, with no possibility of restriction. During this hour I wish you also to accept it as a postulate, whether you think it incontrovertibly established or not; so I beg you to agree with me today in subscribing to the great psycho-physiological formula: *Thought is a function of the brain.*

The question is, then, Does this doctrine logically compel us to disbelieve in immortality? Ought it to force every truly consistent thinker to sacrifice his hopes of an hereafter to what he takes to be his duty of accepting all the consequences of a scientific truth?

---

plete absence of association centers—the sensory centers touch each other. In carnivora and the lower monkeys the latter centers still exceed the association centers in volume. Only in the katarhinal apes do we begin to find anything like the human type (p. 84).

In his little pamphlet, *Die Grenzen geistiger Gesundheit und Krankheit,* Leipzig, 1896, Flechsig ascribes the moral insensibility which is found in certain criminals to a diminution of internal pain-feeling due to degeneration of the *Körperfühlsphäre,* that extensive anterior region first so named by Munk, in which he lays the seat of all the emotions and of the consciousness of self (*Gehirn und Seele,* pp. 62–68; *Die Grenzen,* etc., pp. 31–39, 48). I give these references to Flechsig for concreteness' sake, not because his views are irreversibly made out.—W. J.

Most persons imbued with what one may call the puritanism of science would feel themselves bound to answer this question with a yes. If any medically or psychologically bred young scientists feel otherwise, it is probably in consequence of that incoherency of mind of which the majority of mankind happily enjoy the privilege. At one hour scientists, at another they are Christians or common men, with the will to live burning hot in their breasts; and, holding thus the two ends of the chain, they are careless of the intermediate connection. But the more radical and uncompromising disciple of science makes the sacrifice, and, sorrowfully or not, according to his temperament, submits to giving up his hopes of heaven.[4]

---

[4] So widespread is this conclusion in positivistic circles, so abundantly is it expressed in conversation, and so frequently implied in things that are written, that I confess that my surprise was great when I came to look into books for a passage explicitly denying immortality on physiological grounds, which I might quote to make my text more concrete. I was unable to find anything blunt and distinct enough to serve. I looked through all the books that would naturally suggest themselves, with no effect; and I vainly asked various psychological colleagues. And yet I should almost have been ready to take oath that I had read several such passages of the most categoric sort within the last decade. Very likely this is a false impression, and it may be with this opinion as with many others. The atmosphere is full of them; many a writer's pages logically presuppose and involve them; yet, if you wish to refer a student to an express and radical statement that he may employ as a text to comment on, you find almost nothing that will do. In the present case there are plenty of passages in which, in a general way, mind is said to be conterminous with brain-function, but hardly one in which the author thereupon explicitly denies the possibility of immortality. The best one I have found is perhaps this: "Not only consciousness, but every stirring of life, depends on functions that go out like a flame when nourishment is cut off. . . . The phenomena of consciousness correspond, element for element, to the operations of special parts of the brain. . . . The destruction of any piece of the apparatus involved in, lose if material run or other of the vital operations; and the consequence is that, as far as life extends, we have before us only an organic function, not a *Ding-an-sich*, or an expression of that imaginary entity the Soul. This fundamental proposition . . . carries with it the denial of the immortality of the soul, since, where no soul exists, its mortality or immortality cannot be raised as a question. . . . The function fills its time—the flame illuminates and therein gives out its whole being. That is all; and verily that is enough. . . . Sensation has its definite organic conditions, and, as these decay with the natural decay of life, it is quite impossible for a mind accustomed to deal with realities to suppose any capacity of sensation as surviving when the machinery of our natural existence has stopped." (E. Duhring: *der Werth des Lebens,* 3d edition, pp. 48, 168.)—W. J.

This, then, is the objection to immortality; and the next thing in order for me is to try to make plain to you why I believe that it has in strict logic no deterrent power. I must show you that the fatal consequence is not coercive, as is commonly imagined; and that, even though our soul's life (as here below it is revealed to us) may be in literal strictness the function of a brain that perishes, yet it is not at all impossible, but on the contrary quite possible, that the life may still continue when the brain itself is dead.

The supposed impossibility of its continuing comes from too superficial a look at the admitted fact of functional dependence. The moment we inquire more closely into the notion of functional dependence, and ask ourselves, for example, how many kinds of functional dependence there may be, we immediately perceive that there is one kind at least that does not exclude a life hereafter at all. The fatal conclusion of the physiologist flows from his assuming offhand another kind of functional dependence, and treating it as the only imaginable kind.[5]

---

[5] The philosophically instructed reader will notice that I have all along been placing myself at the ordinary dualistic point of view of natural science and of common sense. From this point of view mental facts like feelings are made of one kind of stuff or substance, physical facts of another. An absolute phenomenism, not believing such a dualism to be ultimate, may possibly end by solving some of the problems that are insoluble when propounded in dualistic terms. Meanwhile, since the physiological objection to immortality has arisen on the ordinary dualistic plane of thought, and since absolute phenomenism has as yet said nothing articulate enough to count about the matter, it is proper that my reply to the objection should be expressed in dualistic terms—leaving me free, of course, on any later occasion to make an attempt, if I wish, to transcend them and use different categories.

Now, on the dualistic assumption, one cannot see more than two really different sorts of dependence of our mind on our brain: Either

(1) The brain brings into being the very stuff of consciousness of which our mind consists; or else

(2) Consciousness pre-exists as an entity, and the various brains give to it its various special forms.

If supposition 2 be the true one, and the stuff of mind pre-exists, there are, again, only two ways of conceiving that our brain confers upon it the specifically human form. It may exist

(a) In disseminated particles; and then our brains are organs of concentration, organs for combining and massing these into resultant minds of personal form. Or it may exist

(b) In vaster unities (absolute "world-soul," or something less); and then

When the physiologist who thinks that his science cuts off all hope of immortality pronounces the phrase, "Thought is a function of the brain," he thinks of the matter just as he thinks when he says, "Steam is a function of the tea-kettle," "Light is a function of the electric circuit," "Power is a function of the moving water-fall." In these latter cases the several material objects have the function of inwardly creating or engendering their effects, and their function must be called *productive* function. Just so, he thinks,

---

our brains are organs for separating it into parts and giving them finite form. There are thus three possible theories of the brain's function, and no more. We may name them, severally,

1. The theory of production;
2a. The theory of combination;
2b. The theory of separation.

In the text of the lecture, theory number 2b (specified more particularly as the transmission theory) is defended against theory number 1. Theory 2a, otherwise known as the mind-dust or mind-stuff theory, is left entirely unnoticed for lack of time. I also leave it uncriticized in these notes, having already considered it, as fully as the so-far published forms of it may seem to call for, in my work, *The Principles of Psychology*, New York, Holt & Co., 1892, Chapter VI. I may say here, however, that Professor W. K. Clifford, one of the ablest champions of the combination theory, and originator of the useful term "mind-stuff" considers that theory incompatible with individual immortality, and in his review of Stewart's and Tait's book, *The Unseen Universe*, thus expresses his conviction:—

"The laws connecting consciousness with changes in the brain are very definite and precise, and their necessary consequences are not to be evaded. . . . Consciousness is a complex thing made up of elements, a stream of feelings. The action of the brain is also a complex thing made up of elements, a stream of nerve-messages. For every feeling in consciousness there is at the same time a nerve-message in the brain. . . . Consciousness is not a simple thing, but a complex; it is the combination of feelings into a stream. It exists at the same time with the combination of nerve-messages into a stream. If individual feeling always goes with individual nerve-message, if combination or stream of feelings always goes with stream of nerve-messages, does it not follow that, when the stream of nerve-messages is broken up, the stream of feelings will be broken up also, will no longer form a consciousness? Does it not follow that, when the messages themselves are broken up, the individual feelings will be resolved into still simpler elements? The force of this evidence is not to be weakened by any number of spiritual bodies. Inexorable facts connect our consciousness with this body that we know; and that not merely as a whole, but the parts of it are connected severally with parts of our brain-action. If there is any similar connection with a spiritual body, it only follows that the spiritual body must die at the same time with the natural one." (*Lectures and Essays*, Vol. i, pp. 247–49. Compare also passages of similar purport in Vol. ii, pp. 65–70.)—W. J.

it must be with the brain. Engendering consciousness in its interior, much as it engenders cholesterin and creatin and carbonic acid, its relation to our soul's life must also be called productive function. Of course, if such production be the function, then when the organ perishes, since the production can no longer continue, the soul must surely die. Such a conclusion as this is indeed inevitable from that particular conception of the facts.[6]

---

[6] The theory of production, or materialistic theory, seldom ventures to formulate itself very distinctly. Perhaps the following passage from Cabanis is as explicit as anything one can find:—

"To acquire a just idea of the operations from which thought results, we must consider the brain as a particular organ specially destined to produce it; just as the stomach and intestines are destined to operate digestion, the liver to filter bile, the parotid and maxillary glands to prepare the salivary juices. The impressions, arriving in the brain, force it to enter into activity; just as the alimentary materials, falling into the stomach, excite it to a more abundant secretion of gastric juice, and to the movements which result in their own solution. The function proper to the first organ is that of receiving [*percevoir*] each particular impression, of attaching signs to it, of combining the different impressions, of comparing them with each other, of drawing from them judgments and resolves; just as the function of the other organ is to act upon the nutritive substances whose presence excites it, to dissolve them, and to assimilate their juices to our nature.

"Do you say that the organic movements by which the brain exercises these functions are unknown? I reply that the action by which the nerves of the stomach determine the different operations which constitute digestion, and the manner in which they confer so active a solvent power upon the gastric juice, are equally hidden from our scrutiny. We see the food-materials fall into this viscus with their own proper qualities; we see them emerge with new qualities, and we infer that the stomach is really the author of this alteration. Similarly we see the impressions reaching the brain by the intermediation of the nerves; they then are isolated and without coherence. The viscus enters into action; it acts upon them, and soon it emits [*renvoie*] them metamorphosed into ideas, to which the language of physiognomy or gesture, or the signs of speech and writing, give an outward expression. We conclude, then, with an equal certitude, that the brain digests, as it were, the impressions; that it performs organically the secretion of thought." [*Rapports du Physique et du Moral*, 8th edition, 1844, p. 137.]

It is to the ambiguity of the word "impression" that such an account owes whatever plausibility it may seem to have. More recent forms of the production theory have shown a tendency to liken thought to a "force" which the brain exerts, or to a "state" into which it passes. Herbert Spencer, for instance, writes:—

"The law of metamorphosis, which holds among the physical forces, holds equally between them and the mental forces. . . . How this metamorphosis takes place; how a force existing as motion, heat, or light can become a mode

But in the world of physical nature productive function of this sort is not the only kind of function with which we are familiar. We have also releasing or permissive function; and we have transmissive function.

The trigger of a crossbow has a releasing function: it removes the obstacle that holds the string, and lets the bow fly back to its natural shape. So when the hammer falls upon a detonating compound. By knocking out the inner molecular obstructions, it lets the constituent gases resume their normal bulk, and so permits the explosion to take place.

In the case of a colored glass, a prism, or a refracting lens, we

---

of consciousness; how it is possible for aerial vibrations to generate the sensation we call sound, or for the forces liberated by chemical changes in the brain to give rise to emotion—these are mysteries which it is impossible to fathom. But they are not profounder mysteries than the transformations of the physical forces into each other." (*First Principles*, 2nd Edition, p. 217.)

So Büchner says: "Thinking must be regarded as a special mode of general natural motion, which is as characteristic of the substance of the central nervous elements as the motion of contraction is of the nerve-substance, or the motion of light is of the universal-ether. . . . That thinking is and must be a mode of motion is not merely a postulate of logic, but a proposition which has of late been demonstrated experimentally. . . . Various ingenious experiments have proved that the swiftest thought that we are able to evolve occupies at least the eighth or tenth part of a second." (*Force and Matter*, New York, 1891, p. 241.)

Heat and light being modes of motion, "phosphorescence" and "incandescence" are phenomena to which consciousness has been likened by the production theory: "As one sees a metallic rod, placed in a glowing furnace, gradually heat itself, and—as the undulations of the caloric grow more and more frequent —pass successively from the shades of bright red to dark red [*sic*], to white, and develop, as its temperature rises, heat and light,—so the living sensitive cells, in presence of the incitations that solicit them, exalt themselves progressively as to their most interior sensibility, enter into a phase of erethism, and at a certain number of vibrations, act [*dégagent*] pain as a physiological expression of this same sensibility superheated to a red while." (*Ì. Luys: Le Cerveau*, p. 91.)

In a similar vein Mr. Percival Lowell writes: "When we have, as we say, an idea, what happens inside of us is probably something like this: the neural current of molecular change passes up the nerves, and through the ganglia reaches at last the cortical cells. . . . When it reaches the cortical cells, it finds a set of molecules which are not so accustomed to this special change. The current encounters resistance, and in overcoming this resistance it causes the cells to glow. This white-heating of the cells we call consciousness. Consciousness, in short, is probably nerve-glow." [*Occult Japan*, Boston, 1895, p. 311.]—W. J.

have transmissive function. The energy of light, no matter how produced, is by the glass sifted and limited in color, and by the lens or prism determined to a certain path and shape. Similarly, the keys of an organ have only a transmissive function. They open successively the various pipes and let the wind in the air-chest escape in various ways. The voices of the various pipes are constituted by the columns of air trembling as they emerge. But the air is not engendered in the organ. The organ proper, as distinguished from its air-chest, is only an apparatus for letting portions of it loose upon the world in these peculiarly limited shapes.

My thesis now is this: that, when we think of the law that thought is a function of the brain, we are not required to think of productive function only; *we are entitled also to consider permissive or transmissive function.* And this the ordinary psychophysiologist leaves out of his account.

Suppose, for example, that the whole universe of material things —the furniture of earth and choir of heaven—should turn out to be a mere surface-veil of phenomena, hiding and keeping back the world of genuine realities. Such a supposition is foreign neither to common sense nor to philosophy. Common sense believes in realities behind the veil even too superstitiously; and idealistic philosophy declares the whole world of natural experience, as we get it, to be but a time-mask, shattering or refracting the one infinite Thought which is the sole reality into those millions of finite streams of consciousness known to us as our private selves.

> Life, like a dome of many-colored glass,
> Stains the white radiance of eternity.

Suppose, now, that this were really so, and suppose, moreover, that the dome, opaque enough at all times to the full super-solar blaze, could at certain times and places grow less so, and let certain beams pierce through into this sublunary world. These beams would be so many finite rays, so to speak, of consciousness, and they would vary in quantity and quality as the opacity varied in degree. Only at particular times and places would it seem that, as a matter of fact, the veil of nature can grow thin and rupturable enough for such effects to occur. But in those places gleams, however finite and unsatisfying, of the absolute life of the universe, are from time to time vouchsafed. Glows of feeling, glimpses of insight, and streams of knowledge and perception float into our finite world.

Admit now that *our brains* are such thin and half-transparent places in the veil. What will happen? Why, as the white radiance comes through the dome, with all sorts of staining and distortion imprinted on it by the glass, or as the air now comes through my glottis determined and limited in its force and quality of its vibrations by the peculiarities of those vocal chords which form its gate of egress and shape it into my personal voice, even so the genuine matter of reality, the life of souls as it is in its fullness, will break through our several brains into this world in all sorts of restricted forms, and with all the imperfections and queernesses that characterize our finite individualities here below.

According to the state in which the brain finds itself, the barrier of its obstructiveness may also be supposed to rise or fall. It sinks so low, when the brain is in full activity, that a comparative flood of spiritual energy pours over. At other times, only such occasional waves of thought as heavy sleep permits get by. And when finally a brain stops acting altogether, or decays, that special stream of consciousness which it subserved will vanish entirely from this natural world. But the sphere of being that supplied the consciousness would still be intact; and in that more real world with which, even whilst here, it was continuous, the consciousness might, in ways unknown to us, continue still.

You see that, on all these suppositions, our soul's life, as we here know it, would none the less in literal strictness be the function of the brain. The brain would be the independent variable, the mind would vary dependently on it. But such dependence on the brain for this natural life would in no wise make immortal life impossible—it might be quite compatible with supernatural life behind the veil hereafter.

As I said, then, the fatal consequence is not coercive, the conclusion which materialism draws being due solely to its onesided way of taking the word "function." And, whether we care or not for immortality in itself, we ought, as mere critics doing police duty among the vagaries of mankind, to insist on the illogicality of a denial based on the flat ignoring of a palpable alternative. How much more ought we to insist, as lovers of truth, when the denial is that of such a vital hope of mankind!

In strict logic, then, the fangs of cerebralistic materialism are drawn. My words ought consequently already to exert a releasing function on your hopes. You *may* believe henceforward, whether you care to profit by the permission or not. But, as this is a very abstract argument, I think it will help its effect to say a word or two about the more concrete conditions of the case.

All abstract hypotheses sound unreal; and the abstract notion that our brains are colored lenses in the wall of nature, admitting light from the super-solar source, but at the same time tingeing and restricting it, has a thoroughly fantastic sound. What is it, you may ask, but a foolish metaphor? And how can such a function be imagined? Isn't the common materialistic notion vastly simpler? Is not consciousness really more comparable to a sort of steam, or perfume, or electricity, or nerve-glow, generated on the spot in its own peculiar vessel? Is it not more rigorously scientific to treat the brain's function as function of production?

The immediate reply is, that, if we are talking of science positively understood, function can mean nothing more than bare concomitant variation. When the brain-activities change in one way, consciousness changes in another; when the currents pour through the occipital lobes, consciousness *sees* things; when through the lower frontal region, consciousness *says* things to itself; when they stop, she goes to sleep, etc. In strict science, we can only write down the bare fact of concomitance; and all talk about either production or transmission, as the mode of taking place, is pure superadded hypothesis, and metaphysical hypothesis at that, for we can frame no more notion of the details on the one alternative than on the other. Ask for any indication of the exact process either of transmission or of production, and science confesses her imagination to be bankrupt. She has, so far, not the least glimmer of a conjecture or suggestion—not even a bad verbal metaphor or pun to offer. *Ignoramus, ignorabimus,* is what most physiologists, in the words of one of their number, will say here. The production of such a thing as consciousness in the brain, they will reply with the late Berlin professor of physiology, is the absolute world-enigma— something so paradoxical and abnormal as to be a stumbling block to nature, and almost a self-contradiction. Into the mode of production of steam in a tea-kettle we have conjectural insight, for the terms that change are physically homogeneous one with another, and we can easily imagine the case to consist of nothing but alterations of molecular motion. But in the production of consciousness by the brain, the terms are heterogeneous natures altogether; and as far as our understanding goes, it is as great a miracle as if we said, Thought is "spontaneously generated," or "created out of nothing."

The theory of production is therefore not a jot more simple or credible in itself than any other conceivable theory. It is only a little more popular. All that one need do, therefore, if the ordinary materialist should challenge one to explain how the brain *can* be an organ for limiting and determining to a certain form a consciousness elsewhere produced, is to retort with a *tu quoque,* asking him in turn to explain how it can be an organ for producing consciousness out of whole cloth. For polemic purposes, the two theories are thus exactly on a par.

But if we consider the theory of transmission in a wider way, we see that it has certain positive superiorities, quite apart from its connection with the immortality question.

Just how the process of transmission may be carried on, is indeed unimaginable; but the outer relations, so to speak, of the process, encourage our belief. Consciousness in this process does not have to be generated *de novo* in a vast number of places. It exists already, behind the scenes, coeval with the world. The transmission theory not only avoids in this way multiplying miracles, but it puts itself in touch with general idealistic philosophy better than the production theory does. It should always be reckoned a good thing when science and philosophy thus meet.[7]

It puts itself also in touch with the conception of a "threshold"— a word with which, since Fechner wrote his book called *Psychophysik*, the so-called "new Psychology" has rung. Fechner imagines as the condition of consciousness a certain kind of psychophysical movement, as he terms it. Before consciousness can come, a certain degree of activity in the movement much be reached. This requisite degree is called the "threshold"; but the height of the threshold varies under different circumstances: it may rise or fall. When it falls, as in states of great lucidity, we grow conscious of things of which we should be unconscious at other times; when it rises, as in drowsiness, consciousness sinks in amount. This rising and lowering of a psychophysical threshold exactly conform to our notion of a permanent obstruction to the transmission of consciousness, which obstruction may, in our brains, grow alternately greater or less.[8]

---

[7] The transmission theory connects itself very naturally with that whole tendency of thought known as transcendentalism. Emerson, for example, writes: "We lie in the lap of immense intelligence, which makes us receivers of its truth and organs of its activity. When we discern justice, when we discern truth, we do nothing of ourselves, but allow a passage to its beams." [*Self-Reliance*, p. 56.] But it is not necessary to identify the consciousness postulated in the lecture, as pre-existing behind the scenes, with the Absolute Mind of transcendental Idealism, although, indeed, the notion of it might lead in that direction. The Absolute Mind of transcendental Idealism is one integral Unit, one single World-mind. For the purposes of my lecture, however, there might be many minds behind the scenes as well as one. All that the transmission theory absolutely requires is that they should transcend *our* minds,—which thus come from *something* mental that pre-exists, and is larger than themselves.—W. J.

[8] Fechner's conception of a "psycho-physical threshold" as connected with his "wave-scheme" is little known to English readers. I accordingly subjoin it, in his own words, abridged:—

"The psychically one is connected with a physically many; the physically many contract psychically into a one, a simple, or at least a more simple. Otherwise expressed: the psychically unified and simple are resultants of physical multiplicity; the physically manifold gives unified or simple results. . . .

"The facts which are grouped together under these expressions, and which

⁸ *Continued*

give them their meaning, are as follows: . . . With our two hemispheres we think singly; with the identical parts of our two retinae we see singly. . . . The simplest sensation of light or sound in us is connected with processes which, since they are started and kept up by outer oscillations, must themselves be somehow of an oscillatory nature, although we are wholly unaware of the separate phases and oscillations. . . .

"It is certain, then, that some unified or simple psychic resultants depend on physical multiplicity. But, on the other hand, it is equally certain that the multiplicities of the physical world do not always combine into a simple psychical resultant,—no, not even when they are compounded in a single bodily system. Whether they may not nevertheless combine into a *unified* resultant is a matter for opinion, since one is always free to ask whether the entire world, as such, may not have some unified psychic resultant. But of any such resultant we at least have no consciousness. . . .

"For brevity's sake, let us distinguish *psychophysical continuity* and *discontinuity* from each other. Continuity, let us say, takes place so far as a physical manifold gives a unified or simple psychic resultant; discontinuity, so far as it gives a distinguishable multiplicity of such resultants. Inasmuch, however, as, within the unity of a more general consciousness or phenomenon of consciousness, there still may be a multiplicity distinguished, the continuity of a more general consciousness does not exclude the discontinuity of particular phenomena.

"One of the most important problems and tasks of Psycho-physics now is this: to determine the conditions (*Gesichtspunkte*) under which the cases of continuity and of discontinuity occur.

"Whence comes it that different organisms have separate consciousnesses, although their bodies are just as much connected by general Nature as the parts of a single organism are with each other, and these latter give a single conscious resultant? Of course we can say that the connection is more intimate between the parts of an organism than between the organisms of Nature. But what do we mean by a more intimate connection? Can an absolute difference of result depend on anything so relative? And does not Nature as a whole show as strict a connection as any organism does—yea, one even more indissoluble? And the same questions come up within each organism. How comes it that, with different nerve-fibers of touch and sight, we distinguish different space-points, but with one fiber distinguish nothing, although the different fibers are connected in the brain just as much as the parts are in the single fiber? We may again call the latter connection the more *intimate,* but then the same sort of question will arise again.

"Unquestionably the problem which here lies before Psycho-physics cannot be sharply unanswered; but we may establish a general point of view for its treatment, consistently with what we laid down in a former chapter on the relations of more general with more particular phenomena of consciousness."

[The earlier passage is here inserted:] "The essential principle is this: That human psycho-physical activity must exceed a certain intensity for any waking consciousness at all to occur, and that during the waking state any particular specification of the said activity (whether spontaneous or due to stimulation), which is capable of occasioning a particular specification of consciousness, must exceed in its turn a certain further degree of intensity for the consciousness actually to arise. . . .

[8] *Continued*

"This state of things (in itself a mere fact needing no picture) may be made clearer by an image or scheme, and also more concisely spoken of. Imagine the whole psycho-physical activity of man to be a wave, and the degree of this activity to be symbolized by the height of the wave above a horizontal basal line or surface, to which every psycho-physically active point contributes an ordinate. . . . The whole form and evolution of the consciousness will then depend on the rising and falling of this wave; the intensity of the consciousness at any time on the wave's height at that time; and the height must always *somewhere* exceed a certain limit, which we will call a *threshold*, if waking consciousness is to exist at all.

"Let us call this wave the *total wave,* and the threshold in question the *principal threshold."*

[Since our various states of consciousness recur, some in long, some in short periods], "we may represent such a long period as that of the slowly fluctuating condition of our general wakefulness and the general direction of our attention as a wave that slowly changes the place of its summit. If we call this the *under-wave,* then the movements of shorter period, on which the more special conscious states depend, can be symbolized by wavelets superposed upon the under-wave, and we can call these *over-waves*. They will cause all sorts of modifications of the under-wave's surface, and the total wave will be the resultant of both sets of waves.

"The greater, now, the strength of the movements of short period, the amplitude of the oscillations of the psycho-physical activity, the higher will the crests of the wavelets that represent them rise above, and the lower will their valleys sink below the surface of the under-wave that bears them. And these heights and depressions must exceed a certain limit of quantity which we may call the *upper threshold,* before the special mental state which is correlated with them can appear in consciousness" [pp. 454–56].

"So far now as we symbolize any system of psycho-physical activity, to which a generally unified or principal consciousness corresponds, by the image of a total wave rising with its crest above a certain 'threshold,' we have a means of schematizing in a single diagram the physical solidarity of all these psycho-physical systems throughout Nature, together with their pyscho-physical discontinuity. For we need only draw all the waves so that they run into each other below the threshold, whilst above it they appear distinct, as in the figure below.

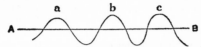

"In this figure *a, b, c* stand for three organisms, or rather for the total waves of psycho-physical activity of three organisms, whilst A B represents the threshold. In each wave the part that rises above the threshold is an integrated thing, and is connected with a single consciousness. Whatever lies below the threshold, being unconscious, separates the conscious crests, although it is still the means of physical connection.

"In general terms: wherever a psycho-physical total wave is continuous with itself above the threshold, there we find the unity or identity of a consciousness, inasmuch as the connection of the psychical phenomena which correspond to the parts of the wave also appears in consciousness. Whenever, on the contrary, total waves are disconnected, or connected only underneath the thresh-

The transmission theory also puts itself in touch with a whole class of experiences that are with difficulty explained by the production theory. I refer to those obscure and exceptional phenomena reported at all times throughout human history, which the "psychical researchers," with Mr. Frederic Myers at their head, are doing so much to rehabilitate; [9] such phenomena, namely, as religious conversions, providential leadings in answer to prayer, instantaneous healings, premonitions, apparitions at time of death, clairvoyant visions or impressions, and the whole range of mediumistic capacities, to say nothing of still more exceptional and incomprehensible things. If all our human thought be a function of the brain, then of course, if any of these things are facts—and to my own mind

[8] *Continued*

old, the corresponding consciousness is broken, and no connection between its several parts appears. More briefly: consciousness is continuous or discontinuous, unified or discrete, according as the psycho-physical total waves that subserve it are themselves continuous or discontinuous above the threshold. . . .

"If, in the diagram, we should raise the entire line of waves so that not only the crests but the valleys appeared above the threshold, then these latter would appear only as depressions in one great continuous wave above the threshold, and the discontinuity of the consciousness would be converted into continuity. We of course cannot bring this about. We might also squeeze the wave together so that the valleys should be pressed up, and the crests above the threshold flow into a line; then the discretely-feeling organisms would have become a singly-feeling organism. This, again, Man cannot voluntarily bring about, but it is brought about in Man's nature. His two halves, the right one and the left one, are thus united; and the number of segments of radiates and articulates show that more than two parts can be thus psycho-physically conjoined. One need only cut them asunder, *i. e.* interpolate another part of nature between them under the threshold, and they break into two separately conscious beings." . . . (*Elemente der Psychophysik,* 1860, Vol. ii, pp. 526–30.)

One sees easily how, on Fechner's wave scheme, a world-soul may be expressed. All psychological activity being continuous "below the threshold," the consciousness might also become continuous if the threshold sank low enough to uncover all the waves. The threshold throughout in general is, however, very high, so the consciousness that gets over it is of the discontinuous form.—W. J.

[9] See the long series of articles by Mr. Myers in the *Proceedings of the Society for Psychical Research,* beginning in the third volume with automatic writing, and ending in the latest volumes with the higher manifestations of knowledge by mediums. Mr. Myers's theory of the whole range of phenomena is, that our normal consciousness is in continuous connection with a greater consciousness of which we do not know the extent, and to which he gives, in its relation to the particular person, the not very felicitous name—though no better one has been proposed—of his or her "subliminal" self.—W. J.

some of them are facts—we may not suppose that they can occur without preliminary brain action. But the ordinary production theory of consciousness is knit up with a peculiar notion of how brain action *can* occur—that notion being that all brain action, without exception, is due to a prior action, immediate or remote, of the bodily sense-organs *on* the brain. Such action makes the brain produce sensations and mental images, and out of the sensations and images the higher forms of thought and knowledge in their turn are framed. As transmissionists, we also must admit this to be the condition of all our usual thought. Sense-action is what lowers the brain-barrier. My voice and aspect, for instance, strike upon your ears and eyes; your brain thereupon becomes more pervious, and an awareness on your part of what I say and who I am slips into this world from the world behind the veil. But, in the mysterious phenomena to which I allude, it is often hard to see where the sense-organs can come in. A medium, for example, will show knowledge of his sitter's private affairs which it seems impossible he should have acquired through sight or hearing, or inference therefrom. Or you will have an apparition of someone who is now dying hundreds of miles away. On the production theory one does not see from what sensations such odd bits of knowledge are produced. On the transmission theory, they don't have to be "produced"—they exist ready-made in the transcendental world, and all that is needed is an abnormal lowering of the brain-threshold to let them through. In cases of conversion, in providential leadings, sudden mental healings, etc., it seems to the subjects themselves of the experience as if a power from without, quite different from the ordinary action of the senses or of the sense-led mind, came into their life, as if the latter suddenly opened into that greater life in which it has its source. The word "influx," used in Swedenborgian circles, well describes this impression of new insight, or new willingness, sweeping over us like a tide. All such experiences, quite paradoxical and meaningless on the production theory, fall very naturally into place on the other theory. We need only suppose the continuity of our consciousness with a mother sea, to allow for exceptional waves occasionally pouring over the dam. Of course the causes of these odd lowerings of the brain's threshold still remain a mystery on any terms.

Add, then, this advantage to the transmission theory—an advantage which I am well aware that some of you will not rate very high—and also add the advantage of not conflicting with a life hereafter, and I hope you will agree with me that it has many points of superiority to the more familiar theory. It is a theory which, in the history of opinion on such matters, has never been wholly left out of account, though never developed at any great length. In the great orthodox philosophic tradition, the body is treated as an essential condition to the soul's life in this world of sense; but after death, it is said, the soul is set free, and becomes a purely intellectual and non-appetitive being. Kant expresses this idea in terms that come singularly close to those of our transmission theory. The death of the body, he says, may indeed be the end of the sensational use of our mind, but only the beginning of the intellectual use. "The body," he continues, "would thus be, not the cause of our thinking, but merely a condition restrictive thereof, and, although essential to our sensuous and animal consciousness, it may be regarded as an impeder of our pure spiritual life." [10] And in a recent book of great suggestiveness and power, less well known as yet than it deserves—I mean *Riddles of the Sphinx*, by Mr. F. C. S. Schiller of Oxford, late of Cornell University—the transmission theory is defended at some length.[11]

---

[10] See *Kritik der reinen Vernunft*, second edition, p. 809.

[11] I subjoin a few extracts from Mr. Schiller's work: "Matter is an admirably calculated machinery for regulating, limiting, and restraining the consciousness which it encases. . . . If the material encasement be coarse and simple, as in the lower organisms, it permits only a little intelligence to permeate through it; if it is delicate and complex, it leaves more pores and exists, as it were, for the manifestations of consciousness. . . . On this analogy, then, we may say that the lower animals are still entranced in the lower stage of brute *lethargy*, while we have passed into the higher phase of *somnambulism*, which already permits us strange glimpses of a lucidity that divines the realities of a transcendent world. And this gives the final answer to Materialism: it consists in showing in detail . . . that Materialism is a hysteron proteron, a putting of the cart before the horse, which may be rectified by just inverting the connection between Matter and Consciousness. Matter is not that which

But still, you will ask, in what positive way does this theory help us to realize our immortality in imagination? What we all wish to keep is just these individual restrictions, these selfsame tendencies and peculiarities that define us to ourselves and others, and constitute our identity, so called. Our finitenesses and limitations seem to be our personal essence; and when the finiting organ drops away, and our several spirits revert to their original source and resume their unrestricted condition, will they then be anything like those sweet streams of feeling which we know, and which even now our brains are sifting out from the great reservoir for our

---

produces Consciousness, but that which *limits* it, and confines its intensity within certain limits: material organization does not construct consciousness out of arrangements of atoms, but contracts its manifestation within the sphere which it permits. This explanation . . . admits the connection of Matter and Consciousness, but contends that the course of interpretation must proceed in the contrary direction. Thus it will fit the facts alleged in favor of Materialism equally well, besides enabling us to understand facts which Materialism rejected as 'supernatural.' It explains the lower by the higher, Matter by Spirit, instead of *vice versa,* and thereby attains to an explanation which is ultimately tenable, instead of one which is ultimately absurd. And it is an explanation the possibility of which no evidence in favor of Materialism can possibly affect. For if, *e. g.,* a man loses consciousness as soon as his brain is injured, it is clearly as good an explanation to say the injury to the brain destroyed the mechanism by which the manifestation of the consciousness was rendered possible, as to say that it destroyed the seat of consciousness. On the other hand, there are facts which the former theory suits far better. If, *e. g.,* as sometimes happens, the man, after a time, more or less, recovers the faculties of which the injury to his brain had deprived him, and that not in consequence of a renewal of the injured part, but in consequence of the inhibited functions being performed by the vicarious action of other parts, the easiest explanation certainly is that, after a time, consciousness constitutes the remaining parts into a mechanism capable of acting as a substitute for the lost parts. And again, if the body is a mechanism for inhibiting consciousness, for preventing the full powers of the Ego from being prematurely actualized, it will be necessary to invert also our ordinary ideas on the subject of memory, and to account for forgetfulness instead of for memory. It will be during life that we drink the bitter cup of Lethe, it will be with our brain that we are enabled to forget. And this will serve to explain not only the extraordinary memories of the drowning and the dying generally, but also the curious hints which experimental psychology occasionally affords us that nothing is ever forgotten wholly and beyond recall." [*Riddles of the Sphinx,* London, Swan Sonnenschein, 1891, p. 293 ff.]

Mr. Schiller's conception is much more complex in its relations than the simple "theory of transmission" postulated in my lecture, and to do justice to it the reader should consult the original work.—W. J.

enjoyment here below? Such questions are truly living questions, and surely they must be seriously discussed by future lecturers upon this Ingersoll foundation. I hope, for my part, that more than one such lecturer will penetratingly discuss the conditions of our immortality, and tell us how much we may lose, and how much we may possibly gain, if its finiting outlines should be changed. If all determination is negation, as the philosophers say, it might well prove that the loss of some of the particular determinations which the brain imposes would not appear a matter for such absolute regret.

But into these higher and more transcendental matters I refuse to enter upon this occasion; and I proceed, during the remainder of the hour, to treat of my second point. Fragmentary and negative it is, as my first one has been. Yet, between them, they do give to our belief in immortality a freer wing.

My second point is relative to the incredible and intolerable number of beings which, with our modern imagination, we must believe to be immortal, if immortality be true. I cannot but suspect that this, too, is a stumbling-block to many of my present audience. And it is a stumbling-block which I should thoroughly like to clear away.

It is, I fancy, a stumbling-block of altogether modern origin, due to the strain upon the quantitative imagination which recent scientific theories, and the moral feelings consequent upon them, have brought in their train.

For our ancestors the world was a small, and—compared with our modern sense of it—a comparatively snug affair. Six thousand years at most it had lasted. In its history a few particular human heroes, kings, ecclesiarchs, and saints stood forth very prominent, overshadowing the imagination with their claims and merits, so that not only they, but all who were associated familiarly with them, shone with a glamour which even the Almighty, it was supposed, must recognize and respect. These prominent personages and their associates were the nucleus of the immortal group; the minor heroes and saints of minor sects came next, and people without distinction formed a sort of background and filling in. The whole scene of eternity (so far, at least, as Heaven and not the nether place was concerned in it) never struck the believer's fancy as an overwhelmingly large or inconveniently crowded stage. One might call this an aristocratic view of immortality; the immortals—I speak of Heaven exclusively, for an immortality of torment need not now concern us—were always an élite, a select and manageable number.

But, with our own generation, an entirely new quantitative imagination has swept over our western world. The theory of evolution now requires us to suppose a far vaster scale of times, spaces, and numbers than our forefathers ever dreamed the cosmic process to involve. Human history grows continuously out of animal history, and goes back possibly even to the tertiary epoch. From this there has emerged insensibly a democratic view, instead of the old aristocratic view, of immortality. For our minds, though in one sense they may have grown a little cynical, in another they have been made sympathetic by the evolutionary perspective. Bone of our bone and flesh of our flesh are these half-brutish prehistoric brothers. Girdled about with the immense darkness of this mysterious universe even as we are, they were born and died, suffered and struggled. Given over to fearful crime and passion, plunged in the blackest ignorance, preyed upon by hideous and grotesque delusions, yet steadfastly serving the profoundest of ideals in their fixed faith that existence in any form is better than non-existence, they ever rescued triumphantly from the jaws of ever-imminent destruction the torch of life, which, thanks to them, now lights the world for us. How small indeed seem individual distinctions when we look back on these overwhelming numbers of human beings panting and straining under the pressure of that vital want! And how inessential in the eyes of God must be the small surplus of the individual's merit, swamped as it is in the vast ocean of the common merit of mankind, dumbly and undauntedly doing the fundamental duty and living the heroic life! We grow humble and reverent as we contemplate the prodigious spectacle. Not our differences and distinctions—we feel—no, but our common animal essence of patience under suffering and enduring effort must be what redeems us in the Deity's sight. An immense compassion and kinship fill the heart. An immortality from which these inconceivable billions of fellow strivers should be excluded becomes an irrational idea for us. That our superiority in personal refinement or in religious creed should constitute a difference between ourselves and our messmates at life's banquet, fit to entail such a consequential difference of destiny as eternal life for us, and for them torment hereafter, or death with the beasts that perish, is a notion too absurd to be considered serious. Nay, more, the very beasts themselves—the wild ones at any rate—are leading the heroic life at all times. And a modern mind, expanded as some minds are by cosmic emotion, by the great evolutionist vision of universal continuity, hesitates to draw the line even at man. If any creature lives forever, why not all?—why not the patient brutes? So that a faith in immortality, if we are to indulge it, demands of us nowadays a scale of representation so stupendous that our imagination faints before it, and our personal feelings refuse to rise up and face the task. The supposition we are swept along to is too vast, and, rather than face the conclusion, we abandon the premise from which it starts. We give up our own immortality sooner than believe that all the hosts of Hottentots and Australians that have been, and shall ever be, should share it with us *in saecula saeculorum*. Life is a good thing on a reasonably copious scale; but the very heavens themselves, and the cosmic times and spaces, would stand aghast, we think, at the notion of preserving eternally such an ever-swelling plethora and glut of it.

Having myself, as a recipient of modern scientific culture, gone through a subjective experience like this, I feel sure that it must also have been the experience of many, perhaps of most, of you who listen to my words. But I have also come to see that it harbors a tremendous fallacy; and, since the noting of the fallacy has set my own mind free again, I have felt that one service I might render to my listeners tonight would be to point out where it lies.

It is the most obvious fallacy in the world, and the only wonder is that all the world should not see through it. It is the result of nothing but an invincible blindness from which we suffer, an insensibility to the inner significance of alien lives, and a conceit that would project our own incapacity into the vast cosmos, and measure the wants of the Absolute by our own puny needs. Our Christian ancestors dealt with the problem more easily than we do. We, indeed, lack sympathy; but they had a positive antipathy for these alien human creatures, and they naïvely supposed the Deity to have the antipathy, too. Being, as they were, "heathen," our forefathers felt a certain sort of joy in thinking that their Creator made them as so much mere fuel for the fires of hell. Our culture has humanized us beyond that point, but we cannot yet conceive them as our comrades in the fields of heaven. We have, as the phrase goes, *no use for them,* and it oppresses us to think of their survival. Take, for instance, all the Chinamen. Which of you here, my friends, sees any fitness in their eternal perpetuation unreduced in numbers? Surely not one of you. At most, you might deem it well to keep a few chosen specimens alive to represent an interesting and peculiar variety of humanity; but as for the rest, what comes in such surpassing numbers, and what you can only imagine in this abstract summary collective manner, must be something of which the units, you are sure, can have no individual preciousness. God himself, you think, can have no use for them. An immortality of every separate specimen must be to him and to the universe as indigestible a load to carry as it is to you. So, engulfing the whole subject in a sort of mental giddiness and nausea, you drift along, first doubting that the mass can be immortal, then losing all assurance in the immortality of your own particular person, precious as you all the while feel and realize the latter to be. This, I am sure, is the attitude of mind of some of you before me.

But is not such an attitude due to the veriest lack and dearth of your imagination? You take these swarms of alien kinsmen as they are *for you:* an external picture painted on your retina, representing a crowd oppressive by its vastness and confusion. As they are

for you, so you think they positively and absolutely are. *I* feel no
call for them, you say; therefore there *is* no call for them. But all
the while, beyond this externality which is your way of realizing
them, they realize themselves with the acutest internality, with the
most violent thrills of life. 'Tis you who are dead, stone-dead and
blind and senseless, in your way of looking on. You open your
eyes upon a scene of which you miss the whole significance. Each
of these grotesque or even repulsive aliens is animated by an inner
joy of living as hot or hotter than that which you feel beating in
your private breast. The sun rises and beauty beams to light his
path. To miss the inner joy of him, as Stevenson says, is to miss the
whole of him.[12] Not a being of the countless throng is there whose
continued life is not called for, and called for intensely, by the
consciousness that animates the being's form. That *you* neither
realize nor understand nor call for it, that you have no use for it,
is an absolutely irrelevant circumstance. That you have a saturation-
point of interest tells us nothing of the interests that absolutely are.
The universe, with every living entity which her resources create,
creates at the same time a call for that entity, and an appetite for
its continuance—creates it, if nowhere else, at least within the heart
of the entity itself. It is absurd to suppose, simply because our
private power of sympathetic vibration with other lives gives out
so soon, that in the heart of infinite being itself there can be such
a thing as plethora, or glut, or supersaturation. It is not as if there
were a bounded room where the minds in possession had to move
up or make place and crowd together to accommodate new occu-
pants. Each new mind brings its own edition of the universe of
space along with it, its own room to inhabit, and those spaces
never crowd each other—the space of my imagination, for example,

---

[12] I beg the reader to peruse R. L. Stevenson's magnificent little essay entitled "The Lantern Bearers," reprinted in the collection entitled *Across the
Plains.* The truth is that we are doomed, by the fact that we are practical
beings with very limited tasks to attend to, and special ideals to look after,
to be absolutely blind and insensible to the inner feelings, and to the whole
inner significance of lives that are different from our own. Our opinion of the
worth of such lives is absolutely wide of the mark, and unfit to be counted at
all.—W. J.

in no way interferes with yours. The amount of possible consciousness seems to be governed by no law analogous to that of the so-
called conservation of energy in the material world. When one
man wakes up, or one is born, another does not have to go to sleep,
or die, in order to keep the consciousness of the universe a constant
quantity. Professor Wundt, in fact, in his *System of Philosophy,* has
formulated a law of the universe which he calls the law of increase
of spiritual energy, and which he expressly opposes to the law of
conservation of energy in physical things.[12] There seems no formal
limit to the positive increase of being in spiritual respects; and
since spiritual being, whenever it comes, affirms itself, expands,
and craves continuance, we may justly and literally say, regardless
of the defects of our own private sympathy, that the supply of
individual life in the universe can never possibly, however im-
measurable it may become, exceed the demand. The demand for
that supply is there the moment the supply itself comes into being,
for the beings supplied demand their own continuance.

I speak, you see, from the point of view of all the other individual
beings, realizing and enjoying inwardly their own existence. If we
are pantheists, we can stop there. We need, then, only say that
through them, as through so many diversified channels of expression,
the eternal Spirit of the Universe affirms and realizes its own infinite life. But if we are theists, we can go farther without altering
the result. God, we can then say, has so inexhaustible a capacity
for love that his call and need is for a literally endless accumulation
of created lives. He can never faint or grow weary, as we should,
under the increasing supply. His scale is infinite in all things. His
sympathy can never know satiety or glut.

I hope now that you agree with me that the tiresomeness of an
over-peopled heaven is a purely subjective and illusory notion, a
sign of human incapacity, a remnant of the old narrow-hearted
aristocratic creed. "Revere the Maker, lift thine eye up to his style
and manners of the sky," and you will believe that this is indeed a

---

[12] W. Wundt: *System der Philosophie,* Leipzig, Engelmann, 1889, p.
315.—W. J.

democratic universe, in which your paltry exclusions play no regulative part. Was your taste consulted in the peopling of this globe? How, then, should it be consulted as to the peopling of the vast City of God? Let us put our hand over our mouth, like Job, and be thankful that in our personal littleness we ourselves are here at all. The Deity that suffers us, we may be sure, can suffer many another queer and wondrous and only half-delightful thing.

For my own part, then, so far as logic goes, I am willing that every leaf that ever grew in this world's forests and rustled in the breeze should become immortal. It is purely a question of fact: are the leaves so, or not? Abstract quantity, and the abstract needlessness in our eyes of so much reduplication of things so much alike, have no connection with the subject. For bigness and number and generic similarity are only manners of our finite way of thinking; and, considered in itself and apart from our imagination, one scale of dimensions and of numbers for the universe is no more miraculous or inconceivable than another, the moment you grant to a universe the liberty to be at all, in place of the non-entity that might conceivably have reigned.

The heart of being can have no exclusions akin to those which our poor little hearts set up. The inner significance of other lives exceeds all our powers of sympathy and insight. If we feel a significance in our own life which would lead us spontaneously to claim its perpetuity, let us be at least tolerant of like claims made by other lives, however numerous, however unideal they may seem to us to be. Let us at any rate not decide adversely on our own claim, whose grounds we feel directly, because we cannot decide favorably on the alien claims, whose grounds we cannot feel at all. That would be letting blindness lay down the law to sight

VII

————•————

THE LAST REPORT

THE FINAL IMPRESSIONS OF
A PSYCHICAL RESEARCHER [1]

The late Professor Henry Sidgwick was celebrated for the rare mixture of ardor and critical judgment which his character exhibited. The liberal heart which he possessed had to work with an intellect which acted destructively on almost every particular object of belief that was offered to its acceptance. A quarter of a century ago, scandalized by the chaotic state of opinion regarding the phenomena now called by the rather ridiculous name of "psychic"— phenomena of which the supply reported seems inexhaustible, but which scientifically trained minds mostly refuse to look at—he established, along with Professor Barrett, Frederic Myers, and Edmund Gurney, the Society for Psychical Research. These men hoped that if the material were treated rigorously and, as far as possible, experimentally, objective truth would be elicited, and the subject rescued from sentimentalism on the one side and dogma-

[1] This essay first appeared in *The American Magazine*, October 1909. It was reprinted in *Memories and Studies*. New York: Longmans Green, 1911. Copyright 1911 by Henry James, Jr. Permission to reprint granted by Paul R. Reynolds & Son.—ED.

tizing ignorance on the other. Like all founders, Sidgwick hoped
for a certain promptitude of result; and I heard him say, the year
before his death, that if anyone had told him at the outset that
after twenty years he would be in the same identical state of doubt
and balance that he started with, he would have deemed the
prophecy incredible. It appeared impossible that that amount of
handling evidence should bring so little finality of decision.

My own experience has been similar to Sidgwick's. For twenty-
five years I have been in touch with the literature of psychical research, and have had acquaintance with numerous "researchers."
I have also spent a good many hours (though far fewer than I
ought to have spent) in witnessing (or trying to witness) phenomena. Yet I am theoretically no "further" than I was at the beginning; and I confess that at times I have been tempted to believe
that the Creator has eternally intended this department of nature
to remain *baffling*, to prompt our curiosities and hopes and sus-
picions all in equal measure, so that, although ghosts and clair-
voyances, and raps and messages from spirits, are always seeming
to exist and can never be fully explained away, they also can never
be susceptible of full corroboration.

The peculiarity of the case is just that there are so many sources
of possible deception in most of the observations that the whole lot
of them *may* be worthless, and yet that in comparatively few cases
can aught more fatal than this vague general possibility of error be
pleaded against the record. Science meanwhile needs something
more than bare possibilities to build upon; so your genuinely scientific inquirer—I don't mean your ignoramus "scientist"—has to remain unsatisfied. It is hard to believe, however, that the Creator
has really put any big array of phenomena into the world merely
to defy and mock our scientific tendencies; so my deeper belief is
that we psychical researchers have been too precipitate with our
hopes, and that we must expect to mark progress not by quarter-
centuries, but by half-centuries or whole centuries.

I am strengthened in this belief by my impression that just at this
moment a faint but distinct step forward is being taken by com-

petent opinion in these matters. "Physical phenomena" (movements of matter without contact, lights, hands and faces "materialized," etc.) have been one of the most baffling regions of the general field (or perhaps one of the least baffling *prima facie*, so certain and great has been the part played by fraud in their production); yet even here the balance of testimony seems slowly to be inclining towards admitting the supernaturalist view. Eusapia Paladino, the Neapolitan medium, has been under observation for twenty years or more. Schiaparelli, the astronomer, and Lombroso were the first scientific men to be converted by her performances. Since then innumerable men of scientific standing have seen her, including many "psychic" experts. Everyone agrees that she cheats in the most barefaced manner whenever she gets an opportunity. The Cambridge experts, with the Sidgwicks and Richard Hodgson at their head, rejected her *in toto* on that account. Yet her credit has steadily risen, and now her last converts are the eminent psychiatrist, Morselli, the eminent physiologist, Botazzi, and our own psychical researcher, Carrington, whose book on *The Physical Phenomena of Spiritualism* (*against* them rather!) makes his conquest strategically important. If Mr. Podmore, hitherto the prosecuting attorney of the S. P. R. so far as physical phenomena are concerned, becomes converted also, we may indeed sit up and look around us. Getting a good health bill from "Science," Eusapia will then throw retrospective credit on Home and Stainton Moses, Florence Cook (Prof. Crookes's medium), and all similar wonder-workers. The balance of *presumptions* will be changed in favor of genuineness being possible at least, in all reports of this particularly crass and low type of supernatural phenomenon.

Not long after Darwin's *Origin of Species* appeared I was studying with that excellent anatomist and man, Jeffries Wyman, at Harvard. He was a convert, yet so far a half-hesitating one, to Darwin's views; but I heard him make a remark that applies well to the subject I now write about. When, he said, a theory gets propounded over and over again, coming up afresh after each time orthodox criticism has buried it, and each time seeming solider and harder to abolish, you may be sure that there is truth in it. Oken and Lamarck and Chambers had been triumphantly dispatched and buried, but here was Darwin making the very same heresy seem only more plausible. How often has "Science" killed off all spook philosophy, and laid ghosts and raps and "telepathy" away underground as so much popular delusion. Yet never before were these things offered us so voluminously, and never in such authentic-seeming shape or with such good credentials. The tide seems steadily to be rising, in spite of all the expedients of scientific orthodoxy. It is hard not to suspect that here may be something different from a mere chapter in human gullibility. It may be a genuine realm of natural phenomena.

Falsus in uno, falsus in omnibus, once a cheat, always a cheat, such has been the motto of the English psychical researchers in dealing with mediums. I am disposed to think that, as a matter of policy, it has been wise. Tactically it is far better to believe much too little than a little too much; and the exceptional credit attaching to the row of volumes of the S. P. R.'s *Proceedings,* is due to the fixed intention of the editors to proceed very slowly. Better a little belief tied fast, better a small investment *salted down,* than a mass of comparative insecurity.

But, however wise as a policy the S. P. R.'s maxim may have been, as a test of truth I believe it to be almost irrelevant. In most things human the accusation of deliberate fraud and falsehood is grossly superficial. Man's character is too sophistically mixed for the alternative of honest or dishonest to be a clean presumption. Scientific men themselves will cheat—at public lectures—rather than let experiments obey their well-known tendency towards failure. I have heard of a lecturer on physics, who had taken over the apparatus of the previous incumbent, consulting him about a certain machine intended to show that, however the peripheral parts of it might be agitated, its center of gravity remained immovable. "It *will* wobble," he complained. "Well," said the predecessor, apologetically, "to tell the truth, whenever *I* used that machine I found it advisable to *drive a nail* through the center of gravity." I once saw a distinguished physiologist, now dead, cheat most shamelessly at a public lecture, at the expense of a poor rabbit, and all for the sake of being able to make a cheap joke about its being an "American rabbit"—for no other, he said, could survive such a wound as he pretended to have given it.

To compare small men with great, I have myself cheated shamelessly. In the early days of the Sanders Theater at Harvard, I once had charge of a heart on the physiology of which Professor Newell Martin was giving a popular lecture. This heart, which belonged to a turtle, supported an index-straw which threw a moving shadow, greatly enlarged, upon the screen, while the heart pulsated. When certain nerves were stimulated, the lecturer said, the heart would act in certain ways which he described. But the poor heart was too far gone and, although it stopped duly when the nerve of arrest was excited, that was the final end of its life's tether. Presiding over the performance, I was terrified at the fiasco, and found myself suddenly acting like one of those military geniuses who on the field of battle convert disaster into victory. There was no time for deliberation; so, with my forefinger under a part of the straw that cast no shadow, I found myself impulsively and automatically imitating the rhythmical movements which my colleague had prophesied the heart would undergo. I kept the experiment from failing; and not only saved my colleague (and the turtle) from a humiliation that but for my presence of mind would have been their lot, but I established in the audience the true view of the subject. The lecturer was stating this; and the misconduct of one half-dead specimen of heart ought not to destroy the impression of his words. "There is no worse lie than a truth misunderstood," is a maxim which I have heard ascribed to a former venerated President of Harvard. The heart's failure would have been misunderstood by the audience and given the lie to the lecturer. It was hard enough to make them understand the subject anyhow; so that even now as I write in cool blood I am tempted to think that I acted quite correctly. I was acting for the *larger* truth, at any rate, however automatically; and my sense of this was probably what prevented the more pedantic and literal part of my conscience from checking the action of my sympathetic finger. To this day the memory of that critical emergency has made me feel charitable towards all mediums who make phenomena come in one way when they won't come easily in another. On the principles of the S. P. R., my conduct on that one occasion ought to discredit everything I ever do, everything, for example, I may write in this article—a manifestly unjust conclusion.

Fraud, conscious or unconscious, seems ubiquitous throughout the range of physical phenomena of spiritism, and false pretense, prevarication, and fishing for clues are ubiquitous in the mental manifestations of mediums. If it be not everywhere fraud simulating reality, one is tempted to say, then the reality (if any reality there be) has the bad luck of being fated everywhere to simulate fraud. The suggestion of humbug seldom stops, and mixes itself with the best manifestations. Mrs. Piper's control, "Rector," is a most impressive personage, who discerns in an extraordinary degree his sitter's inner needs, and is capable of giving elevated counsel to fastidious and critical minds. Yet in many respects he is an arrant humbug—such he seems to me at least—pretending to a knowledge and power to which he has no title, nonplussed by contradiction, yielding to suggestion, and covering his tracks with plausible excuses. Now the non-"researching" mind looks upon such phenomena simply according to their face-pretension and never thinks of asking what they may signify below the surface. Since they profess for the most part to be revealers of spirit life, it is either as being absolutely that, or as being absolute frauds, that they are judged. The result is an inconceivably shallow state of public opinion on the subject. One set of persons, emotionally touched at hearing the names of their loved ones given, and consoled by assurances that they are "happy," accept the revelation, and consider spiritualism "beautiful." More hard-headed subjects, disgusted by the revelation's contemptible contents, outraged by the fraud, and prejudiced beforehand against all "spirits," high

or low, avert their minds from what they call such "rot" or "bosh"
entirely. Thus do two opposite sentimentalisms divide opinion between them! A good expression of the "scientific" state of mind
occurs in Huxley's *Life and Letters:*

"I regret," he writes, "that I am unable to accept the invitation
of the Committee of the Dialectical Society. . . . I take no interest
in the subject. The only case of 'Spiritualism' I have ever had the
opportunity of examining into for myself was as gross an imposture
as ever came under my notice. But supposing these phenomena to
be genuine—they do not interest me. If anybody would endow me
with the faculty of listening to the chatter of old women and curates
in the nearest provincial town, I should decline the privilege, having
better things to do. And if the folk in the spiritual world do not
talk more wisely and sensibly than their friends report them to do,
I put them in the same category. The only good that I can see in
the demonstration of the 'Truth of Spiritualism' is to furnish an
additional argument against suicide. Better live a crossing-sweeper,
than die and be made to talk twaddle by a 'medium' hired at a
guinea a *Seance*." [2]

Obviously the mind of the excellent Huxley has here but two
whole-souled categories, namely revelation or imposture, to apperceive the case by. Sentimental reasons bar revelation out, for
the messages, he thinks, are not romantic enough for that; fraud
exists anyhow; therefore the whole thing is nothing but imposture.
The odd point is that so few of those who talk in this way realize
that they and the spiritists are using the same major premise and
differing only in the minor. The major premise is: "Any spirit-
revelation must be romantic." The minor of the spiritist is: "This *is*
romantic"; that of the Huxleyan is: "This is dingy twaddle"—
whence their opposite conclusions!

Meanwhile the first thing that anyone learns who attends seriously
to these phenomena is that their causation is far too complex for
our feelings about what is or is not romantic enough to be spiritual
to throw any light upon it. The causal factors must be carefully dis-

[2] T. H. Huxley, *Life and Letters,* I, 240.—W. J.

tinguished and traced through series, from their simplest to their strongest forms, before we can begin to understand the various resultants in which they issue. Myers and Gurney began this work, the one by his serial study of the various sorts of "automatism," sensory and motor, the other by his experimental proofs that a split-off consciousness may abide after a post-hypnotic suggestion has been given. Here we have subjective factors; but are not trans-subjective or objective forces also at work? Veridical messages, apparitions, movements without contact, seem *prima facie* to be such. It was a good stroke on Gurney's part to construct a theory of apparitions which brought the subjective and the objective factors into harmonious cooperation. I doubt whether this telepathic theory of Gurney's will hold along the whole line of apparitions to which he applied it, but it is unquestionable that some theory of that mixed type is required for the explanation of all medium-istic phenomena; and that when all the psychological factors and elements involved have been told off—and they are many —the question still forces itself upon us: Are these all, or are there indications of any residual forces acting on the subject from beyond, or of any "metapsychic" faculty (to use Richet's useful term), exerted by him? This is the problem that requires real expertness, and this is where the simple sentimentalisms of the spiritist and scientist leave us in the lurch completely.

"Psychics" form indeed a special branch of education, in which experts are only gradually becoming developed. The phenomena are as massive and widespread as is anything in nature, and the study of them is as tedious, repellent, and undignified. To reject it for its unromantic character is like rejecting bacteriology because *penicillium glaucum* grows on horse-dung and *bacterium termo* lives in putrefaction. Scientific men have long ago ceased to think of the dignity of the materials they work in. When imposture has been checked off as far as possible, when chance coincidence has been allowed for, when opportunities for normal knowledge on the part of the subject have been noted, and skill in "fishing" and following clues unwittingly furnished by the voice or face of by-

standers have been counted in, those who have the fullest acquaintance with the phenomena admit that in good mediums *there is a
residuum of knowledge displayed* that can only be called supernormal: the medium taps some source of information not open to
ordinary people. Myers used the word "telepathy" to indicate that
the sitter's own thoughts or feelings may be thus directly tapped.
Mrs. Sidgwick has suggested that if living minds can be thus tapped
telepathically, so possibly may the minds of spirits be similarly
tapped—if spirits there be. On this view we should have one distinct theory of the performances of a typical test-medium. They
would be all originally due to an odd *tendency to personate,* found
in her dream life as it expresses itself in trance. (Most of us reveal
such a tendency whenever we handle a "ouija-board" or a "planchette," or let ourselves write automatically with a pencil.) The result is a "control," who purports to be speaking; and all the resources of the automatist, including his or her trance faculty of
telepathy, are called into play in building this fictitious personage
out plausibly. On such a view of the control, the medium's *will to
personate* runs the whole show; and if spirits be involved in it at all,
they are passive beings, stray bits of whose memory she is able to
seize and use for her purposes, without the spirit being any more
aware of it than the sitter is aware of it when his own mind is
similarly tapped.

This is one possible way of interpreting a certain type of psychical phenomenon. It uses psychological as well as "spiritual" factors,
and quite obviously it throws open for us far more questions than
it answers, questions about our subconscious constitution and its
curious tendency to humbug, about the telepathic faculty, and
about the possibility of an existent spirit world.

I do not instance this theory to defend it, but simply to show
what complicated hypotheses one is inevitably led to consider, the
moment one looks at the facts in their complexity and turns one's
back on the *naïve* alternative of "revelation or imposture," which is
as far as either spiritist thought or ordinary scientist thought goes.
The phenomena are endlessly complex in their factors, and they are

so little understood as yet that offhand judgments, whether of "spirits" or of "bosh," are the one as silly as the other. When we complicate the subject still farther by considering what connection such things as rappings, apparitions, poltergeists, spirit photographs, and materializations may have with it, the bosh end of the scale gets heavily loaded, it is true, but your genuine inquirer still is loath to give up. He lets the data collect, and bides his time. He believes that "bosh" is no more an ultimate element in nature, or a really explanatory category in human life than "dirt" is in chemistry. Every kind of "bosh" has its own factors and laws; and patient study will bring them definitely to light.

The only way to rescue the "pure bosh" view of the matter is one which has sometimes appealed to my own fancy, but which I imagine few readers will seriously adopt. If, namely, one takes the theory of evolution radically, one ought to apply it not only to the rock-strata, the animals and the plants, but to the stars, to the chemical elements, and to the laws of nature. There must have been a far-off antiquity, one is then tempted to suppose, when things were really chaotic. Little by little, out of all the haphazard possibilities of that time, a few connected things and habits arose, and the rudiments of regular performance began. Every variation in the way of law and order added itself to this nucleus, which inevitably grew more considerable as history went on; while the aberrant and inconstant variations, not being similarly preserved, disappeared from being, wandered off as unrelated vagrants, or else remained so imperfectly connected with the part of the world that had grown regular as only to manifest their existence by occasional lawless intrusions, like those which "psychic" phenomena now make into our scientifically organized world. On such a view, these phenomena ought to remain "pure bosh" forever, that is, they ought to be forever intractable to intellectual methods, because they should not yet be organized enough in themselves to follow any laws. Wisps and shreds of the original chaos, they would be connected enough with the cosmos to affect its periphery every now and then, as by a momentary whiff or touch or gleam, but not enough ever to be followed up and hunted down and bagged. Their relation to the cosmos would be tangential solely.

Looked at dramatically, most occult phenomena make just this sort of impression. They are inwardly as incoherent as they are outwardly wayward and fitful. If they express anything, it is pure "bosh," pure discontinuity, accident, and disturbance, with no law apparent but to interrupt, and no purpose but to baffle. They seem like stray vestiges of that primordial irrationality, from which all our rationalities have been evolved.

To settle dogmatically into this bosh-view would save labor, but it would go against too many intellectual prepossessions to be adopted save as a last resort of despair. Your psychical researcher therefore bates no jot of hope, and has faith that when we get our data numerous enough, some sort of rational treatment of them will succeed.

When I hear good people say (as they often say, not without show of reason), that dabbling in such phenomena reduces us to a sort of jelly, disintegrates the critical faculties, liquefies the character, and makes of one a *gobe-mouche* generally, I console myself by thinking of my friends Frederic Myers and Richard Hodgson. These men lived exclusively for psychical research, and it converted both to spiritism. Hodgson would have been a man among men anywhere; but I doubt whether under any other baptism he would have been that happy, sober, and righteous form of energy which his face proclaimed him in his later years, when heart and head alike were wholly satisfied by his occupation. Myers's character also grew stronger in every particular for his devotion to the same inquiries. Brought up on literature and sentiment, something of a courtier, passionate, disdainful, and impatient naturally, he was made over again from the day when he took up psychical research seriously. He became learned in science, circumspect, democratic in sympathy, endlessly patient, and above all, happy. The fortitude of his last hours touched the heroic, so completely were the atrocious sufferings of his body cast into insignificance by his interest in the cause he lived for. When a man's pursuit gradually makes his face shine and grow handsome, you may be sure it is a worthy one. Both Hodgson and Myers kept growing ever handsomer and stronger-looking.

Such personal examples will convert no one, and of course they ought not to. Nor do I seek at all in this article to convert anyone to my belief that psychical research is an important branch of science. To do that, I should have to quote evidence; and those for whom the volumes of S. P. R. *Proceedings* already published count for nothing would remain in their dogmatic slumber, though one rose from the dead. No, not to convert readers, but simply to *put my own state of mind upon record publicly* is the purpose of my present writing. Someone said to me a short time ago that after my twenty-five years of dabbling in "Psychics," it would be rather shameful were I unable to state any definite conclusions whatever as a consequence. I had to agree; so I now proceed to take up the challenge and express such convictions as have been engendered in me by that length of experience, be the same true or false ones. I may be dooming myself to the pit in the eyes of better-judging posterity; I may be raising myself to honor; I am willing to take the risk, for what I shall write is *my* truth, as I now see it.

I began this article by confessing myself baffled. I *am* baffled, as to spirit return, and as to many other special problems. I am also constantly baffled as to what to think of this or that particular story, for the sources of error in any one observation are seldom fully knowable. But weak sticks make strong faggots; and when the stories fall into consistent sorts that point each in a definite direction, one gets a sense, of being in presence of genuinely natural types of phenomena. As to there being such real natural types of phenomena ignored by orthodox science, I am not baffled at all, for I am fully convinced of it. One cannot get demonstrative proof here. One has to follow one's personal sense, which, of course, is liable to err, of the dramatic probabilities of nature. Our critics here obey their sense of dramatic probability as much as we do. Take "raps," for example, and the whole business of objects moving without contact. "Nature," thinks the scientific man, is not so unutterably silly. The cabinet, the darkness, the tying, suggest a sort of human rat-hole life exclusively and "swindling" is for him the dramatically sufficient explanation. It probably is, in an indefinite majority of instances; yet it is to me dramatically improbable that the swindling should not have accreted round some originally genuine nucleus. If we look at human imposture as a historic phenomenon, we find it always imitative. One swindler imitates a previous swindler, but the first swindler of that kind imitated someone who was honest. You can no more create an absolutely new trick than you can create a new word without any previous basis. You don't know how to go about it. Try, reader, yourself, to invent an unprecedented kind of "physical phenomenon of spiritualism." When *I* try, I find myself mentally turning over the regular medium-stock, and thinking how I might improve some item. This being the dramatically probable human way, I think differently of the whole type, taken collectively, from the way in which I may think of the single instance. I find myself believing that there is "something in" these never ending reports of physical phenomena, although I haven't yet the least positive notion of the something. It becomes to my mind simply a very worthy problem for investigation. Either I or the scientist is of course a fool, with our opposite views of probability here; and I only wish he might feel the liability, as cordially as I do, to pertain to both of us.

I fear I look on nature generally with more charitable eyes than his, though perhaps he would pause if he realized, as I do, how vast the fraudulency is which in consistency he must attribute to her. Nature is brutal enough, Heaven knows; but no one yet has held her non-human side to be *dishonest,* and even in the human sphere deliberate deceit is far rarer than the "classic" intellect, with its few and rigid categories, was ready to acknowledge. There is a hazy penumbra in us all where lying and delusion meet, where passion rules beliefs as well as conduct, and where the term "scoundrel" does not clear up everything to the depths as it did for our forefathers. The first automatic writing I ever saw was forty years ago. I unhesitatingly thought of it as deceit, although it contained vague elements of supernormal knowledge. Since then I have come to see in automatic writing one example of a department of human activity as vast as it is enigmatic. Every sort of person is liable to it, or to something equivalent to it; and whoever encourages it in himself finds himself personating someone else, either signing what he writes by fictitious name, or spelling out, by ouija board or table-tips, messages from the departed. Our subconscious region seems, as a rule, to be dominated either by a crazy "will to make-believe," or by some curious external force impelling us to personation. The first difference between the psychical researcher and the inexpert person is that the former realizes the commonness and typicality of the phenomenon here, while the latter, less informed, thinks it so rare as to be unworthy of attention. *I wish to go on record for the commonness.*

The next thing I wish to go on record for is *the presence,* in the midst of all the humbug, *of really supernormal knowledge.* By this I mean knowledge that cannot be traced to the ordinary sources of information—the senses, namely, of the automatist. In really strong mediums this knowledge seems to be abundant, though it is usually spotty, capricious, and unconnected. Really strong mediums are rarities; but when one starts with them and works downwards into less brilliant regions of the automatic life, one tends to interpret many slight but odd coincidences with truth as possibly rudimentary forms of this kind of knowledge.

What is one to think of this queer chapter in human nature? It is odd enough on any view. If all it means is a preposterous and inferior monkey-like tendency to *large messages, systematically* embedded in the soul of all of us, it is weird, and weirder still that it should then own all this supernormal information. If on the other hand the supernormal information be the key to the phenomenon, it ought to be superior; and then how ought we to account for the "wicked partner," and for the undeniable mendacity and inferiority of so much of the performance? We are thrown, for our conclusions, upon our instinctive sense of the dramatic probabilities of nature. My own dramatic sense tends instinctively to picture the situation as an interaction between slumbering faculties in the automatist's mind and a cosmic environment of *other consciousness* of some sort which is able to work upon them. If there were in the universe a lot of diffuse soul-stuff, unable of itself to get into consistent personal form, or to take permanent possession of an organism, yet always craving to do so, it might get its head into the air, parasitically, so to speak, by profiting by weak spots in the armor of human minds, and slipping in and stirring up there the sleeping tendency to personate. It would induce habits in the subconscious region of the mind it used thus, and would seek above all things to prolong its social opportunities by making itself agreeable and plausible. It would drag stray scraps of truth with it from the wider environment, but would betray its mental inferiority by knowing little how to weave them into any important or significant story.

This, I say, is the dramatic view which my mind spontaneously takes, and it has the advantage of falling into line with ancient human traditions. The views of others are just as dramatic, *for the phenomenon is actuated by will of some sort anyhow,* and wills give rise to dramas. The spiritist view, as held by Messrs. Hyslop and Hodgson, sees a "will to communicate," struggling through inconceivable layers of obstruction in the conditions. I have heard Hodgson liken the difficulties to those of two persons who on earth should have only dead-drunk servants to use as their messengers. The scientist, for his part, sees a "will to deceive," watching its chance in all of us, and able (possibly?) to use "telepathy" in its service.

Which kind of will, and how many kinds of will are most inherently probable? Who can say with certainty? The only certainty is that the phenomena are enormously complex, especially if one includes in them such intellectual flights of mediumship as Swedenborg's, and if one tries in any way to work the physical phenomena in. That is why I personally am as yet neither a convinced believer in parasitic demons, nor a spiritist, nor a scientist, but still remain a psychical researcher waiting for more facts before concluding.

Out of my experience, such as it is (and it is limited enough), one fixed conclusion dogmatically emerges, and that is this, that we with our lives are like islands in the sea, or like trees in the forest. The maple and the pine may whisper to each other with their leaves, and Conanicut and Newport hear each other's foghorns. But the trees also commingle their roots in the darkness underground, and the islands also hang together through the ocean's bottom. Just so there is a continuum of cosmic consciousness, against which our individuality builds but accidental fences, and into which our several minds plunge as into a mother-sea or reservoir. Our "normal" consciousness is circumscribed for adaptation to our external earthly environment, but the fence is weak in spots, and fitful influences from beyond leak in, showing the otherwise unverifiable common connection. Not only psychic research, but metaphysical philosophy, and speculative biology are led in their own ways to look with favor on some such "panpsychic" view of the universe as this. Assuming this common reservoir of consciousness to exist, this bank upon which we all draw, and in which so many of earth's memories must in some way be stored, or mediums would not get at them as they do, the question is, What is its own structure? What is its inner topography? This question, first squarely formulated by Myers, deserves to be called "Myers's problem" by scientific men hereafter. What are the conditions of individuation or insulation in this mother-sea? To what tracts, to what active systems functioning separately in it, do personalities correspond? Are individual "spirits" constituted there? How numerous, and of how many hierarchic orders may there then be? How permanent? How transient? And how confluent with one another may they become?

What, again, are the relations between the cosmic consciousness and matter? Are there subtler forms of matter which upon occasion may enter into functional connection with the individuations in the psychic sea, and then, and then only, show themselves?—so that our ordinary human experience, on its material as well as on its mental side, would appear to be only an extract from the larger psychophysical world?

Vast, indeed, and difficult is the inquirer's prospect here, and the most significant data for his purpose will probably be just these dingy little mediumistic facts which the Huxleyan minds of our time find so unworthy of their attention. But when was not the science of the future stirred to its conquering activities by the little rebellious exceptions to the science of the present? Hardly, as yet, has the surface of the facts called "psychic" begun to be scratched for scientific purposes. It is through following these facts, I am persuaded, that the greatest scientific conquests of the coming generation will be achieved. *Kühn ist das Mühen, herrlich der Lohn!*

IN RETROSPECT[1]

By Gardner Murphy

William James's active interest in psychical research extended through the last thirty years of his life and was not something apart from his main activities; rather for him it was an integral part of the whole. He was a corresponding member of the Society for Psychical Research (London) from 1884–89, a vice-president from 1890–1910, and president during the years 1894 and 1895. His essay "What Psychical Research Has Accomplished" must be regarded as the most powerful and convincing of all apologies for the work of this society.

James did four important things for psychical research. First, he gave it a certain status, a certain intellectual respectability, which only his own immense prestige could have given it in the United States, in the era in which he flourished. Second, he played a major role in founding official psychical research in the United States, keeping it, properly, very close indeed to the S. P. R. of London, but in an administratively independent place which helped pave

---

[1] Adapted from an essay in the *Journal of the Society for Psychical Research* (London), December 1958.

the way for a later fully independent American S. P. R. Third, he
discovered the extraordinary mediumistic powers of Mrs. L. E.
Piper, who was, one might well say, the major research instrument
of psychical research from the middle eighties until the end of the
century, and continued for another decade into the twentieth century as one of the major sources of information regarding those
paranormal processes which are related to the issue of communication from the deceased. Fourth, he presented a "radical empiricism" regarding the position which a serious facer of facts must
assume when what seem to be unassimilable data must somehow
be faced, thought through, and correlated.

James's restless and ruthless search for facts, or, even more
broadly, his search for new experience, appears as a reflection of
the pioneer openness and ruggedness of spirit so characteristic of
American thought in the era. It reflects the mottled texture of
James's efforts in France, Switzerland, Germany, and Britain, to
achieve, through painting, through medicine, through science, and
through philosophy, a sort of conglomerate of experience from
which he could ultimately make a life perspective for himself. And
it reflects that deeply personal nervousness which showed itself repeatedly in huge physical discomforts and illnesses from which he
thought he had saved himself in a new philosophy of life, but which
again and again upset his equanimity and forced upon him new
efforts at serenity and personal poise.

In and through all this turbulence, James was identified intensely
with the new spirit of science as represented by the evolutionary
outlook on the one hand and the laboratory studies of physiology
on the other. When he was asked by President Eliot of Harvard
to teach undergraduate students the rudiments of physiology, he
used this as an entering wedge for the development of a psychological laboratory; later a department of psychology; later still an
effort at the understanding of man in which no barrier between
psychology and philosophy can be discovered. Philosophy, however, did not mean a divine detachment from human affairs. It

meant the grubbiest concern with particular details, findable facts, verifiable working principles. The only person not at home in such a laboratory approach is he who has an utterly systematic scientific outlook, with no ghosts, no skeletons in cupboards, no strange and deviant phenomena, demanding to be examined. Everyone soon knew that when James took a subject seriously there was something there worthy of a vigorous and inquiring mind. Psychical research received this endorsement as a tremendous push.

Specifically, he responded with eager sympathy to the organization of the S. P. R. in 1882 by the Cambridge, England, group to which we owe so much, and helped to persuade the American astronomer Simon Newcomb to assume the presidency of an American Society for the same purpose. He remained spiritually and personally close to both the British and the American groups—and especially to Frederic W. H. Myers.

In this setting it is utterly natural and credible that William James should grasp the religious as well as the scientific challenge. Just as he offered a listening ear to many a new religious movement, so he responded to that extraordinary cult, the use of human mediators between the deceased and the living, which was so dramatically represented in the professional mediums, resident or itinerant, known to every large American community.

But what did psychic phenomena *mean* to James? For James, of course, the gap between the paranormal and the normal psychology of the day was less immense than it must have appeared to most of his contemporaries, because he had himself given such deep and sustained thought to problems of double personality and of strange healings—realities so personal for him that, as has been seen, he made his way to the Boston State House in the interests of getting a fair hearing for "unorthodox" healers.

As, with the turn of the century, he moved into his sixties and the last decade of his life, his thought was evidently more and more concerned with the empirical realities of religious experiences, in which the concept of a "window" into the unknown bound together for him the sense of unutterable revelation and some aspects of the world of paranormal sensitivity. The term religion, however, had for James the same rugged empirical meaning that the terms philosophy and science conveyed. Religion was not an "easy escape." It was a tough world calling for analysis in terms of empirical realities. In this decade his volume on *A Pluralistic Universe* reminded us that the world does not necessarily hang together in tightly joined architectural fashion, but may be composed of somewhat disparate parts; while a year or two later, in his lectures on *Pragmatism,* he was struggling to show that the philosopher's reality can never get far from the kind of truth that is directly testable in human living.

These are fundamental background components if one is to understand James's own most extensive empirical study in psychical research, namely his "Report on Mrs. Piper's Hodgson-Control."

James feels his way to the position that it is not essentially the mass of evidential material, but something about the exquisite rendering of the personal quality of the Hodgson individuality, as it deals gently with certain Hodgson memories, that constitutes the best evidence of its survival. James was groping toward the view expressed by many since his time, that there is something about the style or personality modulation that properly carries its own conviction, as in our recognizing a voice over the telephone or in recognizing the style of a master in the arts when sheer analysis of content or structure must fail. In view of the unknown riches of histrionic skill which a medium like Mrs. Piper may have been able to command, this argument does not carry today the weight which James attached to it fifty years ago, but it is of interest to see that James was willing to go so far as to accord the Hodgson control a significant place among the factors inclining him to consider seriously the belief in survival. He tells us, in the end, that he is convinced that he had either been talking with Richard Hodgson or with a "spirit counterfeit" of him.[2] Although this is a very psycho-

---

[2] See p. 209.

logical study, a study that a professional psychologist is gratified to make, it is not, in my judgment, the highest type of psychical research of that period or of the present.

But I believe that the highest contribution which James was able to give to psychical research was a disciplined, unfearing, ever inquiring, nervously revolving and reconsidering mind. I will choose as documentation of this point James's review of Frederic W. H. Myers's *Human Personality and Its Survival of Bodily Death* (London: Longmans, 1903, two volumes), the fruit of twenty years' profound study, investigation, and reflection, which Myers and his group had given to the subject since the founding of the S. P. R. in 1882. James, as a frequent visitor to Britain and devoted admirer of Frederic Myers's amazing sensitivity, scholarship, creativeness, and courage, was eager to hail this work as a crowning achievement properly marking the culmination of its author's extraordinary life. Yet even in this moment of warmth and pathos, reminding one of Shelley's greeting to Keats upon his death, James cannot quite give up the empiricist's bitter task of criticism, reserve, caution: "*But is it really so?*" Flying with Myers through the vast spaces in which the immortal soul roams as it did in the Orphic mysteries and in the world of Dante and Blake, James has to ask the impertinent question: But do all the evidences of psychopathology, dissociation, double personality, the evidence of the weak, the sick, the frightened, the undisciplined, the savage, that you find in the deeper strata of the mind, really turn out, my dear friend, to come from the same region in which the sublime, the ecstatic, the potentially immortal reside? Can we really accept psychopathology on the same dish, so to speak, with the glowing message of those extraordinary last pages in Myers's book, entitled "Trance, Possession, and Ecstasy"? It was as if James, like Icarus, tried to fly but got nearer to the sun than any empiricist can safely allow himself, and fell back to earth.

But after all, the empiricist's fate can be a magnificent one if he is allowed to define it in his own terms; that is, if he is allowed to wander in all meadows and over all mountaintops; if he is a seeker who never really expects either final discovery or final peace. It was this restlessness to which William James was wedded, and it is this view, as a modern intellectual's approach to psychical research, with which he must be identified permanently in his role as a pioneer in psychical research.

INDEX

INDEX

Agassiz, Louis, 5, 225
American Society for Psychical Research, 14, 31, 241, 328, 329
"Amherst Mystery," 62
Animal magnetism, 27, 28
Apparitions, 35–36
Aristotle, 243
"Astral body," 92–94
Australian recollections, Hodgson's, 194–97
Automatic writing, 34, 49–51, 54–55, 220, 229
Automatism, 61, 112, 113, 220, 222, 233, 237
Ayer, J. C., 73, 74–75, 77

Balch, Alfred W., 82
Baldwin, Professor, 130
Balfour, Arthur, 29, 32
Bancroft, Margaret, 123, 125, 126, 153, 158–69
Barrett, William, 14, 29, 212, 309
Bayley, Dr., 149, 160, 162, 166, 168–69, 181
Bergman, Miss R., 189–94, 196
Berkeley, George, 244
Berry, Helen, 95, 96

Bible, 267
Binet, Alfred, 219, 220, 227
Blavatsky, Madame, 37, 64, 165
Blodgett, Mrs., 108
Botazzi, 311
Briggs, Henry L., 75
Brown, Thomas, 188
Büchner, Friedrich, 290n.

Carnochan, Gouverneur M., 71
Carrington, H., 311
Child, F. J., 201–202
Christian Science, 10, 14
Clairvoyance, 72–88, 229
Cleghorn, Allen H., 82
Clifford, W. K., 288n.
Consciousness, 222, 249
Cook, Florence, 311
Cranch, C. P., 252
Creery sisters, 32–33
Crystal-gazing, 37–38, 109, 229, 233

Darwin, Charles, 42, 311–12
Davey, Mr., 36, 61
Davidson, Thomas, 63, 256, 258
Dean, Sidney, 49

335